THE LIVERY HALLS OF THE CITY OF LONDON

WE ARE ONE
1914
1919
The gift of Robert Allen Brown Master 1918-19
THE WAR OF 1939 - 1945

THE LIVERY HALLS OF THE CITY OF LONDON

ANYA LUCAS & HENRY RUSSELL

Foreword by
ALDERMAN CHARLES BOWMAN
THE RT HON. THE LORD MAYOR OF THE CITY OF LONDON

Preface by
BARRY MUNDAY
MASTER OF THE WORSHIPFUL COMPANY
OF CHARTERED ARCHITECTS

Photography by
Andreas von Einsiedel

MERRELL
LONDON • NEW YORK

IN ASSOCIATION WITH
THE WORSHIPFUL COMPANY OF
CHARTERED ARCHITECTS

DIRIGE
DOMINE NOS

CONTENTS

Frontispiece: The main staircase, Armourers' Hall; *see pp. 148–51.*

Opposite: A stained-glass window in the Banqueting Hall, Carpenters' Hall; *see pp. 164–67.*

FOREWORD

The Livery Halls of the City of London are unique jewels that greatly enhance the City's rich architectural heritage. They represent the significance of the livery in the governance of the Square Mile, and they reflect the long history of trade and commerce that defines the historic heart of the capital.

The Halls, and the Companies that inhabit them, symbolize the City's resilience across the centuries, its ability to reinvent itself and to respond to the commercial needs of the time. It is remarkable that these ancient guilds – the oldest tracing their history back some 800 years – remain a vibrant part of a community that today includes some of the most technologically advanced businesses on the globe.

Although I have spent my professional life as a chartered accountant, I read architecture at university, and therefore am most grateful to the Worshipful Company of Chartered Architects for compiling this magnificent record of the Livery Halls. This book reveals the unique relationship between past and present reflected in the City's architecture, ranging from Apothecaries' Hall, built in 1672 (sadly, most of the earlier Halls were destroyed in the Great Fire of London), to the new Leathersellers' Hall, opened in 2017.

The Chartered Architects' Company is a modern Company, and has produced this book to mark the thirty years since it achieved full livery status. The publication is particularly appropriate since members of the Company are professionally involved in designing the modern City, creating buildings that provide the offices and the leisure, cultural and public spaces that are so crucial to the City of London's continuing role as the trusted driver of the nation's economy.

I congratulate the Worshipful Company on its important anniversary, and thank the Master Architect and Merrell Publishers for producing this vital record of the City's evolving history.

Alderman Charles Bowman, *The Rt Hon. the Lord Mayor of the City of London 2017–18*

The Chief Commoner's Parlour, Guildhall. The office of Chief Commoner, first established in 1444, is unique in that it is the only role now directly elected by the whole Court of Common Council (the governing body of the City of London Corporation), and serves to recognize the contribution that the office holder has made to the City Corporation over a number of years. A Past Master of the Worshipful Company of Chartered Architects, Michael Welbank, MBE, held this post in 2016.

PREFACE

Temple Bar, designed by Sir Christopher Wren, has been the symbol of the Worshipful Company of Chartered Architects since the WCCA's formation. The Bar's chequered history reflects many characteristics of the City, those of growth, change, destruction and rebirth. For the time being, Temple Bar serves as our spiritual home rather than a physical one, but being a peripatetic Company has its advantages. We have the opportunity to see and marvel at the Halls of other Companies as we conduct our Court meetings, banquets and dinners, and note what a unique and eclectic group of buildings they are.

As we approached the thirtieth anniversary of our receiving full livery status, it seemed to us that the history and architecture of Livery Halls would form a wholly appropriate subject for a celebratory book. Surprisingly, no such book has been undertaken since the W.A.D. Englefield and Peter Lubbock volume published in 1981, the charming pencil illustrations of which were drawn by Richard Howard Penton, the father of our late Past Master John Howard Penton.

We were fortunate enough to find two excellent and expert writers in Anya Lucas and

Henry Russell. Anya was already well known to us and other Companies through her doctoral thesis on Livery Halls and her fascinating lecture on the effect of the Great Fire on the Livery Halls and their Companies. Her Introduction sets the scene against which building and rebuilding have played out, while her essay on pp. 225–57 considers those Halls that, for a variety of reasons, have been lost over the centuries. Henry's herculean task has been to visit every extant Hall and to describe not only its architecture but also the origins and purpose of its associated Company, as well as its waxing and waning fortunes. All of this is richly illustrated by the wonderful original photography of Andreas von Einsiedel and the carefully researched historical drawings and plans, some of which have been newly discovered.

Among the forty extant Halls featured in this book, we are delighted to include two modern Halls (Haberdashers' Hall and Leathersellers' Hall) and one heavily remodelled Hall (Salters' Hall) designed by leading contemporary architects – respectively, Michael Hopkins and Partners (now Hopkins Architects), Eric Parry Architects and de Metz Forbes Knight Architects. These Halls demonstrate that the values of quality of design and construction are as important to the Livery Companies today as in the past.

To bring this book to completion has been a huge task, made possible only by the cooperative spirit that has existed between the writing and photography team and the Livery Companies that have opened their doors to us; and, of course, by those who have generously contributed towards the publication. We hope you will enjoy reading this volume and that it will remain the definitive work on this subject for many years to come.

Barry Munday, *Master of the Worshipful Company of Chartered Architects 2018*

The Worshipful Company of Chartered Architects uses Temple Bar, designed by Sir Christopher Wren, as its logo and the centrepiece of its coat of arms. The monument was the last surviving gateway into the City until it was removed in 1878 to improve traffic flow along Fleet Street. The Company helped to secure its return, and has worked with other Companies to ensure that the room above the arch is usable for occasional events.

Overleaf: The Livery Hall, Stationers' Hall; see pp. 192–95.

MASTERS OF THE COMPANY

FIRE EXIT

Chas. Fredk. Angell

MINCING LANE.

A Catalogue

Of all the valuable

BUILDING MATERIALS

Fixtures, remaining Furniture, & Fittings-up

OF

CLOTHWORKERS' HALL,

And several HOUSES adjoining, in Mincing Lane, extending to the Corner of Fenchurch Street,

COMPRISING ABOUT

500,000 CAPITAL BRICKS,

50,000 Plain Tiles, 30 Square of nearly New Slates,

2500 *Feet of Sheet Copper, Eight Tons of Lead,*

In Gutters, Flats, Cisterns, and Pipes; **Stout Oak & Fir Timber,** in Roofs, Floors, and Quartering; Modern Sashes and Frames (some with Plate Glass), 4 and 6-panelled, Sash, and other Doors; elegant Statuary and other Chimney Pieces, **300 Sq. of Flooring & Slating Boards,**

The OAK SCREEN in Hall, with Pilasters and Capitals,

15,000 FEET of OAK and other PANELLING,

Oak and other Lobby Doors (some with Plate Glass), Handsome Register and other Stoves, Kitchen Ranges, Hot Plates, **Large Copper Boilers and Steamers,** and Expensive Fittings-up of the Kitchens, Large Lead and Slate Cisterns, the Ornamental Fountain with Pipes, &c., complete,

7000 FEET SUPER OF STONE PAVING,

700 Feet run of Stone Coping, Stone Portico Entrance and Columns, with Carved Capitals, Stone Window Cills, Iron Columns, Wrought-iron Gates, Railing and Gratings, Iron Doors and Erection of Strong Room, and a great variety of Useful Materials and Fittings-up of a superior description, also the remaining

FURNITURE

Of the Hall and Court Rooms, including

12 Handsome Solid Brass Chandeliers (from 12 to 24 lights each),

Large Turkey and Brussels Carpets, Chimney and Pier Glasses, 11 elegant richly Gilt Girandoles, 8 Sets of rich Crimson Cloth Curtains, and handsome Cornices, Mahogany Dining and other Tables and Sideboards, Fenders and Fire Irons, Stools, Forms, Gas Fittings, Lamps, &c.,

Which will be Sold by Auction, by

PULLEN & SON,

ON THE PREMISES,

On Tuesday, Sept. 30, 1856, & following Day, at 12 o'Clk.

By Order of the Worshipful Company of Clothworkers.

May be Viewed on Saturday and Monday previous. Catalogues had on the Premises; of ROBERT BECKWITH TOWSE, Esq., at the Offices of the Clothworkers' Company, Barbers' Hall, Monkwell Street; of SAMUEL ANGELL, Esq., Architect, 16, Russell Square; and of PULLEN & SON, 80, Fore Street, Cripplegate.

[W. DEWICK, Printer, 46, Barbican.

INTRODUCTION

Anya Lucas

On Tuesday, 30 September 1856, an auction was held in Mincing Lane in the City of London. The sale catalogue advertises 'the valuable Building Materials, Fixtures, remaining Furniture, & Fittings-up of Clothworkers' Hall', including, among other lots, '500,000 Capital Bricks', 'Eight Tons of Lead', 'Stout Oak & Fir Timber', 'elegant Statuary and other Chimney Pieces', 'The Oak Screen in Hall, with Pilasters and Capitals', '15,000 Feet of Oak and other Panelling', 'Large Lead and Slate Cisterns', '7000 Feet Super of Stone Paving', 'Stone Portico Entrance and Columns, with Carved Capitals', and 'Wrought-iron Gates' (fig. 1).[1] Clothworkers' Hall, rebuilt for the fourth time after the Great Fire of London in 1666, was now, in the mid-nineteenth century, to be rebuilt once more, and lay, deconstructed, on its site at the corner of Fenchurch Street. This bricolage of dismembered building parts, strangely reminiscent of the heaps of melted and charred materials noted by observers of the ruined sites of the City Livery Halls in the days following the Great Fire, is a fitting frontispiece to the study of an architectural type characterized by repeated destruction and reconstitution (fig. 2).

This volume on the City of London's Livery Halls explores the architectural development of a nationally significant yet under-researched group of buildings. The Livery Halls have shaped and been shaped by the City's commercial activities and social–political hierarchies for more than 600 years. Collectively, they represent an identifiable building type matched in scale and ambition only by the Venetian *scuole*, and, as Simon Bradley and Nikolaus Pevsner have pointed out, the guild houses of the Southern Netherlands (figs. 3 and 4).[2] Of the forty Halls standing today, half remain on their medieval sites, but all of these have been rebuilt several times.[3]

From their earliest days, the Livery Halls played an important part in the City's civic culture, characterized as it was by a 'complex pattern of separate but interdependent institutions'; they were critical to the Companies, whose survival depended on a 'capacity to provide an environment where the flexible forms of association and exchange conducive to doing business could prosper'.[4] The Companies were established as trade or craft fraternities from the fourteenth century onwards; by the seventeenth, their

Fig. 1 Title page of the catalogue for the auction of building materials, fittings and fixtures from the demolished post-Fire Clothworkers' Hall, 1856.

Fig. 2 (above) Detail of A true and exact prospect of the famous citty of London … before the fire [and] … after the sad calamitie and destruction by fire in the yeare MDCLXVI, *etching by Wenceslaus Hollar, 1666.*

Fig. 3 (below) The 15th-century Scuola Grande di San Marco, Venice.

Fig. 4 (below, right) Guild houses in the Grand Place, Brussels.

authority and stability were being challenged by general economic and social trends such as the growth of extramural London, where guild control could be evaded,[5] and by specific events, such as enforced loans to the Crown, the Civil War, the Great Fire and the *quo warranto* proceedings against corporate Charters instigated by Charles II (fig. 6).[6] These threats had important architectural implications at the mid-point of the Halls' development as a building type. Since these were structures that proclaimed the Livery Companies' physical presence in the City, the reinforcement of this presence and the provision of a physical environment persuasive enough to retain and enhance Company numbers, even at great expense, became arguably more important than ever for these institutions.[7]

The challenges in subsequent centuries have been no less formidable. Even after the reconstruction that followed the Great Fire, more minor fires, structural problems and changes to the City's street pattern, combined with fierce inter-Company rivalry and the need to accommodate new functional requirements (both industrial and ceremonial), precipitated more building activity in the eighteenth and nineteenth centuries. Many of the Restoration Halls did not survive these years and, where they did, alterations, additions and repairs continued apace. By 1939, thirty-six Companies retained Halls (eight of these had had their Hall on the same site for more than 500 years, and the majority had occupied their site since the Great Fire). Only three remained untouched by enemy action in 1940–41, however, and yet another wave of rebuilding was the result (fig. 5). These post-war rebuildings predominate among the extant Halls (see Henry Russell's accounts, pp. 39–223).

For centuries, the very process of Hall-building – which has typically been funded and managed collaboratively – has helped the Companies to promote cohesion, fashion a coherent corporate self-image, and perpetuate the minutely differentiated political culture to which they belong. A Hall, newly repaired, beautified or reconstructed, has always placed a financial burden on its Company, but it has also functioned as a powerful reputational asset by upholding corporate honour. As capacious gathering places in an urban polity known across the centuries for the radical tendencies and assertiveness of its citizens – by 1657, for example, James Howell was describing a populace divided by 'rents, factions, and feuds' that was 'prone to riot at the slightest provocation' – the Halls have also been spaces on which numerous

Fig. 5 Plaques marking the site of six successive Cordwainers' Halls and that of the post-Fire Parish Clerks' Hall, destroyed in 1940.

Fig. 6 Detail of Charles II's Cavalcade through the City of London, 22 April 1661*, oil on canvas by Dirck Stoop, 1662.*

Fig. 7 (above) Stephen Harrison's 'Londinium' arch, erected for James I's coronation entry of 1604.

Fig. 8 (above, right) Tallow Chandlers' Hall, Dowgate Hill, *built 1668–75, watercolour by Samuel Ireland, c. 1794.*

actors have sought to stamp authority (fig. 7).[8] These have included aldermanic grandees and wealthy benefactors within the Companies' own ranks and, beyond the Hall gate and City walls, even monarchs. Indeed, Crown interest in and politicization of these buildings in the seventeenth century – discussed further in the 'Lost Halls' chapter (pp. 225–57) – represent one of the most fascinating but little-known episodes in their history.

The Livery Halls have always been elusive and paradoxical buildings: semi-public spaces that have both promoted jointness (often in chaotic and fractured times) and yet proclaimed their distinctness within the finely grained City polity; which have looked backwards to medieval London in their conservative plan and yet embraced changing tastes in ornament and decoration; which have usually receded, architecturally speaking, from the street and yet asserted their presence there; which have been both frugally built and richly adorned. Today the oldest survivals are those from the post-Fire period. None of the seventeenth-century Halls remains wholly intact; substantial fabric from this period survives in only five today (figs. 8 and 9).[9] The Clothworkers' auction catalogue is also, then, an appropriate introduction to what is in large part an account of lost buildings: the forerunners of those that stand today.

Why were the Livery Companies such active builders in what is traditionally regarded as their pivotal moment of decline, the seventeenth century? Such economic historians as George Unwin and Stella Kramer once argued that the Companies of seventeenth-century London were corporate bodies already reconciled to decline and loss of power: 'gothic remnants of a bygone age' and 'hotbeds of economic conservatism'.[10] Starting in the 1980s, a new wave of scholarship argued that the 'evidence adduced for guild decline in this period is ambiguous'.[11] Such recent studies challenge the orthodox chronology of decline, and recast the seventeenth century as one in which the Livery Companies, institutions that possessed greater flexibility and stronger survival instincts than was previously thought, retained both their economic and social–symbolic relevance (fig. 10).[12] Indeed, it is worth remembering that membership of the livery continued to confer economic

Fig. 9 The Court Room of Tallow Chandlers' Hall.

privileges in the Square Mile as late as 1856, when an Act of Common Council admitted all to retail trade. Curiously, the link between building activity and continuing status has not been the subject of any sustained analysis by historians; architectural patronage is arguably the last area of Company life to be interrogated. The evidence suggests that building activity was not merely a result of the Companies' continuing status, but was critical to it.

THE HISTORIOGRAPHY OF THE LIVERY COMPANIES AND THEIR HALLS

If the sixteenth century has been regarded as the high-water mark of Livery Company power and influence, the historiography of the seventeenth-century Companies is one of difficulties compounded and blows upon blows. The study of guilds in London, other British cities and continental cities is currently active, however, and this well-trodden narrative of decline has begun to change.

The 'decline' narrative can be traced back to William Herbert, whose two-volume *History of the Twelve Great Livery Companies of London* (1837) presented, as the revisionist guild historian Michael Berlin has noted, 'colourful, if somewhat longwinded accounts of feasts, pageants, heraldry and regalia' of the later medieval period, while ignoring evidence of guild vitality well after their supposed demise in the seventeenth century.[13] For Herbert, the Great Fire was 'the consummation' of the Companies' 'miseries' and marked the end of twenty-six years of 'intolerable exaction, spoliation, and calamity'.[14] What Herbert the antiquarian began, new economic historians of the early twentieth century entrenched. George Unwin's landmark *The Gilds and Companies of London* (1908) amplified the narrative of guild decline and romanticized a pre-modern world of artisanal free association lost to the ravages of capitalism.[15] After Unwin, Berlin has argued, 'historians tended to assume rather than demonstrate the absence of guild powers in the eighteenth century, concentrating instead on the seventeenth century as the key period for their demise. As a result a contradictory and often vague chronology of the loss of guild regulatory powers developed.'[16]

Twentieth-century economic historians variously identified the onset of the decline of the Companies' powers with the English Civil War, the lifting of monopolies on the building trades after the Great Fire and, most notably, as in the case of Stella Kramer in *The English Craft Gilds: Studies in Their Progress and Decline* (1927), with the Restoration.[17] The shared assumption was that, by the seventeenth century, guild control was increasingly running counter to a proto-capitalist grain. Since the 1980s, however, scholarship has challenged dominant assumptions about the role of early modern European guilds, and placed new emphasis on more tacit functions and powers. Berlin has presented evidence of the London Livery Companies' capacity for survival and flexibility. He argues that the Companies' roles had never been confined to economic control, but were 'polymorphous' and more 'deeply entrenched'.[18] Citing the important work of Steve Rappaport and Ian Archer, Berlin underlines the extent to which the question of economic control has been a distraction, since this was never the sole *raison d'être* of these institutions.[19]

Fig. 10 Liverymen with banners stand to attention on the north side of Cheapside for Marie de' Medici's processional entry to the City in 1638; detail of an engraving by Wenceslaus Hollar from Jean Puget de la Serre's Histoire de l'entree de la reyne mere du roy tres-chrestien, dans la Grande-Bretaigne, *1639.*

So what other functions did the Companies have, and how might these be relevant to buildings? Here, too, scholarship has moved on. That by Rappaport and Archer, in particular, has shed light on how the City's layered social and political structure allowed multiple and fluid networks of association while at the same time preserving and promoting stability.[20] Rappaport argues that the Companies provided one of many interconnected and overlapping 'worlds within worlds' within the polity and were vital to its commercial success, social stability and even its law and order: '[Along with] parishes, precincts, and wards ... livery companies ... formed the substructure of society, a complex and highly organised network of social organisations which provided London with a stable foundation and its people with communal associations through which they participated in the social, economic, and political life of the city.'[21]

Ian Gadd and Patrick Wallis's 2002 edited collection of essays sheds further light on the role of the Companies in the social fabric and political life of the City; for those authors and their contributors – Perry Gauci, in particular – the seventeenth century was, socially, economically and politically, the apotheosis of the London Companies, despite obvious challenges in the form both of 'the specific crises of the reformation, the civil war, the great fire, and the purges and charter surrenders of the 1680s [and of] more general shifts in terms of London's size, social structure and economy'.[22] The Companies' undoubted commitment to rebuilding and beautifying their Halls in the light of these challenges becomes all the more intriguing. Gadd and Wallis suggest, rightly in this writer's view, that the Companies achieved impact and influence through a formula in which image was as crucial as wealth and regulatory powers. However, their volume neglects to consider material culture and the ways in which the Companies used the Halls to project their corporate images to themselves, one another and to different constituents within and without the City walls. In seeking to answer the question 'How did the Companies manage to endure?', historians have so far neglected one of the most obvious answers: architecture.[23]

Fig. 11 Charter of Incorporation of the Haberdashers' Company, granted by Henry VI in 1448.

Publications that consider the Livery Companies and the Halls themselves have varied considerably in quality and approach, from monographs and lengthy, expensively produced 'house' histories to articles and essays. Henry Lennox Hopkinson's *The History of Merchant Taylors' Hall* (1931), printed for private circulation, is typical of the kind of in-house publishing that the Livery Companies used to, and in some cases still, undertake. More recently, professional historians have taken on Company histories.[24] Ian Archer's *The History of the Haberdashers' Company* (1991), Ian Doolittle's *The Mercers' Company, 1579–1959* (1994) and *The History of the Merchant Taylors' Company* by Matthew Davies and Ann Saunders (2004) all set a high standard for the genre. Company histories have often neglected the Halls, however. The publication of Priscilla Metcalf's *The Halls of the Fishmongers' Company: An Architectural History of a Riverside Site* (1977) was, therefore, a milestone. Metcalf charts the evolution of three successive Fishmongers' Halls on the same riverside plot, observing that, unlike country houses, for example, Livery Halls are not 'isolated set-pieces' but 'fit, like pieces of a jigsaw, into a finely-grained urban environment'.[25] Jean Imray's *The Mercers' Hall* (1991) offers a minutely detailed and very valuable account of the post-Fire rebuilding of Mercers' Hall, but, as one reviewer commented, it 'tends to pile up information, while offering relatively little by way of overall interpretative frameworks or comparison with other company experiences'.[26]

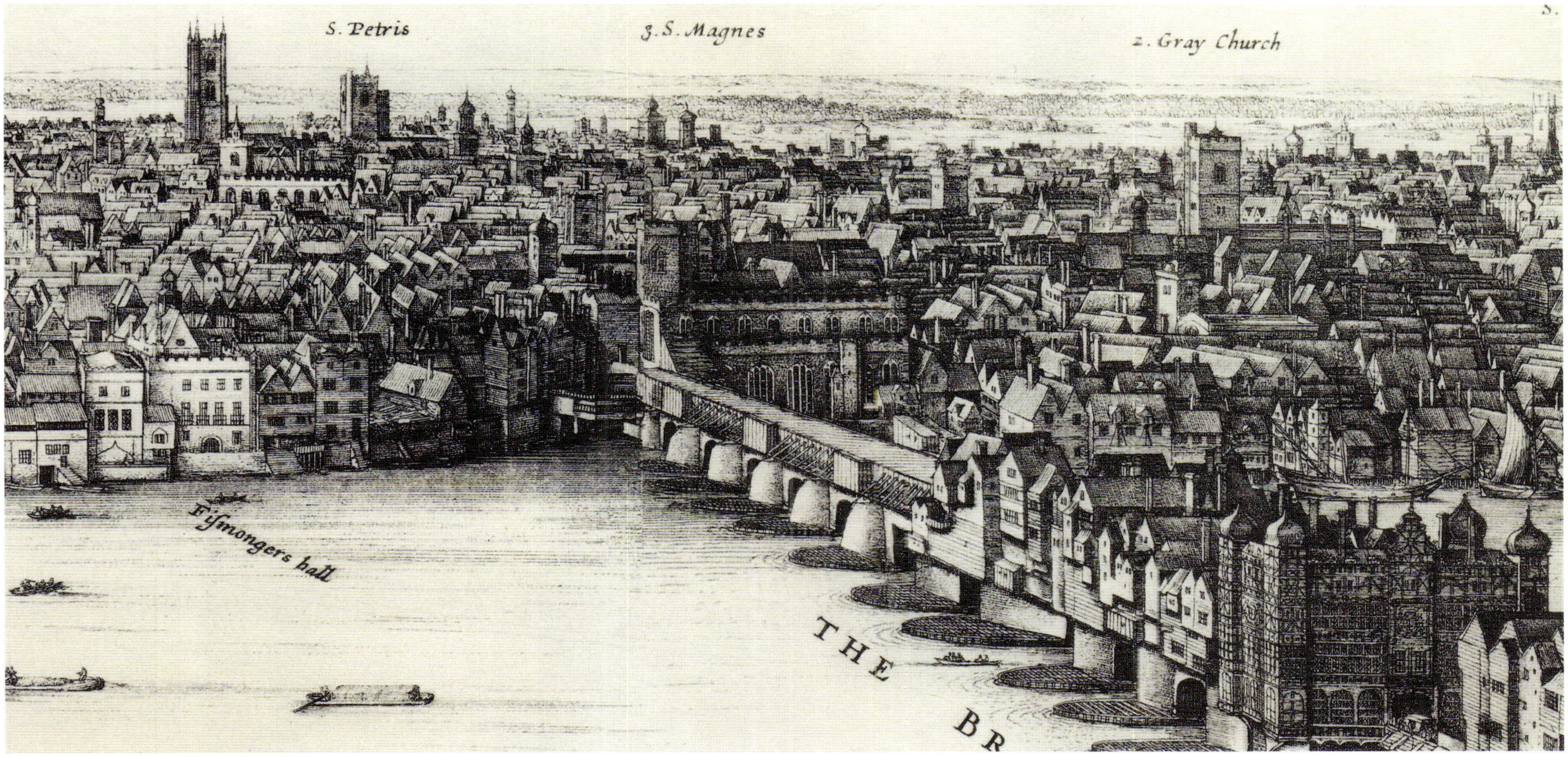

Fig. 12 The Fishmongers' pre-Fire Hall; detail of an engraved view of London by Wenceslaus Hollar, 1647.

Archer has suggested that 'The effect of individually-commissioned company histories, often works of *pietas* or corporate legitimation, has been the ghettoisation of the subject', and identified a 'crying need for works of synthesis and comparison'.[27] It is our hope that this book will go some way towards filling the gap.

LIVERY HALLS: WORLDS WITHIN WORLDS

The Livery Companies had their origins in medieval guilds that in some cases may even have antedated the mayoralty of London (1189).[28] These were a combination of religious fraternities and mutual benefit societies, the functions of which included regulating the practices and standards of a trade or craft; charity; sociability; and the organization of funerals and Masses for the dead. Many of the ancient Companies were established and incorporated by Royal Charter in the fourteenth and fifteenth centuries, and began acquiring and adapting buildings from which to operate with particular intensity from *c.* 1390 (fig. 11). By the reign of Richard III (1483–85), there were twenty-eight Livery Halls; when John Stow wrote his *Survey of London* in 1598, he was able to record forty-six.[29] At least fifty-three were standing by the time of the Great Fire (figs. 12 and 13).

An order of precedence was agreed in 1515, when the most senior Companies, headed by the Mercers, became known as the 'Great Twelve'. Every Company was engaged in a continual process of competitive comparison, emulation and assuring its place in the order. The Company order of precedence, in which the Great Twelve were followed by the newer, more junior, Companies, ingrained a sense of rank or degree that often dictated corporate behaviour. The Mercers' Company, for example, referred to its dealings

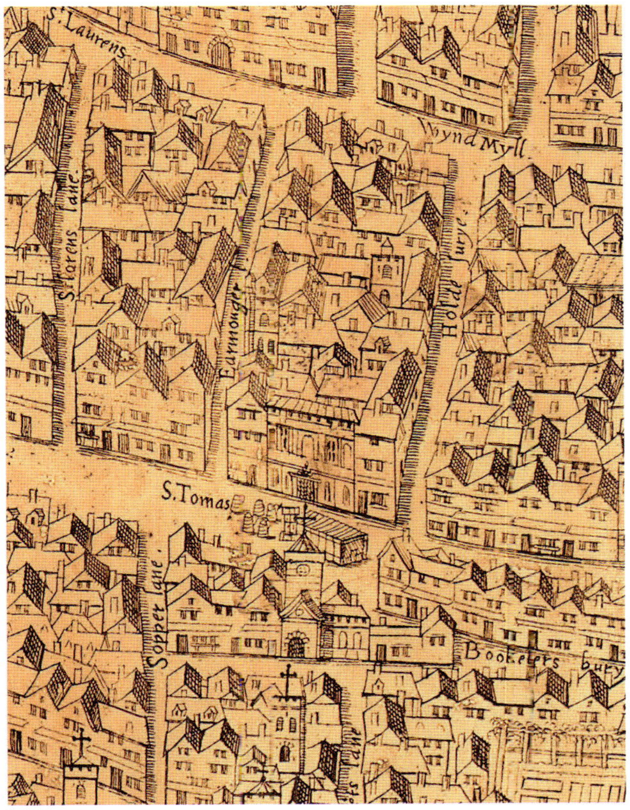

Fig. 13 Mercers' Hall in Cheapside, c. 1550 and as it would still have appeared in 1632; detail of a surviving plate of the Copperplate Map of London, c. 1560.

Fig. 14 View of the lands belonging to the City of London, from 'A Survey of the Estate of the Plantation of the County of Londonderry Taken in 1624', Lambeth Palace MS *634, fols. 1v–2.*

with 'the inferior Companies' in the negotiations it led in the 1630s regarding the plantation of Ulster (fig. 14).[30] The question of relative and correct placement preoccupied those who governed the Companies not only at an abstract level but also because it dictated, not least, where a particular Company stood when required to line the City's streets for civic and royal processions.

In this way, precedence was conceived of spatially as well as metaphorically. City authorities called on the Companies to form the front line of the crowd that was 'the inevitable and necessary frame' for such public rituals as the Lord Mayor's Show; they were a 'validating presence needed to legitimate the civic values being performed'.[31] The honour and responsibility this implied made the Companies particularly sensitive to slights on such occasions. Typical of this concern is an episode in the records of the Barber-Surgeons' Company, whose Court of Assistants complained to the Corporation of London's Court of Aldermen in June 1604 that at 'the passage of the King and Queen and Prince of Wales through the city with gentry and nobility of the land' their liverymen had been 'misplaced'.[32]

The Mercers' Company, the City's premier guild, was just as conscious of its position at the top of the order of precedence; this translated into a prime position at the top of Cheapside nearest to St Paul's on civic occasions, as an engraving by William Hogarth shows (fig. 16).

Order also governed corporate organization. Each Company had ranks or degrees of men: freemen, liverymen and members of the Court of Assistants. At the top of the structure was the Master, the chief officer, who was elected annually, having first served his years on the Court of Assistants and as Renter and Upper Warden. These Wardens were also annually elected officers, with responsibility for keeping account books, collecting money and paying creditors (fig. 15).[33] The Assistants, selected from among the liverymen, were the oligarchic grandees of the Company, and alone voted on elections and elected freemen for the livery, using as their base the Court room or Court parlour typically adjoining the dais end of the hall room. The liverymen were a Company's economic and social elite; their status was reflected in their right to wear distinctive gowns trimmed with satin and fur. The more senior the Company, the smaller the ratio of liverymen to ordinary freemen.

Beneath the liverymen were the freemen or yeomanry, who were in turn responsible for the apprentices contracted to the Company for seven years to learn a trade, and the journeymen, who worked for wages. The administrative officer who ran Company business for the Master, Wardens and Court of Assistants was the Clerk. As Adrian Johns has observed, the Clerk was 'no mere amanuensis. In his office at the hall, he was a conventionally invisible agent who in fact wielded much influence.'[34] The Beadle, whose accommodation

Fig. 15 Portrait of Clement Pargeter, William Peacock and Thomas Babb, all of whom served as Wardens of the Painter-Stainers' Company; oil on canvas by an unknown artist, 1623/24.

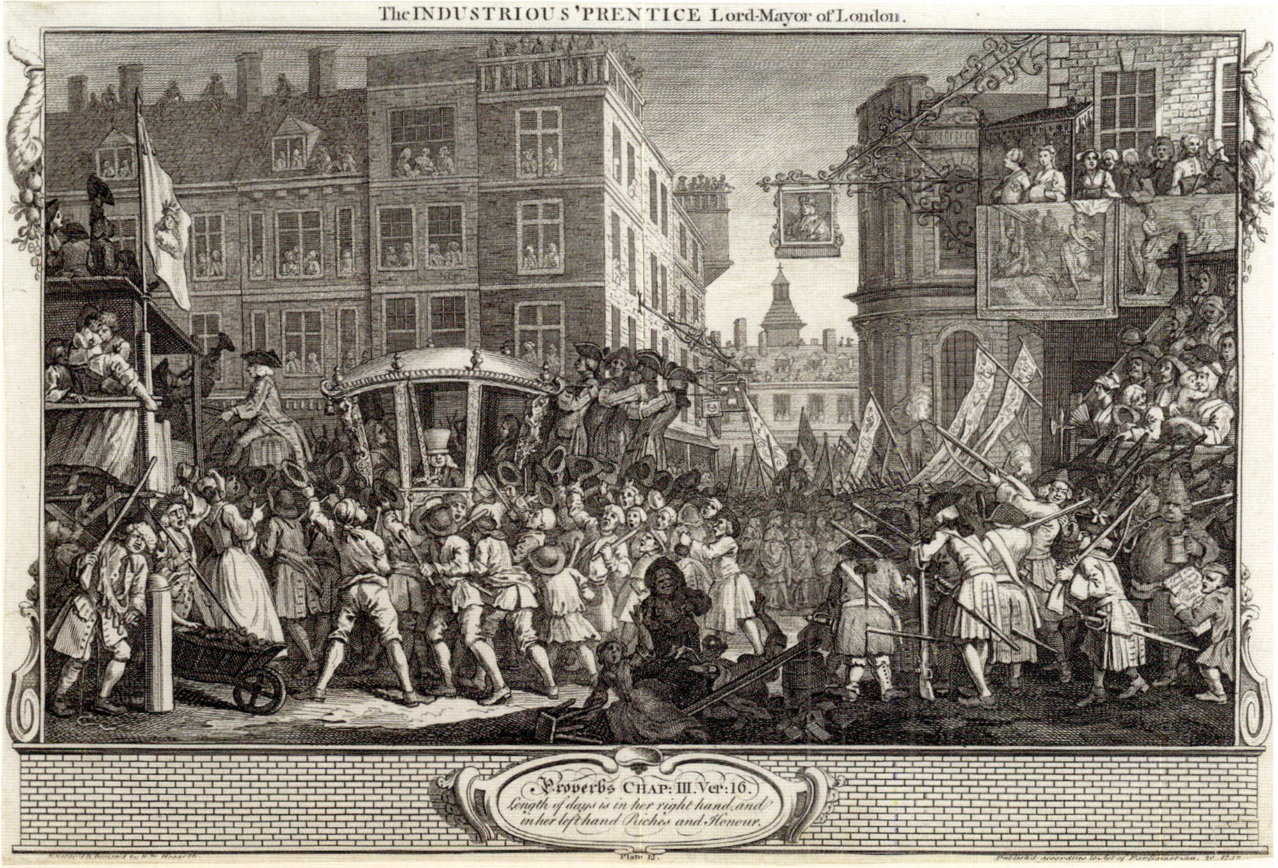

Fig. 16 The Industrious 'Prentice Lord-Mayor of London*: the Lord Mayor's carriage enters the top of Cheapside and is met by the Maiden's head banner of the Mercers' Company, just visible at top left; etching and engraving by William Hogarth, 1747.*

Fig. 17 The Industrious 'Prentice grown rich, & Sheriff of London at Fishmongers' Hall*; etching and engraving by William Hogarth, 1747.*

Fig. 18 Guildhall, London; 17th-century engraving.

was often to be found in the street range of the Hall, acted as porter, oversaw security and also had an important ceremonial role. Foreigners (that is, men from the provinces) and aliens (men from other countries) were permitted to join a Livery Company, although the latter could not be freemen of the City. Three methods of entry to a Livery Company were available: by patrimony, whereby an adult male could join his father's Company (provided that the father had taken the livery prior to his son's birth); by redemption, which entailed a one-off payment; or by apprenticeship (otherwise known as servitude). Once part of the Company, the freeman was able to participate in the rituals of Company life, including the dinners and feasts that characterized liveried social activity in the popular imagination and 'enhanced harmonious relations' within the Company (fig. 17).[35]

It was through the Companies that men became enfranchised in the body politic as citizens or freemen and gained a range of economic rights and privileges.[36] These men had basic access to political process in the form of wardmotes for the election of Aldermen and Common Councillors. Liverymen, however, attended Common Hall at Guildhall, where they played a role in the election of the Lord Mayor, Sheriffs, Chamberlain and the City's MPs (fig. 18).

A historical account of the Companies is incomplete without reference to their relationship with the Crown and the subject of Royal Charters. In his *Survey of London* (1598; revised edition 1603), John Stow gave a straightforward account of the Companies' origins, noting merely that they had 'severally, at sundry times, purchased the King's favour and license ... to associate themselves in brotherhoods, with Master and Wardens for their government'.[37] In his expanded version of Stow's *Survey* printed in 1633, however, Anthony Munday found an explanation of the Companies' status and function much more awkward. He offered a tortuous and contradictory argument concerning the nature of City government, claiming first that 'London is ... no place endowed with any distinct or absolute power', and yet later examining in detail 'such causes as have heretofore moved the Princes ... to seize the liberties of the City'.[38] 'The public Armour and munition of the City remaineth in the Halls of the Companies', he assured his reader, 'onely for obedience of the law which commandeth it'.[39] This laborious account of the City's status in relation to the monarch – part embarrassed apology, part spirited defence – indicates awareness of a new tension that had formed between these two centres of power in the thirty-year interval since the final Elizabethan edition of the *Survey*.

Munday's insistence that no significance should be attached to the Halls' function as City armouries is revealing. The Halls were used as repositories for weapons and gunpowder, but – as Munday was no doubt aware – they also held significant political firepower in the form of liverymen who were able to vote in parliamentary, mayoral and shrieval elections at Guildhall. Furthermore, in the absence of a Mansion House before the eighteenth century, the larger Halls were frequently used for entertaining by Lord Mayors and Sheriffs in their year of office, conferring on them additional political significance (fig. 21).[40]

The relationship between the Crown and the Companies (as with the City more generally)

Fig. 19 The Leathersellers' second Charter, issued by James I in 1604.

was complex; it could be coercive and mutually beneficial, antagonistic and reciprocal. The practice whereby monarchs took the freedom of a particular Company further illustrates how nuanced the power dynamic could be: who was honouring whom? When Charles II accepted the freedom of the Grocers' Company in 1674, the poet and courtier the Earl of Rochester sneered, 'Monarchs rank themselves with Grocers. / Cringe, scrape no more, ye City Fops'.[41] Mutual mistrust often prevailed between these centres of power, and the Crown sometimes had good reason to be suspicious. Despite these tensions, there has always been a cultural affinity between Whitehall and Guildhall.[42]

In the early modern period (when the Halls were most numerous), the Square Mile had developed into a variegated place that saw the 'divers fair houses ... meet for merchants' of Aldermanbury jostle with 'filthy' Aldgate (fig. 22).[43] As John Schofield has shown, 'there was no social segregation into rigidly divided areas of rich and poor quarters; this lack of differentiation, a feature of the medieval city, was still the case in 1638 ... Poor streets or lanes were interspersed between the larger mansions or prosperous districts' (fig. 23).[44] It was on to this finely grained urban environment that the Companies grafted themselves, acquiring property in which to operate from and often, in addition, property portfolios that developed as a result of bequests from wealthy members.

The Livery Halls, the centrepieces of these dispersed estates, were rarely purpose-built and sometimes occupied awkward and constrained sites. Land within the confines of the City walls was much prized and freeholds relinquished reluctantly.[45] The Companies tended to acquire medieval courtyard town houses, and it was primarily around this type – with a dominating hall and withdrawing apartments opening off it – that their corporate activities and rituals evolved (fig. 24).[46] The whole complex came to be known as a Hall after the room at its centre, and this range typically sat behind the principal elevation of the inner courtyard at ground, or sometimes first-floor, level. The courtyard was accessed from the street through a row of shops or tenements belonging to the Company. At the back of the site, furthest from the street and beyond the hall range, there

Fig. 20 (opposite, top) *Frontispiece to Richard Wallis,* Londons Armory, *1677.*

Fig. 21 (opposite, bottom) Perspective view of Goldsmiths' Hall in Foster Lane; watercolour by John Ward, 1692.

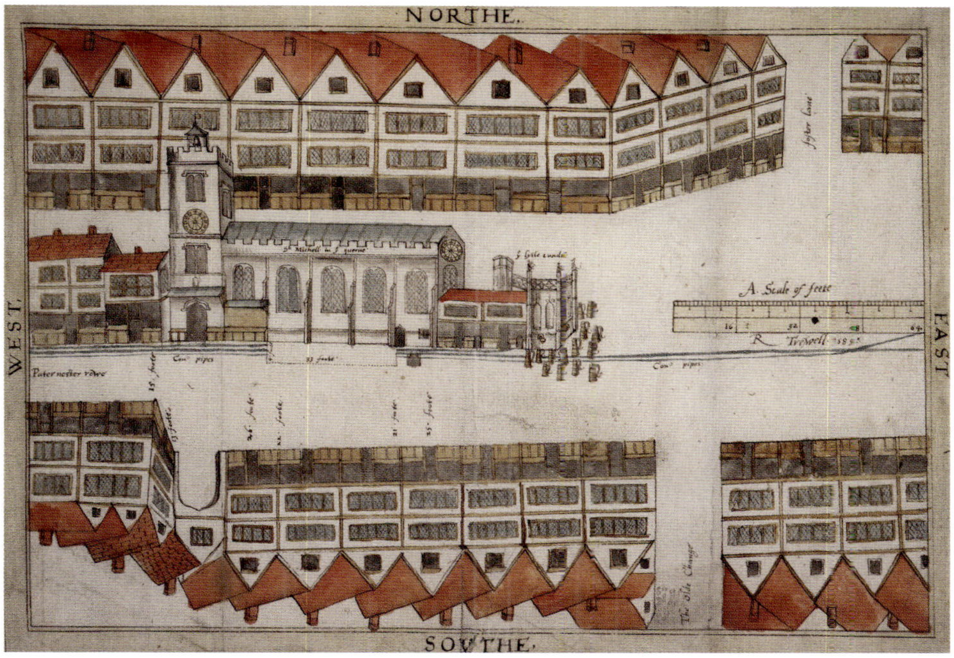

Fig. 22 (above) A guide for Cuntrey men In the famous Cittey of LONDON by the helpe of wich plot they shall be able to know how farr it is to any Street ..., *1593, from the 1653 edition of John Norden's* Speculum Britanniae.

Fig. 23 (left) Bird's-eye view of the west end of Cheapside, Foster Lane, Goldsmiths' Row and Paternoster Row; watercolour by Ralph Treswell, c. 1585.

Fig. 24 (right) Plan of Stationers' Hall off Ave Maria Lane, made by William Leybourn on completion in 1674; fol. 3 of a plan book in the Company's possession.

Fig. 25 (far right) Watercolour plan of the Clothworkers' pre-Fire Hall in Mincing Lane by Ralph Treswell, 1612.

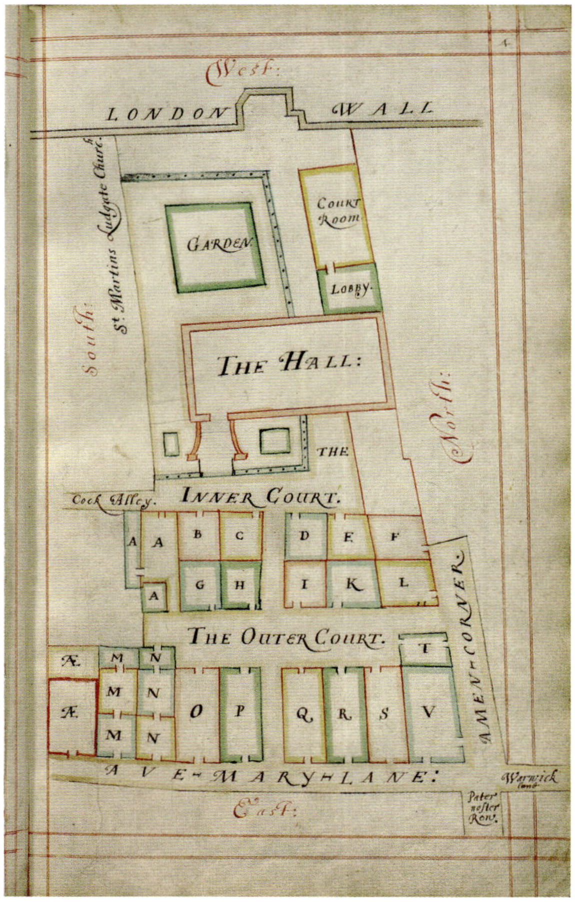

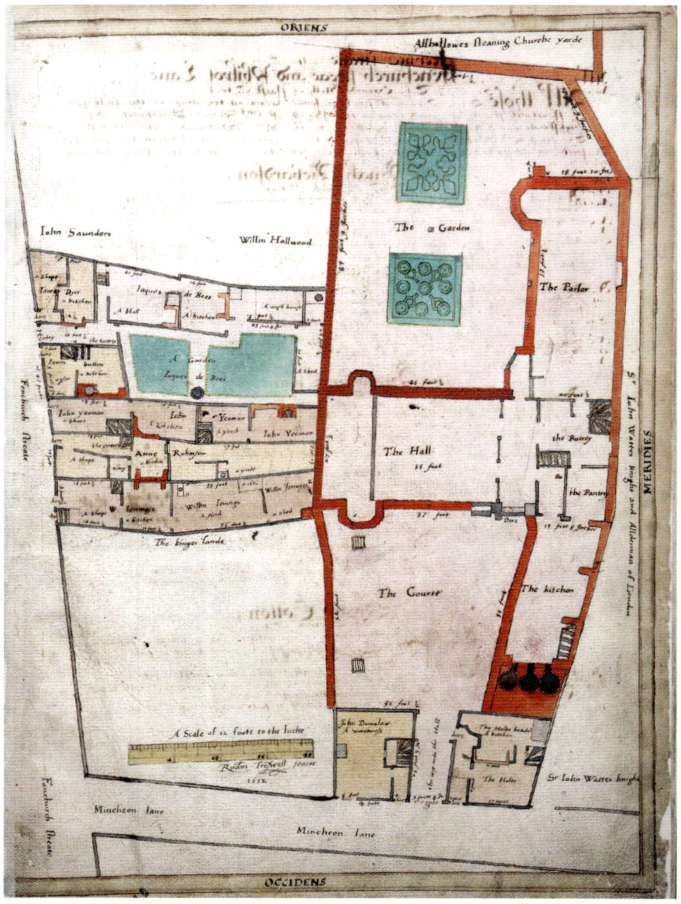

Fig. 26 Reconstruction by Peter Jackson of Clothworkers' Hall in Mincing Lane before its rebuilding in 1633.

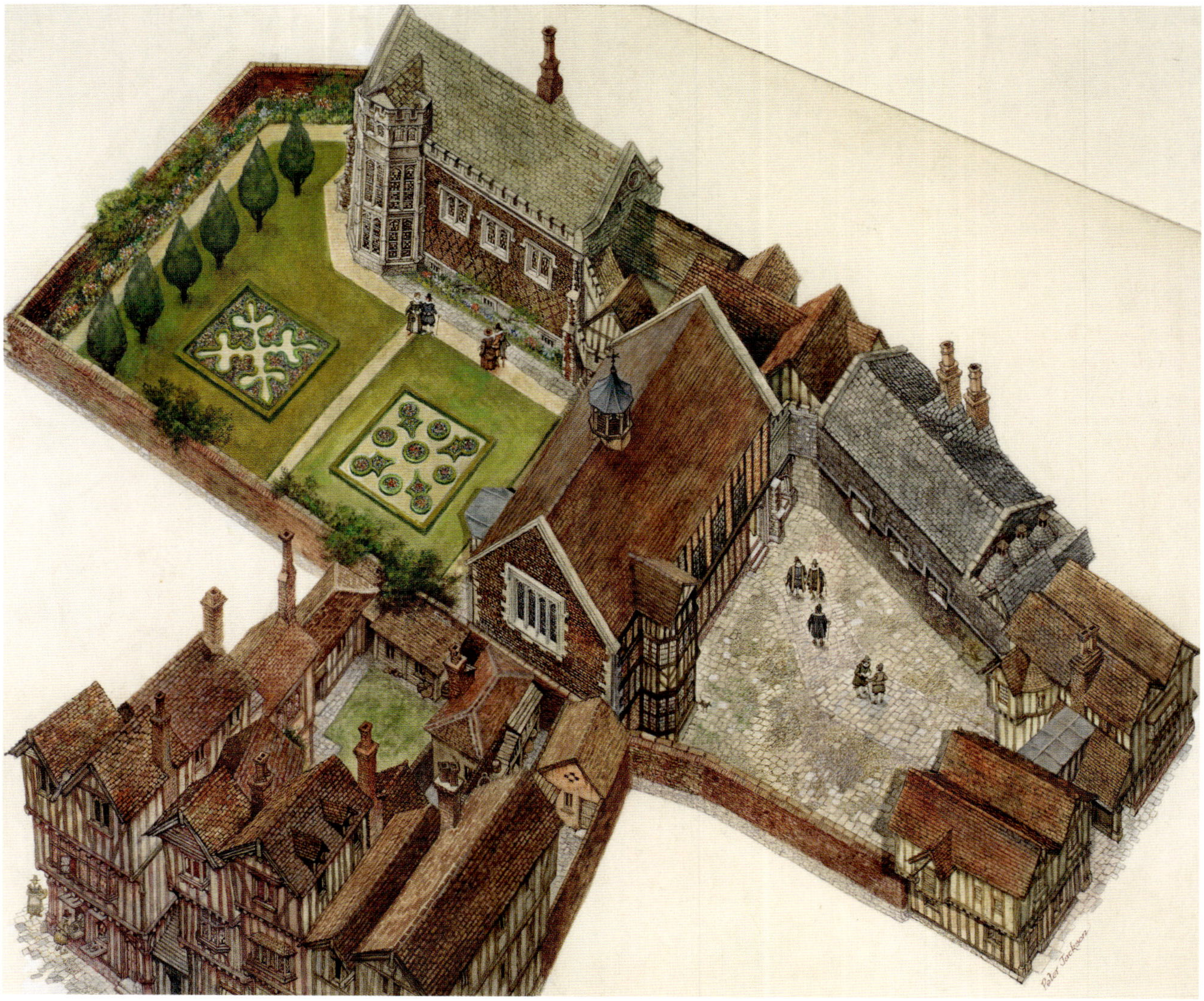

was usually a garden or simply a yard in the case of the more modest Halls. The sixteenth-century Hall of the Clothworkers' Company followed such an arrangement (figs. 25 and 26). Not all Companies adapted domestic buildings. Nine took advantage of the Dissolution and acquired ranges of monastic complexes (fig 27).[47] Around the courtyard, in addition to the Court room or parlour, might be disposed a variety of other reception rooms adorned with tapestries, portraits, plate, Turkey carpets and fine furniture; the Halls were 'theatres of memory' in which acts of charity were memorialized through such artefacts (fig. 28).[48] Inventories remind us, too, of the areas and items such as 'pissing places', ovens and lead cisterns that kept the Halls functioning (fig. 29).[49]

Ultimately, the Hall became synonymous with the group of men who formed the Company. We find, for example, the Barber-Surgeons' Court of Assistants in 1609 ordering that 'no master [is] to ever sell or impawne the tapestry hangings which were bought for the use and credit of *this house*'.[50] The elision of buildings with bodies – both corporate and human – was more than a convenient shorthand; it is revealing of the Halls' vital function as containers.

Fig. 27 (top, left) Section showing Leathersellers' Hall and the vaults of the former Benedictine priory of St Helen's, 1799.

Fig. 28 (top, right) The Court Room of Brewers' Hall, completed in 1673 to designs by Thomas Whiting (now destroyed).

Fig. 29 (above) Painters' Hall, Little Trinity Lane, *showing the garden and a lead cistern beneath the open windows of the Hall; watercolour by Samuel Ireland,* c. *1794.*

THE LIVERY HALL AS TYPE

In her monograph on the Master Carpenter Edward Jerman (the builder of several post-Fire Halls), Helen Collins discourages typological examination of the Halls, asserting that they 'always were, and still are today, a miscellaneous group, not

Fig. 30 Barber-Surgeons' Hall from the churchyard of St Giles' Cripplegate, c. 1800.

Fig. 31 Portrait of Sir Joseph Sheldon, Master of the Tallow Chandlers' Company in 1667 (translated to the Drapers' Company as Lord Mayor Elect, 1675), by Gerard Soest, 1677. Sheldon donated oak wainscoting to the Tallow Chandlers' post-Fire Hall.

easily categorised'.[51] Bradley and Pevsner compare the Halls with the guild houses of Antwerp and Brussels, but these uniformly tall and slender buildings ranged side by side in the same locations, and with similar gables and sculptural stonework, present much more homogeneous groupings (fig. 4).[52]

It is true that the structural diversity of the corporate system was to some extent mirrored in built fabric; no two Livery Halls – either before or after the Great Fire – have shared an identical plan, the same disposition of rooms or precisely the same relationship between function and space, but to suggest they were a miscellany is not accurate.[53] Nor is the assertion that in the mid-seventeenth century the buildings were 'united only by their incorporation of a livery hall'.[54] By this time it was the rule rather than the exception for Livery Hall complexes to have a parlour or Court room, a kitchen and ovens, an armoury, a garden or yard and accommodation for the Beadle, as well as the large hall room from which they took their name.[55] The shape of each Hall site inevitably controlled the development of each Hall complex and directed the precise arrangement of the core elements described above. This resulted in variations in morphology: the incorporation of bastion 13 of London Wall in Barber-Surgeons' Hall, for example, or the river quay of Fishmongers' Hall (figs. 30 and 32). It was also typical, as we have seen, for the complexes to be set back from the line of the street, behind a row of shops or tenements belonging to the Company and across a courtyard. Nevertheless, these were variations on a single theme and implicitly point to the existence of an underlying type that was being evoked on each rebuilding, if not fully replicated. The Livery Hall may not be a rigidly defined type, but it has proved a resilient one.

A final word on those aspects of the Halls and the Companies' material culture not covered in this volume but which the reader may find it useful to bear in mind. The headquarters of the City's trading companies do not come within the scope of this study, although they provide a useful point of comparison with the Halls, especially in the early modern period (fig. 33). Moveable objects that formed part of the Companies' wider material culture, such as plate (loving cups, salts, rosewater dishes and ewers, etc.), tapestries,

Fig. 32 River front of the post-Fire Fishmongers' Hall, built 1667–69; engraving by Bernard Lens, early to mid-18th century.

Fig. 33 The old East India House, Leadenhall Street, headquarters of the East India Company; 17th-century engraving.

Fig. 34 Arms of Samuel Pepys in a window of the post-Fire Clothworkers' Hall (destroyed 1941). Pepys was Master Clothworker in 1677 and donated a rosewater dish, a ewer and a loving cup to the Company.

painted glass and portraiture, are discussed only in so far as they illuminate the role of the Halls as containers; built fabric, fixtures and fittings are the chief focus (figs. 31 and 34). The acquisition, repair and beautification of barges and barge-houses preoccupied Livery Courts from the early modern period to the nineteenth century and beyond; in several instances this activity appears to have coincided with Hall-building (fig. 35).[56] The Livery Halls formed the centrepiece of what were often very significant property portfolios; through charitable bequests the Companies came to own a wide range of buildings both within the City and outside it, including tenements, almshouses, school buildings and farms. The seventeenth century also saw the Companies pressed by the Crown to invest in the plantation of Ulster, and the requirement to build houses and churches in their portions there placed an additional strain on finances (fig. 14).[57] Though these wider property portfolios cannot be discussed here, it is important to remember that the Companies' building activity was by no means confined to the Halls. Finally, the Halls' gardens should not be overlooked. Throughout their long history, the laying-out of a new garden or renovation of a neglected garden has often taken place alongside repairs to and beautification of the Hall, and they remain an essential part of the overall complex (fig. 36).

Fig. 35 The Triumphall Entertainment of ye King and Queenes Matie by ye … Lord Maior and Cittizens of London, at their coming from Hampton Court to Whitehall (on ye River of Thames) Aug: ye 23 1662; *the barges of the 'Great Twelve' Companies in an etching by Dirck Stoop depicting the marriage of Charles II and Catherine of Braganza.*

Fig. 36 Garden Front of Stationers' Hall, *watercolour by Samuel Ireland,* c. *1794.*

Until 1752, the civil calendar began on Lady Day (25 March). To avoid ambiguity, dates between 1 January and 24 March are here given using both the old-style and the new-style year, e.g., 24 February 1671/72.

BS Archives of the Worshipful Company of Barbers

CL Archives of the Clothworkers' Company

GL Guildhall Library, London

MC Archives of the Worshipful Company of Mercers

1 The catalogue is in the Archives of the Clothworkers' Company: CL G/Angell/1.
2 Simon Bradley and Nikolaus Pevsner, *London 1: The City of London* (Pevsner Architectural Guides: Buildings of England), Harmondsworth (Penguin) 1997, pp. 373–412, on p. 373.
3 Writing in 1997, Bradley and Pevsner, *London 1*, list thirty-five Halls. The present volume includes HQS *Wellington*, which is the floating home of the Honourable Company of Master Mariners; two Halls – Glaziers' Hall and the Proof House – that are located outside the area covered by the Pevsner City of London volume; and two new Halls, those of the Furniture Makers' and Information Technologists' Companies.
4 Derek Keene, 'Livery Companies: What, When and Why?', in *Guilds, Society and Economy in London, 1450–1800*, ed. Ian Anders Gadd and Patrick Wallis, London (Centre for Metropolitan History, Institute of Historical Research in association with Guildhall Library) 2002, pp. 171–74, on pp. 172–73.
5 See J.R. Kellett, 'The Breakdown of Gild and Corporation Control over the Handicraft and Retail Trade in London', *The Economic History Review*, vol. 10, no. 3, April 1958, pp. 381–94.
6 See Ian Anders Gadd and Patrick Wallis, 'Introduction', in *Guilds, Society and Economy in London, 1450–1800*, ed. Ian Anders Gadd and Patrick Wallis, London (Centre for Metropolitan History, Institute of Historical Research in association with Guildhall Library) 2002, pp. 1–14, on p. 3.
7 *Ibid.*, p. 5.
8 James Howell, *Londinopolis*, London (printed for H. Twiford *et al.*) 1657, p. 47; Tim Harris, 'Perceptions of the Crowd in Later Stuart London', in *Imagining Early Modern London: Perceptions and Portrayals of the City from Stow to Strype, 1598–1720*, ed. J.F. Merritt, Cambridge and New York (Cambridge University Press) 2001, pp. 250–72, on p. 251.
9 Those of the Skinners', Vintners', Tallow Chandlers', Stationers' and Apothecaries' Companies. In addition, ceilings of the period survive at the Drapers', Goldsmiths' and Innholders' Halls.
10 S.R. Epstein and Maarten Prak, 'Introduction', in *Guilds, Innovation and the European Economy, 1400–1800*, ed. S.R. Epstein and Maarten Prak, Cambridge and New York (Cambridge University Press) 2008, pp. 1–24, on p. 1. See, for example, George Unwin, *The Gilds and Companies of London*, London (Methuen) 1908, and S. Kramer, *The English Craft Gilds: Studies in Their Progress and Decline*, New York (Columbia University Press) 1927.
11 Michael Berlin, 'Guilds in Decline? London Livery Companies and the Rise of a Liberal Economy, 1600–1800', in *Guilds, Innovation and the European Economy, 1400–1800*, ed. S.R. Epstein and Maarten Prak, Cambridge and New York (Cambridge University Press) 2008, pp. 316–41, on p. 327.
12 *Ibid.*, pp. 322–25.
13 *Ibid.*, p. 318.
14 William Herbert, *The History of the Twelve Great Livery Companies of London*, London (W. Herbert) 1837, vol. 1, p. 176.
15 See Berlin, 'Guilds in Decline?', p. 320.
16 *Ibid.*, p. 321.
17 *Ibid.*
18 *Ibid.*, p. 325.
19 *Ibid.*
20 Steve Rappaport, *Worlds within Worlds: Structures of Life in Sixteenth-Century London*, Cambridge and New York (Cambridge University Press) 1989; Ian W. Archer, *The Pursuit of Stability: Social Relations in Elizabethan London*, Cambridge and New York (Cambridge University Press) 1991.
21 Rappaport, *Worlds within Worlds*, p. 214.
22 Gadd and Wallis, 'Introduction', p. 3.
23 *Ibid.*
24 *Ibid.*, p. 2.
25 Priscilla Metcalf, *The Halls of the Fishmongers' Company: An Architectural History of a Riverside Site*, London (Phillimore) 1977, p. 4.
26 Ian Archer, review of *The Mercers' Hall*, *Urban History*, vol. 21, no. 1, April 1994, pp. 154–55; Jean Imray, *The Mercers' Hall*, ed. Ann Saunders, with an introduction by Derek Keene, London (London Topographical Society) 1991.
27 Ian Archer, 'The Livery Companies and Charity in the Sixteenth and Seventeenth Centuries', in *Guilds, Society and Economy in London, 1450–1800*, ed. Ian Anders Gadd and Patrick Wallis, London (Centre for Metropolitan History, Institute of Historical Research in association with Guildhall Library) 2002, pp. 15–28, on p. 15.
28 See Gadd and Wallis, 'Introduction', p. 4.
29 See John Schofield, *The Building of London: From the Conquest to the Great Fire*, London (British Museum Publications in association with the Museum of London) 1984, p. 115.
30 MC, Acts of Court 1631–37, fol. 242r, February 1636/37.
31 Ian Munro, *The Figure of the Crowd in Early Modern London: The City and Its Double*, New York and Basingstoke (Palgrave Macmillan) 2005, p. 53.
32 BS B/1/3, fols. 196–97, June 1604.
33 See Joseph P. Ward, *Metropolitan Communities: Trade Guilds, Identity, and Change in Early Modern London*, Stanford, Calif. (Stanford University Press) 1997, p. 83.
34 Adrian Johns, *The Nature of the Book: Print and Knowledge in the Making*, Chicago (University of Chicago Press) 1998, p. 198.
35 Robert Tittler, 'Portraiture, Precedence and Politics amongst the London Liveries, *c.* 1540–1640', *Urban History*, vol. 35, no. 3, December 2008, pp. 349–62, on p. 349.
36 See Phil Withington, *The Politics of Commonwealth: Citizens and Freemen in Early Modern England*, Cambridge (Cambridge University Press) 2005, p. 10.
37 John Stow, *A Survey of London: Written in the Year 1598*, with an introduction by Antonia Fraser, Stroud (Sutton) 2005, p. 415.
38 John Stow, *The Survey of London*, London 1633, pp. 600–701.
39 *Ibid.*, p. 698.

40 See Sally Jeffery, *The Mansion House*, Chichester (Phillimore for the Corporation of London) 1993, p. 1.
41 Lord Rochester, 'The History of Insipids; A Lampoon', 1676; see Withington, *Politics of Commonwealth*, p. 12.
42 See Tittler, 'Portraiture, Precedence and Politics', p. 358.
43 John Stow, quoted in M.J. Power, 'The Social Topography of Restoration London', in *London, 1500–1700: The Making of the Metropolis*, ed. A.L. Beier and Roger Finlay, Harlow (Longman) 1986, pp. 199–223, on p. 199.
44 John Schofield, 'The Topography and Buildings of London, ca. 1600', in *Material London, ca. 1600*, ed. Lena Cowen Orlin, Philadelphia (University of Pennsylvania Press) 2000, pp. 296–321, on p. 310.
45 See *The City of London: A Record of Destruction and Survival … Presented in 1947*, London (Architectural Press for the Corporation of London) 1951, pp. 130–34. The Brewers' Company, for example, purchased the freehold of its site from the Dean and Chapter of St Paul's Cathedral as late as 1860, more than 400 years after it first occupied premises there.
46 See John Schofield, *Medieval London Houses*, New Haven, Conn., and London (Yale University Press) 1995, p. 44; Katherine Giles, 'The "Familiar" Fraternity: The Appropriation and Consumption of Medieval Guildhalls in Early Modern York', in *The Familiar Past? Archaeologies of Later Historical Britain*, ed. Sarah Tarlow and Susie West, London and New York (Routledge) 1999, pp. 87–102, on p. 90.
47 See Robert Scourfield, 'The Livery Company Hall, 1536–1666', MA diss., Courtauld Institute of Art, University of London, 1993, pp. 2–5.
48 See Ian W. Archer, 'The Arts and Acts of Memorialization in Early Modern London', in *Imagining Early Modern London: Perceptions and Portrayals of the City from Stow to Strype, 1598–1720*, ed. J.F. Merritt, Cambridge and New York (Cambridge University Press) 2001, pp. 89–113, on pp. 98–99.
49 GL MS 5445/21, fol. 55r, 24 February 1671/72.
50 BS B/1/4, fol. 78, October 1609; my italics.
51 Helen Collins, *Edward Jerman, 1605–1668: The Metamorphosis of a Master-Craftsman*, Cambridge (Lutterworth) 2004, p. 20.
52 Bradley and Pevsner, *London 1*, p. 373.
53 See Withington, *Politics of Commonwealth*, p. 87.
54 Collins, *Edward Jerman*, p. 19.
55 See Schofield, *The Building of London*, pp. 117–18.
56 See MC, Acts of Court 1631–37, fol. 36r, 25 June 1632; GL MS 6153/4, fol. 10r, 11 August 1668.
57 See James Stevens Curl, *The Honourable the Irish Society and the Plantation of Ulster, 1608–2000*, Chichester (Phillimore) 2000.

Overleaf: The Great Hall, Guildhall. This vast, Grade I-listed space has been the setting for the annual Lord Mayor's Banquet since 1502. The Court of Common Council convenes here nine times a year, and it is also where liverymen meet biannually in gatherings known as Common Hall to elect the new Sheriffs and the new Lord Mayor.

MAP OF THE CITY OF LONDON

showing extant Livery Halls

Contains OS data © Crown copyright and database right 2016

KEY

1 APOTHECARIES' HALL
Black Friars Lane, EC4

2 ARMOURERS' HALL
81 Coleman Street, EC2

3 BAKERS' HALL
9 Harp Lane, EC3

4 BARBER-SURGEONS' HALL
Monkwell Square, Wood Street, EC2

5 BREWERS' HALL
Aldermanbury Square, EC2

6 BUTCHERS' HALL
87 Bartholomew Close, EC1

7 CARPENTERS' HALL
1 Throgmorton Avenue, EC2

8 CLOTHWORKERS' HALL
Dunster Court, Mincing Lane, EC3

9 COOPERS' HALL
13 Devonshire Square, EC2

10 CUTLERS' HALL
4 Warwick Lane, EC4

11 DRAPERS' HALL
Throgmorton Avenue, EC2

12 DYERS' HALL
11–13 Dowgate Hill, EC4

13 FARMERS' AND FLETCHERS HALL, 3 Cloth Street, EC1

14 FISHMONGERS' HALL
London Bridge, EC4

15 FOUNDERS' HALL
1 Cloth Fair, EC1

16 FURNITURE MAKERS' HALL
12 Austin Friars, EC2

17 GIRDLERS' HALL
Basinghall Avenue, EC2

18 GLAZIERS' HALL
9 Montague Close, SE1

19 GOLDSMITHS' HALL
Foster Lane, EC2

20 GROCERS' HALL
Princes Street, EC2

21 HABERDASHERS' HALL
18 West Smithfield, EC1

22 HQS *WELLINGTON*
(Master Mariners' Company)
Temple Stairs, Victoria Embankment, WC2

23 INFORMATION TECHNOLOGISTS' HALL
39a Bartholomew Close, EC1

24 INNHOLDERS' HALL
30 College Street, EC4

25 IRONMONGERS' HALL
Shaftesbury Place, EC2

26 LEATHERSELLERS' HALL
7 St Helen's Place, EC3

27 MERCERS' HALL
Ironmonger Lane, EC2

28 MERCHANT TAYLORS' HALL
30 Threadneedle Street, EC2

29 PAINTERS' HALL
9 Little Trinity Lane, EC4

30 PEWTERERS' HALL
Oat Lane, EC2

31 PLAISTERERS' HALL
1 London Wall, EC2

32 THE PROOF HOUSE
(Gunmakers' Company)
48–50 Commercial Road, E1

33 SADDLERS' HALL
40 Gutter Lane, EC2

34 SALTERS' HALL
4 London Wall Place, EC2

35 SKINNERS' HALL
8½ Dowgate Hill, EC4

36 STATIONERS' HALL
Ave Maria Lane, EC4

37 TALLOW CHANDLERS' HALL
4 Dowgate Hill, EC4

38 VINTNERS' HALL
68 Upper Thames Street, EC4

39 WATERMEN'S HALL
16–18 St Mary at Hill, EC3

40 WAX CHANDLERS' HALL
6 Gresham Street, EC2

THE LIVERY HALLS

Henry Russell

The forty extant Livery Halls that follow are arranged in order of Company precedence. (Note that each year the Merchant Taylors' Company and the Skinners' Company swap their positions – sixth or seventh – in the order of precedence.) The information given at the head of each entry lists the name of the Livery Hall, the name of the Livery Company (or Companies) that resides there, the Company's position in the order of precedence, and the listed and/or scheduled ancient monument status of the Hall, if applicable.

References to Bradley and Pevsner are to *London 1: The City of London* (pp. 373–412), by Simon Bradley and Nikolaus Pevsner, originally published by Penguin in 1997 as part of the 'Buildings of England' series.

MERCERS' HALL

THE WORSHIPFUL COMPANY OF MERCERS
ORDER OF PRECEDENCE: 1ST

The stained-glass windows on the Grand Staircase feature full-length figures depicting Elizabeth I and Richard II on either side of an image of Thomas Becket.

The earliest mercers were traders in any commodity – the English word comes via medieval French from the Latin noun *merx*, meaning 'merchandise' – but eventually they specialized in the exportation of English wool and the importation from Europe of silk, velvet and other luxurious fabrics.

There is known to have been a prosperous mercer named Serlo working from London premises, possibly in Cheapside, in 1235, and some indications that other organized practitioners of the trade were in the City as early as 1137. The oldest surviving evidence of a mercers' organization is a record of a meeting in 1348 in which they refer to themselves as a 'company' and a 'mistery'.[1]

Over the following two years the Black Death killed around 40 per cent of the population of England; many if not most of the mercers were among its victims. The company's recovery, though slow, was achieved through an astute recruitment policy aimed at attracting the well heeled and men of good birth. By 1394 the Mercers had distanced themselves sufficiently from hawkers, pedlars and other disreputable pliers of cognate trades for Richard II to award them a Royal Charter, under the terms of which they were allowed to conduct themselves as a business known as a perpetual commonality and to own and manage land. (The Charter also stipulated that the Company should make adequate provision for those of its members who fell on hard times.)

By the end of the Middle Ages the Mercers had expanded into the retail selling of almost anything that could be weighed on their 'little beam'; anything too big for these scales had to be balanced on the 'great beam' (aka the King's Beam) of the Grocers' Company.

The Mercers' late fourteenth-century meetings were held in a building at what is now the junction of Old Jewry and Poultry that was then part of the Hospital of the Knights of St Thomas of Canterbury at Acre. The link between the holy order and the Company requires some explanation. The Knights formed their society after helping Richard I to capture the Levantine city in 1191 during the Third Crusade. They named themselves in honour of Thomas Becket, the Archbishop of Canterbury martyred in 1170 (killed by soldiers of Henry II) and canonized only two years later. In 1228 the Knights set up their London headquarters at the church that had been constructed on the site of the house where Becket

was born. In 1330 the Knights demilitarized and became Augustinian friars who divided their time between pious contemplation and charitable work. The Mercers used the Hospital as a meeting place until the early sixteenth century, when they concluded negotiations with the Hospital, which they were subsidizing financially, to purchase a small plot in Cheapside next to the Hospital church. There, from 1517, they built a Hall of their own with a Chapel beneath it: the former was completed in 1522, and the latter was consecrated in 1524. Monks and merchants then coexisted until 1538, at the height of the Protestant Reformation. The cult of St Thomas of Canterbury was particularly distasteful to Henry VIII because Becket had challenged royal authority. As a consequence, not only was the Hospital of St Thomas of Acre forfeit to the Crown – such seizures were routine during the Dissolution of the monasteries – but the monks also had to remove every likeness of Becket, who was proclaimed a rebel and a traitor and desanctified. His festivals (29 December and 7 July) were banned and images of him destroyed.

Almost immediately the Mercers tried to buy the property. Negotiations were protracted, and it was not until 1542 that the Company acquired the church of St Thomas, the Hospital precinct, the cloisters and the rest of the monastery buildings, as well as some tenements nearby. The purchase also included the church and rectory of St Mary Colechurch on the corner of Cheapside and Old Jewry. The monastic church became the Mercers' Company Chapel. This was the only chapel attached to a Livery Hall that survived the English schism from Rome. The Chapel that the Mercers had built eighteen years previously was converted into two shops. Much of the rest of the site was sold to finance the purchase.

The frontage on the north side of Cheapside was rebuilt in 1632–33, but then the whole Hall was destroyed in the Great Fire of 1666. Work on rebuilding the detached shops in Cheapside began almost immediately; plans for the Hall and Chapel were drawn up in 1668 by Edward Jerman (see p. 27), and they might have been yet another of his projects had he not died later that same year. John Oliver took over as architect. The stonemasons were Thomas Cartwright, Snr, until 1672, and then John and Nicholas Young to the completion of the works in 1682 (see fig. 5 on p. 227). The Chapel porch on Cheapside was rebuilt first, then the Chapel itself, then the Ambulatory and the Hall and the other rooms above. The first court was held on 4 May 1676, while work was still going on.

The splendid mid-19th-century chandeliers in the Livery Hall, with the circular stained-glass window at the east end.

The new Hall was built on top of an aisled Ambulatory where the old church's nave had been; the new Chapel was constructed on the footprint of the former chancel. Money was tight in the eighteenth century, and the buildings were left to deteriorate to such an extent that by the start of the nineteenth century

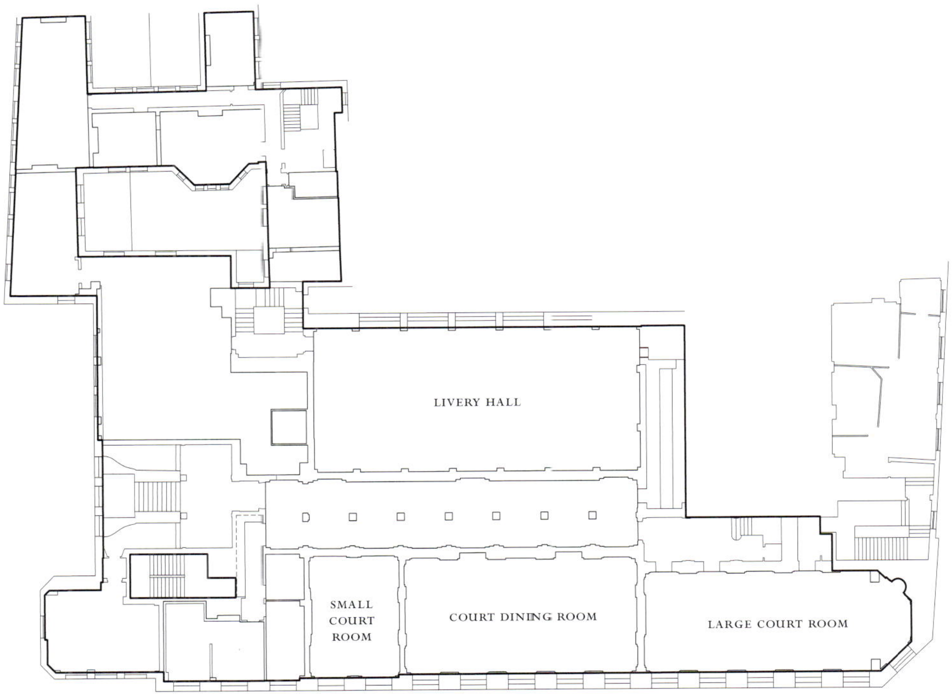

FIRST-FLOOR PLAN

The Livery Hall is notable for its unusual modified barrel-vault ceiling.

Two views of the Court Dining Room, the lower one from the Large Court Room.

The Chapel viewed, below, through the wrought-iron gates at its entrance off the Ambulatory and, opposite, from the gallery off the reception landing.

they were a serious cause for concern, and the consensus view was that the Mercers should demolish the premises and start again. Eventually, a more modest programme of works was implemented. Between 1878 and 1881 George Barnes Williams rebuilt the Cheapside façade, the seventeenth-century frontispiece of which was moved to Swanage, Dorset, where it was re-erected as the entrance to the town hall and remains *in situ* to this day (see fig. 30 on p. 247). Meanwhile, the interiors of Mercers' Hall were redecorated by J.G. Crace (1809–1889), a leading designer of the period who had been responsible for the Waterloo Chamber at Windsor Castle and who worked with Augustus Pugin on the Houses of Parliament and the Medieval Court at the Great Exhibition of 1851. Also at this time, the Grand Staircase was installed to the west of the Cheapside entrance.

In 1926 a survey of the Hall conducted by Sir Frank Baines found deathwatch beetle and dry rot running amok in the Hall's timbers; their removal involved major structural works that were not completed until 1930.

And then the second Hall was almost totally obliterated by fire during a Luftwaffe air raid on the night of 10–11 May 1941. All that escaped the flames were the furniture, artworks and archives, which had been presciently removed from the building at the start of the conflict.

Reconstruction after the Second World War, begun in 1954 and completed in 1958, adhered to the broad seventeenth-century outline, but modern measurement devices, more accurate than those of the Carolean age, regularized its dimensions. The most noticeable change was the relocation of the main entrance and the Grand Staircase from Cheapside to Ironmonger Lane. The new exterior was by E. Noel Clifton of Gunton & Gunton; the interiors were the work of H.H. Martyn & Co., of Cheltenham, Gloucestershire.

On the ground floor of the modern building are the Ambulatory and the Chapel. The second floor contains the Library, the Master's flat, the Clerk's flat and six guest bedrooms. Along the length of the first floor is a broad-aisled reception corridor with Doric columns lined up noticeably off-centre. Above this walkway on the southern side is a gallery; on the northern side is the Livery Hall, with mahogany-panelled walls, a circular stained-glass window at one end, a minstrels' gallery at the other end and a plasterwork ceiling that is an unusual variation of the classic barrel vault – a shape that more resembles an upturned bowl than the traditional keg. In the centre of the roof is a rectangular skylight. Also here are ten late eighteenth-century carved swags of unknown origin in the style of Grinling Gibbons.

Enfiladed along the southern side of the corridor are three other public rooms, overlooking Cheapside: the Large Court Room; the Court Dining Room, with mahogany panelling; and the Small Court Room, with white sycamore panelling.

Off the reception landing a gallery overlooks the Chapel, the double height and square ground plan of which broadly replicate the layout of the seventeenth-century Hall. Here are two great monuments that have survived from the previous buildings. One is a limestone effigy of the dead Christ recumbent on an Imperial robe. Discovered in 1953 beneath ancient overlying debris, this work is possibly early sixteenth-century Flemish (and indeed is, if its resemblance to a sculpture in Mainz Cathedral is anything to go by). The other is a recumbent alabaster male effigy inscribed with the legend 'Richard Fishborne Mercer A Worthy Benefactor Dyed 3 April 1625'.

Most of the Chapel's other features are post-war creations in seventeenth-century style; the most striking part of it that is unmistakably and unapologetically modern is the font, a big cylindrical creation designed by H.O. Corfiato and Sidney Loweth and installed in 1958.

A more recent round of Chapel refurbishment in 2008 included new seats, in every one of which was incorporated an individually carved representation by Colin Mantripp of the Mercers' emblem, the Maiden.

On the landing of the ceremonial stairs are three stained-glass windows that were part of Crace's nineteenth-century restoration programme: two full-length figures of monarchs and an image of Becket. The upper part of the latter is a 1957 resetting by H.L. Pawle of the 1880 work by Heaton, Butler & Bayne that was in the pre-war Livery Hall. On the half-landing of the staircase to the upper gallery a marquetry overmantel stands inside a thickly carved frame with garlands held in the beaks of twin eagles. In the centre is a further image of the Maiden, here in the form of a badge carved in 1682–83 by John Baker.

NOTE

1 Anne F. Sutton, *The Mercery of London: Trade, Goods and People, 1130–1578*, Aldershot (Ashgate) 2005.

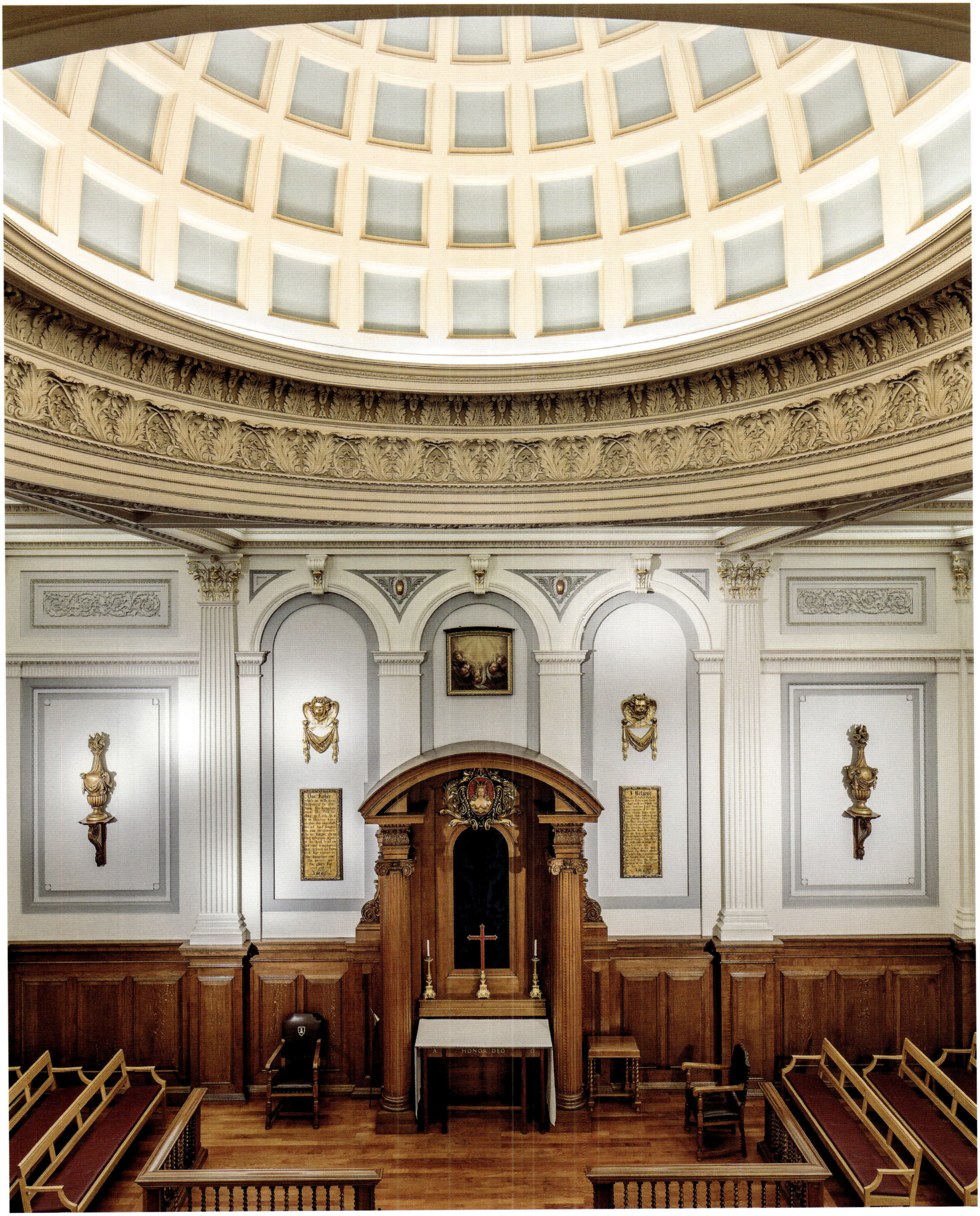

GROCERS' HALL

THE WORSHIPFUL COMPANY OF GROCERS
ORDER OF PRECEDENCE: 2ND

The earliest reference to what became the Grocers' Company is in 1180, during the reign of Henry II, when the Guild of Pepperers was entrusted with the duty of *garbling* (in its original sense, preventing the adulteration of spices and drugs; the modern sense of mixing up or confusing language is much later, *c.* 1680). In 1345 these Pepperers established a fraternity, which in 1376 became the Worshipful Company of Grocers of London. Their trade's new name, derived from the medieval Latin *grossarius*, is a reference to practitioners' responsibility for the King's Beam – scales that weighed goods by *aver-do-poys* or *peso gross*. A grocer was one concerned with gross weight long before the word acquired its current meaning, according to the *Oxford English Dictionary*: 'A person who sells food and small household goods.'

The Grocers' earliest meeting places included the house of the Abbot of Bury (Bury St Edmunds, Suffolk) in St Mary Axe and later the house of the Abbot of St Cross. In 1383 they settled in Bucklersbury, where they rented offices until 1427. In the latter year they purchased the land on which they have remained ever since, where at the time stood a town house with a large garden. In order to own property the Company required incorporation, and this was granted to it by Henry VI in 1429.

Above: A cameo camel on a doorknob. Images of the ship of the desert are featured throughout the Hall; they are inspired by the creature that surmounts the Grocers' heraldic blazon (see also p. 48).

Right: The main entrance to Grocers' Hall is in a large secluded courtyard off Princes Street. The rebuild in the late 1960s incorporated the remaining part of the 19th-century façade.

The Grocers then demolished the existing building, which had previously belonged to the Fitz-Walter family, and by 1433 had built in its place a new Hall entirely to their own specifications. This was an unusual practice for Livery Companies of the period, most of which modified or adapted themselves to whatever buildings they acquired. The principal construction material was ragstone from Merstham, Surrey, with Flanders bricks and stone from Stapleton, Yorkshire, in the window jambs and sills.[1]

Over the next 200 years the Grocers made various embellishments and improvements to their Hall, including the replacement of the stone around the windows with an expensive equivalent specially imported from Caen, Normandy. But the most noteworthy – and with the benefit of hindsight most bitterly ironic – change was the installation in 1631 of wooden floorboards in the Great Parlour because the rushes that had previously been strewn underfoot there had come to be regarded as a fire hazard. The conflagration of September 1666 made no such fine material distinctions, destroying most things in its path, including 'every particle'[2] of the Grocers' Hall and their rental properties; all that survived were the Company records, which were stored in a turret in the garden.

The Grocers struggled to finance reconstruction, but their second Hall was eventually rebuilt in the shell of its fifteenth-century predecessor by the stonemasons Edward Pearce (or Pierce; *c.* 1635–1695) and Richard Crooke. It was completed in the autumn of 1681 and further enlarged in the following year. In 1694 the Company leased the building to the newly formed Bank of England, of which the first governor was a grocer, Sir John Houblon (1632–1712). Forty years later the tenants moved to a new place of their own in Threadneedle Street, but the Grocers' joy at reoccupying their home lasted only until they discovered the extent of its decay. After years of prevarication, during which various renovation proposals were shelved on grounds of cost, a crisis came in 1798, when the roof and lantern were found to be in imminent danger of collapse.

Thomas Leverton (*c.* 1743–1824), the Company Surveyor, immediately set about turning the post-Fire Hall into what was later described as 'a brick building

The foot of the main staircase in the reception area.

with stone facings (including a rusticated basement level and Tuscan pilasters)'.[3] It was during these works that the Grocers gave up much of their garden, some of which was covered by John Soane's Bank of England extension and some of which was subsumed by a realignment of Princes Street.

Leverton completed his task in 1802. What at first seemed remarkable alacrity was re-evaluated as undue haste when only six years later great cracks were discovered where the new buildings had been mounted on the foundations of the old. Cost-conscious and cash-strapped, the Grocers carried out only cosmetic repairs that did nothing to arrest further deterioration of the Hall. For their quincentenary celebrations in 1845 they spent considerable sums on plate (inter alia) that would perhaps have been better directed into reinforcing the fabric of their buildings, but in 1864 they finally addressed the most pressing matter on their agenda and invited some of the most distinguished architects of their era to outline their visions for a new Hall.

Among the respondents were George Gilbert Scott (1811–1878), then working on the Midland Grand Hotel at St Pancras railway station, and Edward Barry (1830–1880), designer in 1857 of the theatre of the Royal Italian Opera (now the Royal Opera House, Covent Garden), which replaced Robert Smirke's building destroyed by fire in the previous year. For whatever reason, the Grocers decided that none of these plans was viable or desirable, and in 1875 began investigating the possibility of a move to new premises; this scheme, too, came to naught.

In 1887 the Grocers finally resolved to stop squandering their financial resources on superficial repairs and to clear the ground for an all-new Hall. This work, supervised by the Company Surveyor, Henry Cowell Boyes (1846/47–1900), began in the following year, and the foundation stone of the new structure was laid in 1889. The first dinner in the completed Livery Hall was held on 18 January 1893.

On 19 July 1944 the fourth Hall was hit by a German flying bomb, which destroyed the offices of the Clerk and the Beadle, the Library, the Inner Drawing Room and some of the back rooms: the damage was fearful but nevertheless, by the standards that obtained in the City of London during the Second World War, the Grocers got off comparatively lightly.

What the Nazis failed to manage was later achieved by an oversight. On the night of 22 September 1965, an

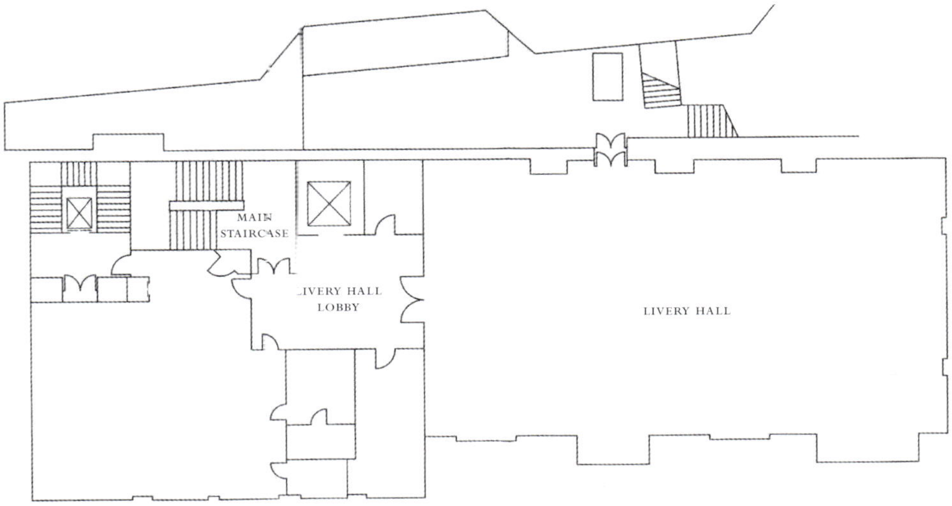

FIRST-FLOOR PLAN

The Livery Hall. The wrought-iron screen by Thomas Collins (opposite), dating from the early 1680s, is the only surviving remnant of the Stuart-period furnishings.

electric light left on beneath an oak lintel in a cupboard under the Grand Staircase[4] caused what has been described as the biggest fire in the City of London since the Blitz: 82 fire engines and up to 200 firemen took more than two hours to bring it under control; four firefighters were injured, a dog was suffocated and the building was almost completely destroyed.

For the next five years the Grocers were homeless; they held events in other Companies' Halls, most frequently those of the Mercers and the Saddlers. Meanwhile, a new Grocers' Hall, the Company's fifth, was constructed on the site of the old one. Designed by Beard, Bennett, Wilkins & Partners and built by A.E. Symes Ltd, it incorporated an upper floor of offices. Opened in 1970 by Queen Elizabeth The Queen Mother, it is a synthesis of ancient and modern – surviving medieval and Renaissance artefacts in late twentieth-century frames.

This juxtaposition is evident from the outset: the frontage incorporates part of Boyes's Victorian red-brick façade, with pedimented flat bays and stone dressings in seventeenth-century Netherlandish style, alongside the modern part of plain stone. By the entrance, the statue of St Anthony the Great is also a survivor from the previous Hall.

The Piper Room, off the Entrance Hall, is named after the creator of the tapestries that line its walls. John Piper first came to prominence in the 1950s as the designer, with Patrick Reyntiens, of the stained-glass Baptistery window in Coventry Cathedral.

Adjacent to the Entrance Hall is a reception room named after the artist John Piper (1903–1992), creator in 1968 of the three colourful Aubusson tapestries therein that depict the foreign foodstuffs and spices of which the Grocers were wholesalers in the Middle Ages. On the lower ground floor are cloakrooms, the Wine Cellar and the Plate Room.

On the first floor, the walls of the Livery Hall are lined with crimson silk; the ceiling is hung with three Venetian chandeliers; Simon Bradley and Nikolaus Pevsner fairly describe the overall effect as 'discreetly modern'. Near the entrance, the remains of a wrought-iron screen by Thomas Collins date from 1682–83.

On the second floor are three rooms. The Library has a fireplace dating from around 1800 and featuring the Company's arms; it was rediscovered in 1966 and is believed to come from Leverton's Hall. Among the books here are copies of three historic versions of the Bible: the so-called Bug Bible of 1537, in which the unfortunate Richard Grafton misprinted Psalm 91:5; and the Great Bibles of 1540 and 1541, the first authorized versions of the text after the English Reformation.

The highlights of the Court Room are a coloured marble fireplace of around 1800, a bust of William Pitt the Younger by Joseph Nollekens (1737–1823), an oval table of Honduras mahogany and the restored Master's chair of carved Spanish mahogany.

The Court Dining Room has segment-headed blind recesses. It contains the Master's small chair of 1750 and some furniture that strictly pre-dates the 1965 fire but which has been extensively restored. Also worthy of note are the Rockingham porcelain pieces and glassware from the Walter Hale collection. On the landing are fragments of the Company's Charters; on the walls of the staircase are cases containing other damaged Charters.

NOTES

1 See John Schofield, 'The Construction of Medieval and Tudor Houses in London', *Construction History*, vol. 7, 1991, p. 3.
2 Helen Clifford, *The History of the Grocers' Company Through Its Collection of Silver and Glass*, London (The Worshipful Company of Grocers) 2014.
3 Thomas Allen and Thomas Wright, *The History and Antiquities of London, Westminster, Southwark and Parts Adjacent*, vol. 3, London (George Virtue) 1839.
4 The bitter irony of this is that during the previous refurbishment of the Grocers' Hall, the old marble staircase had been replaced by a wooden structure on cost grounds.

The main staircase is decorated with further tapestries and some of the Company's historic Royal Charters.

DRAPERS' HALL

THE WORSHIPFUL COMPANY OF DRAPERS
ORDER OF PRECEDENCE: 3RD
GRADE II* LISTED

The modern Drapers' Hall stands on the site of a turreted stone mansion that the Company purchased from Henry VIII in 1543, three years after its original owner, Thomas Cromwell, was beheaded. It had been privately built in 1532 for the soon-to-be Chancellor of the Exchequer by James Nedeham (or Needham), Master Carpenter of the Royal Works, designer of the roof of the Great Hall at Hampton Court.

Of this structure and its contents, all that survived the Great Fire of 1666 were the plate and the archives, which were stored in a sewer out of the blaze. The replacement buildings, with a spacious quadrangle, an ambulatory of intricately ornamented arches, and views to the distant hills of Hampstead and Highgate, were commenced in 1668 by the bricklayer Thomas Netheway, working to designs by Edward Jerman, the architect of, among numerous replacement Livery Company buildings, the recently rebuilt Fishmongers' Hall. Extensive further damage was caused by a fire in 1772 that broke out in the vaults beneath the Hall, which were at the time being leased to tenants as storage cellars.

Above: The shield of the Drapers' coat of arms, as depicted in the alabaster-and-marble decoration on the main landing.

Right: The main entrance to Drapers' Hall, on Throgmorton Street. Designed by Sir Thomas Graham Jackson, it incorporates mighty atlantes by Henry Pegram.

Part of the Hall's frontage was rebuilt in the 1860s to an Adam-style design by the Company Surveyor, Herbert Williams (1812/13–1873). The remainder of the frontage was modified in the 1860s and 1890s into polished shop fronts in order to maximize the lettable street frontage. The overall result is a nostalgic iteration of the style of the free commercial Northern Renaissance. Continuity between the two nineteenth-century projects was provided by Charles Reilly, Snr (1844/45–1928), who worked on both of them, designing the red-brick and Portland stone façade of the Hall himself, and incorporating the Hall's front door by Sir Thomas Graham Jackson (1835–1924).

This gated entrance on Throgmorton Street, framed by a grand aedicule, comprises an open pediment with the Drapers' coat of arms supported by two massive atlantes. The work of Henry Pegram (1862–1937), a leading figure in the New Sculpture movement, these male caryatids wear turbans that represent the Company's main trade, woollen cloth. (It is noteworthy that the English word 'draper' is derived from the Old French *draperie*, which meant 'clothwork'.)

The Hall is built around a small courtyard, at the centre of which a pond with a statue – of a boy pulling a thorn from the sole of his foot – reputedly occupies the same position as a water feature in the pre-Great Fire layout. This quadrangle was rebuilt in 1869 to another Williams design. The allegorical carvings by Edward Wyon (1811–1885) in the tympana of the arches depict Commerce, the Continents, Religion and Science. Behind the Hall is a garden with mulberry trees; the gates, railings and walls of this area were designed in the 1970s by the Gothic Revivalist Stephen Dykes Bower (1903–1994).

Inside the building there is first a long corridor, designed again by Jackson. The dark oak panelling along its length is lit via a stained-glass window bearing the coats of arms of four great English mariners: Sir Francis Drake, Vice Admiral Viscount Nelson, Sir Walter Raleigh and John Jervis, 1st Earl of St Vincent. The portraits along the walls depict various descendants of William Lambarde (1536–1601), founder in 1576 of the Queen Elizabeth College almshouses in Greenwich.

Jackson's magnificent Italianate staircase is lined with Ionic columns of breccia marble and walls of green-and-white banded cipollino from the Greek island of Euboea; the doorcases are of Portuguese encarnado marble, and the balustrade is of finely carved alabaster.

The main staircase and landing. The central feature is a stained-glass window by Burlison & Grylls depicting the royal, City and Drapers' coats of arms, surrounded by the arms of several significant medieval Drapers and benefactors of the Company.

At the foot of the stairwell is an 1818 statue by Rudolph Schadow (1786–1822) of a girl fastening her sandal; this is a version of another in Berlin (*Die Sandalenbinderin*) by the same sculptor. On the landing are an 1825 fireplace with a frieze, and busts by John Francis (1780–1861), acquired by the Drapers in 1852, of William IV; his brother Frederick, Duke of York; Queen Victoria and Prince Albert. From the ceiling of the staircase hangs a 5000-piece glass chandelier.

The stained-glass window – damaged by enemy action during the Second World War but fully restored thereafter – bears various coats of arms: those of the Company, the City and the British sovereign, together with the heraldic devices of benefactors and of Drapers who became Lord Mayor of London.

At the top of the stairs, three rooms lead off the landing: straight ahead, the Court Room; to the right, the Court Drawing Room; to the left, the Court Dining Room.

In the Court Room – a happy synthesis of old and new – details seem to vie for the viewer's attention. The eighteenth-century wainscot was effectively complemented, first by chandeliers by John Blades (*c.* 1751–1829), purchased and installed in 1797; then with marble chimney pieces and a cornice based by Williams and J.D. Crace (1838–1919) on a design of the 1770s by George Richardson (d. *c.* 1813); and then in the 1970s by the green-and-gold ceiling with

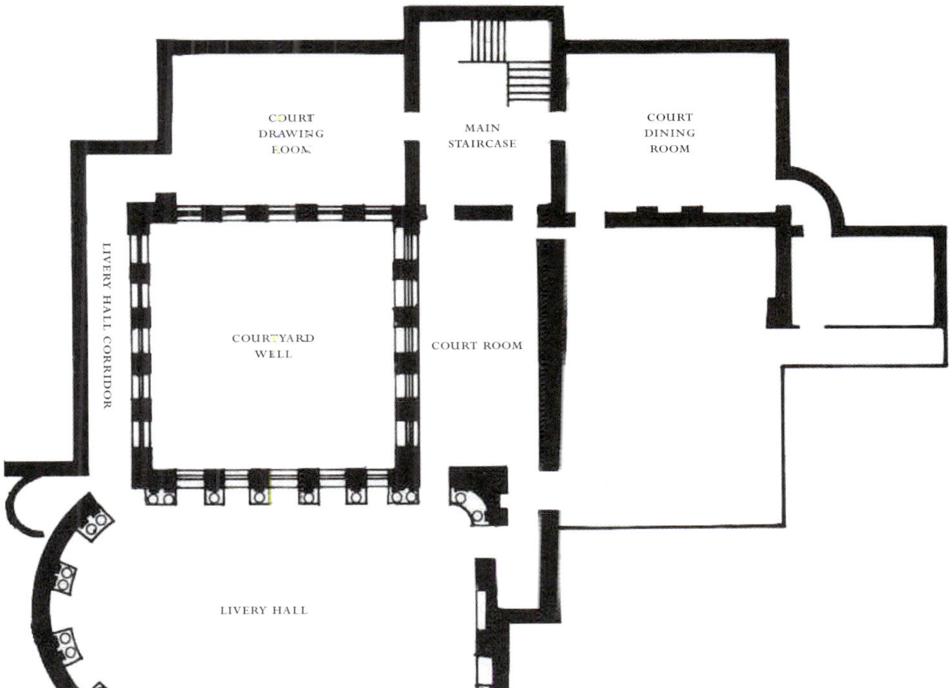

FIRST-FLOOR PLAN

The Livery Hall was altered in size and form in the 1860s and 1890s. The ceiling paintings by Herbert James Draper (top), completed between 1903 and 1910, depict scenes from A Midsummer Night's Dream *and* The Tempest. *The sequence of royal portraits (above) starts with William III and finishes with Edward VII.*

The Court Drawing Room was designed by J.D. Crace in 1868. Here hang The Gates of Dawn *by Herbert James Draper and a pair of magnificent Perry & Co. chandeliers. The room also features the sculpture* The Shepherd Boy *by Bertel Thorvaldsen (bottom).*

Jacobeanesque pendants. The late eighteenth-century-style panelling (between the dado rail and the frieze) was installed between 1910 and 1915 by White, Allom & Company. On the walls are portraits of Nelson, the Duke of Wellington, and an unknown lady and child. Also here are two tapestries of Gobelin silk, woven in 1773–74 and depicting episodes from the legend of Jason and the Golden Fleece.

The Court Drawing Room remains much as Crace designed, decorated and furnished it in the 1860s, although the light green-and-gold colour scheme is again the work of White, Allom. The ornate pulvinated frieze, reminiscent of and possibly inspired by that of the Pantheon in Rome, is surmounted by blind lunettes beneath a coffered stucco ceiling. The white marble chimney piece is the highest of High Victorian in the manner of Michelangelo. The Aubusson-style carpet is a 1925 commission by Morris & Co. *The Gates of Dawn*, by the Classicist Herbert James Draper (1863/64–1920), was painted in 1900 to mark the start of the twentieth century. Among the sculpture here are busts of Elizabeth II (by Lorne McKean) and Prince Charles (by Anita Lafford), and *The Shepherd Boy* by Bertel Thorvaldsen.

Another of Jackson's alterations to the seventeenth-century buildings, the Livery Hall Corridor – a corridor between the Court Drawing Room and the Livery Hall – is flanked by oak panels with carved depictions of drapers and associated crafts. At the western end, a stained-glass window bears the coats of arms of four future monarchs who were granted the Freedom of the Company: Prince William of Orange (later William III), Prince Albert (George VI) and Princess Elizabeth (Elizabeth II) of England or the United Kingdom, and Prince Carl of Denmark (Haakon VII of Norway). (The glass also gives the dates on which each royal was admitted: purely by chance, at the time of their birth none of these inductees was first in line to their nation's throne.) The glass pane bearing the Company's coat of arms was engraved by Laurence Whistler (1912–2000) in 1964 to commemorate the 600th anniversary of the grant of the Company's first Royal Charter.

The double-height Livery Hall is a composite work of three architects. Williams enlarged the room to its present size in the 1860s and is responsible for everything between the floor and the upper entablature. Jackson and Reilly supplied the arcaded upper walls and the ceiling. The latter, inspired by the work of Inigo

The Court Dining Room was redesigned by Crace in 1869. The story of Jason and the Golden Fleece forms the subject of both the ceiling painting by Félix-Joseph Barrias (commissioned in 1869) and the Gobelin tapestries (woven in 1773–74 and purchased by the Company in 1881).

Jones, is an elliptical, low-relief plaster structure pieced out with rectangular end panels, painted by Herbert James Draper between 1903 and 1910 with scenes from Shakespeare's *A Midsummer Night's Dream* and *The Tempest*: the overall theme is the movement of the day.

Around the walls of the Livery Hall, and arranged in pairs around the apsed south end, are twenty-eight Corinthian columns of Devonshire red Ipplepen marble on low pedestals, with capitals in fifteenth-century Italian style. The columns support a balustraded gallery bearing urns and the Company's coat of arms. The room also features a green Genoa marble dado, panelled walls, and full-length royal portraits in the blind bays. At the north end are two sculptures: *Venus* by John Gibson (1790–1866) and *Hypatia* by Richard Belt (1851–1920).

Off the landing to the north is the Court Dining Room. Some of the ceiling fabric is original, from around 1670, but the painting on it of Jason and the Golden Fleece by Félix-Joseph Barrias (1822–1907) and further adornments by Crace were completed in 1869. At the same time, the coving was filled with painted coats of arms; Bradley and Pevsner describe the ceiling cove as having been 'elaborated crashingly insensitively' by Williams, but this seems a harsh assessment of embellishments that are well assimilated into the whole.

The wall tapestries here, like those in the Court Room, are of Gobelin silk, and depict further scenes from the voyages of the *Argo*. Above the chimney piece is a portrait of Elizabeth II by the Russian-born artist Sergei Pavlenko, commissioned by the Drapers in 1998 and unveiled by Her Majesty in 2000. Also worthy of note in this room is the long-case clock of 1715 by Daniel Quare (1648/49–1724), the inventor of the repeating watch mechanism.

The south door of the Court Dining Room leads back on to the landing, thus completing the fourth side of the Drapers' Hall quadrangle.

On the ground floor, to the north of the Hall, is the Wardens' Room, which was converted in 1844 from two counting-houses into a single lounge area. The artefacts displayed here include Richard Roberts's late eighteenth-century design for a Drapers' state barge and group portraits of distinguished Drapers by Norman Hepple (1908–1994) and Andrew Festing (b. 1941). Carefully preserved behind the panelling in the frame of the door from the Wardens' Room corridor into the Clerk's office is some vestigial 1670s brickwork.

FISHMONGERS' HALL

THE WORSHIPFUL COMPANY OF FISHMONGERS
ORDER OF PRECEDENCE: 4TH
GRADE II* LISTED; SCHEDULED ANCIENT MONUMENT

The Fishmongers' arms in stained glass above the main staircase.

There have been administrative bodies of fishmongers since before the Norman Conquest. In the twelfth century there were several such entities, and on his accession in 1154, Henry II granted patents to two of them: the Stock Fishmongers, otherwise known as wet fishmongers, who dealt with cod that had been wind-cured; and the Pessoners, who salted their catches and sold dried fish. A unified, consolidated Company was granted its first Royal Charter by Edward I in 1272; it split into two again in 1364 (*sub regno* Edward III); was reunited in 1433 or 1434, during the reign of Henry VI; divided again in 1512, despite having been granted conjoined Company arms by Henry VIII in the same year; and finally reunited forever in 1536 under the same monarch.

Before their first unification, the two main societies of fishmongers had at various times had six halls – two each in Thames Street, Old Fish Street (now Knightrider Street) and New Fish Street (now the site of the Monument) – but from 1434 their main base was at the north-western corner of London Bridge, on land gifted to them by Sir John Cornwall, 1st Baron Fanhope.

In the sixteenth century the original buildings were reconfigured as a square, three-storey structure with crenellations, turrets and a central gateway on its southern side, facing the Thames; the Livery Hall, on the north side, had a hammer-beam roof and a tall bay window. All of this was burnt down on the first day of the Great Fire of London, 2 September 1666, but thanks to the building's proximity to the water, the Company's most important documents, its iron money chest and its silver were borne away to safety by boat.

The design for a new Hall had to be granted special dispensation by Dr (as he then was) Christopher Wren, Surveyor General to Charles II, because it infringed the river quay in a way proscribed by the 1667 Act for Rebuilding. Completed in 1669, the new Fishmongers' Hall, along with Wren's Custom House at Barking, became one of the first major works of post-Fire reconstruction along the riverside. Larger than its predecessor, the red-brick Hall, with stone dressings, a pedimented centre and twin flights of steps to the riverbank, was designed by Edward Jerman and Thomas Lock, with assistance from Edward Pearce (*c.* 1635–1695) and possibly Robert Hooke or Peter Mills (see fig. 32 on p. 29).

This Hall was modernized between 1788 and 1791 by John Gorham, whose programme of works featured

The riverside façade viewed from Hibernia Chambers, the home of three other Livery Companies (Glaziers, Scientific Instrument Makers and Launderers), on the south bank of the River Thames.

a host of innovations. A terrace replaced the steps, and the roof became one of the first in England to be made of copper rather than of lead. The long upstairs gallery was divided into three rooms: a ladies' tea room, a card room (aka a coffee room) and a drawing room. A new main staircase was installed at the parlour end of the Great Hall, but the 'carved bolection, mouldings [and] raised pannels' of 1670 were retained unaltered.[1]

In 1827 an Act of Parliament empowered the City to take a strip of ground 20 feet (6 m) wide from the eastern edge of the Fishmongers' premises in order to build a new London Bridge 180 feet (55 m) to the west of the troublesome structure that in various forms had straddled the river since the thirteenth century. Prima facie, all that the Company had to sacrifice was the east wall of its dining hall, but the liverymen feared collateral damage during the works, and were unwilling to dwell in future in the shadow of a vast new bridge. What was more, they were already aware that chronic water damage to the interior of their existing premises had made renewal necessary and probably disproportionately expensive. In view of all that, they decided to demolish their Hall and build an entirely new one a little further upstream.

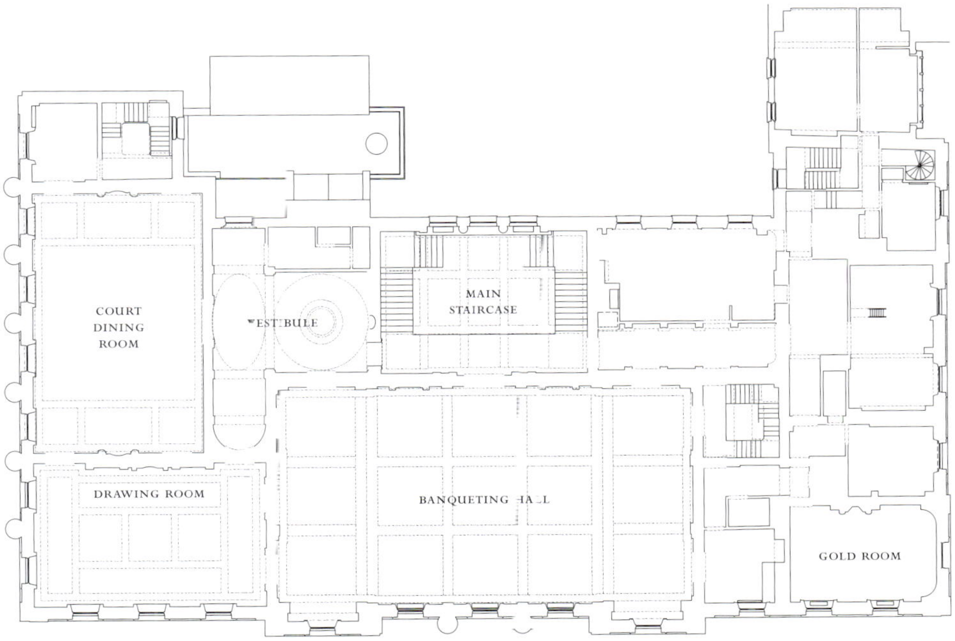

FIRST-FLOOR PLAN

The Banqueting Hall. The stained-glass windows at both ends of the room are post-war replacements for originals destroyed in German air raids. A Charles X bronze-and-ormolu clock sits at the head of the Hall (left), surrounded by some of the Company's finest plate.

Above: *In the Vestibule, the Millennium Chandelier, commissioned by the Company to celebrate the year 2000, is designed to resemble an old light fitting that was damaged in the Blitz.*

Right: *The walls of the Fish Passage, on the ground floor, are lined with Arnold van Haecken's eight-canvas* Wonders of the Deep, *purchased in 1767.*

Opposite: *The Entrance Hall (bottom) leads to the foot of the main staircase (top). The chandelier features 743 fish, one for every year between the granting of the Company's first Royal Charter (1272) and the work's completion (2015). Each fish is made of fine bone china and coated in 24-carat gold.*

A competition in 1831 for the best design was won in the following year by twenty-eight-year-old Henry Roberts (1803–1876), a pupil of Sir Robert Smirke (1780–1867). Smirke had briefly studied under Sir John Soane, and when construction of the new Fishmongers' Hall began, Roberts was assisted by a pupil of his own, twenty-year-old George Gilbert Scott (1811–1878), who would go on to design the Midland Grand Hotel at St Pancras railway station and the Albert Memorial – three linked generations of great British architects.

Constructed by W. & L. (William and Lewis) Cubitt & Co., the new building featured an arcaded base in the manner of a Roman aqueduct, a riverside terrace and a Greek-style main edifice on an iron-girder framework that was similar to that used by Smirke in his façade of the British Museum. The principal building materials were to be Portland stone and the same Devon granite that was used in the new London Bridge. The Hall was completed in spring 1835 and, with the architect supervising the acquisition and installation of fixtures and furnishings, was in use from June of that year.

After the Prime Minister Neville Chamberlain's Munich Agreement with Adolf Hitler in September 1938, the Fishmongers made contingency plans for what to do in the event of armed conflict with Germany. On the day that Britain declared war, 3 September 1939, two pantechnicons removed many articles of value to safe storage in the Kent countryside, while paintings and other treasures too difficult to move were protected in the Hall.

Wise precautions: at around 3.30 am on 9 September 1940, an incendiary bomb fell on Seal House, the next-door building to the west of the Hall; the flames soon spread and took hold of the Fishmongers' roof. By the time the blaze was put out, the riverside range was gutted from the ground up, reduced to no more than a smouldering shell. But otherwise damage was slight – a testament in part to Roberts's solid brick-vaulted floor construction.

Although the damage caused to Fishmongers' Hall by the Nazis was considerably less than that caused to it by the Great Fire, restoration took disproportionately longer: three years in the seventeenth-century case, fourteen years in the post-war period. The process was slowed partly by nationwide economic privations, partly by the requirement that works could proceed only once a Building Licence had been obtained (this form of 'rationing' was finally removed in 1954) and partly also by the sheer complexity of the task.

At the time of publication of the present volume, Fishmongers' Hall remains largely as it was when restoration was completed in 1954. Along the riverfront of Roberts's Hall, the former wharf is surmounted by a granite plinth with seven arches, the central five protruding, the two end structures set back; on top of them is a seven-bay façade punctuated by six giant columns that rise two storeys to a crowning pediment. On the London Bridge Approach side is a symmetrical, two-storey front of Portland stone with eleven bays, five of which protrude slightly beneath the first-floor Banqueting Hall and in one of which (the fourth from the right when viewed from the east) is the main entrance. Above a balustrade is an attic with the Company's arms carved in stone. On the northern flank of the building, along Upper Thames Street, is a gated tradesmen's entrance, behind which are offices by Holford Associates, completed in 1977.

Although the interiors have been several times redecorated, most recently in 1954 by Herbert Austen Hall (1881–1968) of Whinney, Son & Austen Hall, they remain largely as Roberts designed them: neo-Greek. The Court Room, though extensively remodelled in 1951, retains a 1741 broken pediment by Charles Easton above a fireplace with a triton mask and seashell garlands. The fireplace in the adjacent Library has portrait medallions, including an image of Inigo Jones; this piece is eighteenth century, but imported from another building.

The Entrance Hall issues on to a main staircase with iron balusters; one flight divides halfway up at right angles and doubles back on itself to the first floor. On the half-landing is a statue by Edward Pearce of Sir William Walworth, Fishmongers' liveryman and Lord Mayor of London, who helped to suppress the Peasants' Revolt of 1381 by wounding Wat Tyler after the rebel leader had threatened Richard II. Also on the stairs are eighteenth-century wooden panels with carvings of boys on dolphins and stained glass by Hugh Easton (1951).

In the Banqueting Hall, off the landing, the yellow scagliola Corinthian pilasters are modelled on the Choragic Monument of Lysicrates near the Acropolis in Athens. Mounted on them is a coffered elliptical vault that matches the arches of London Bridge. Also noteworthy here are the heraldic glass by Hancock & Rixon, the large mirrors, the reliefs of sea gods in the lunettes, and the minstrels' gallery.

Beyond the T-shaped Vestibule, partly domed and partly tunnel-vaulted in a design that recalls the work of Soane, Roberts's teacher's teacher, are the Drawing Room and the Court Dining Room. Both badly damaged by the Luftwaffe, these rooms are now fully restored and offer wonderful views across and along the Thames. Pride of place in the former space goes to the famous 1955 portrait of Elizabeth II by Pietro Annigoni (1910–1988). Although the roadway over London Bridge is in plain sight and within a stone's throw, there is little or no discernible traffic noise, which, according to the current Head of Collection, is again attributable to the robust design and construction.

NOTE

1 From a billbook of the time, quoted in Priscilla Metcalf, *The Halls of the Fishmongers' Company: An Architectural History of a Riverside Site*, London (Phillimore) 1977, p. 105.

GOLDSMITHS' HALL

THE WORSHIPFUL COMPANY OF GOLDSMITHS
ORDER OF PRECEDENCE: 5TH
GRADE I LISTED

The main façade, on Foster Lane. The palace-like Hall, with its giant columns, occupies an entire block.

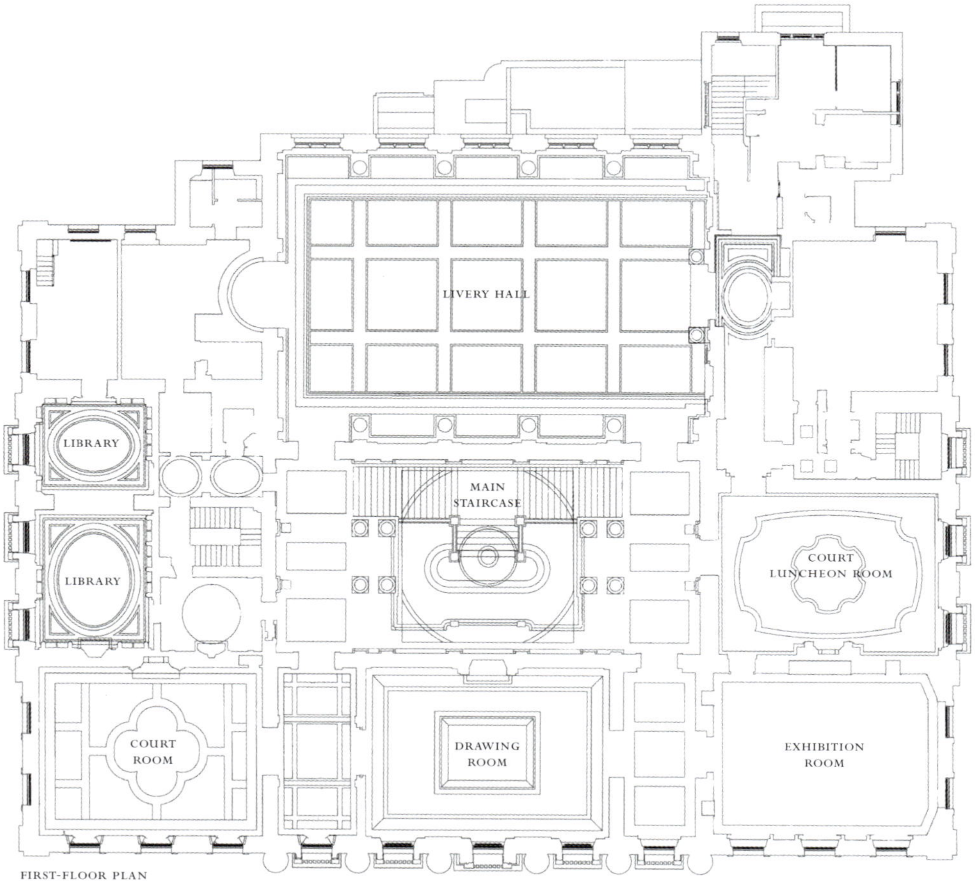

FIRST-FLOOR PLAN

The Goldsmiths have occupied this site, on land now bounded on the north by Gresham Street (formerly Maiden Lane), on the south by Carey Lane, on the east by Gutter Lane and on the west by Foster Lane, since the early Middle Ages. They have been in a single location for longer than any other Livery Company; the current Hall is their third. It is unique in housing the Company's large London Assay Office, which tests and hallmarks precious metals. The term 'hallmark' originates from the marks struck in Goldsmiths' Hall.

The Company was granted its first Royal Charter in 1327 by Edward III. By then the Goldsmiths had been established as a fraternity since no later than the reign of Henry II (1154–89). In 1300 Edward I empowered them to judge the fineness of gold and silver wares: nothing without the Goldsmiths' hallmark (an image of a 'leopart', or part of a lion, which later evolved into a leopard's head) could be classified as genuine. The test at first involved the use of touchstones – small tablets of black stone on which genuine gold and silver would leave traces of a particular shade when rubbed, while base metals and other counterfeit materials would leave traces slightly different in colour. The process was later improved by the addition of acid to the streaks ('the acid test'). Although other assaying techniques such as cupellation became predominant in later centuries, touchstone testing is still carried out at the Assay Office today.

The Goldsmiths would also take a central role in testing the coinage from the Royal Mint through the Trial of the Pyx. Held annually since 1282, originally in Westminster Abbey and since 1871 in Goldsmiths' Hall, the trial is now mainly a ceremonial ritual (although the coinage is still assayed); but for hundreds of years, until the standardization of modern minting methods, it was an important safeguard against debasement of the currency.

The original Hall in Foster Lane was purchased in 1339 by nineteen goldsmiths. They bought it from William de Clyf, who had purchased it from the executors of Sir Nicholas de Segrave, brother of the Bishop of London. Situated near the 'Goldsmithery', or goldsmiths' area of the City, details of this property are few. By the mid-fifteenth century, some rebuilding work had taken place, and in addition to the obligatory Great Hall it contained a parlour, a chapel, a chamber, a granary, an armoury and cellars with a courtyard and a garden. It also featured what was termed a Saye-house: a room or separate building in which gold and silver were 'sayed' (assayed; tested for purity).

Right: The dome of the Staircase Hall has painted coffering.

Right, bottom: An 18th-century gilded wooden statue of St Dunstan, the patron saint of English goldsmiths, stands on the first-floor landing.

Something of the wealth and prestige of the early Company may be gauged from its purchase in 1530 of a vast tapestry, woven to order and imported from Flanders, depicting the life of St Dunstan, the patron saint of English goldsmiths. It was draped around the walls of the Great Hall, but not for long: at some time during the Reformation of the following decade it was either destroyed or removed for safekeeping; either way, it was never seen again. Another great treasure of the first Hall that was lost forever during the Church of England's split from Roman Catholicism was a jewel-encrusted silver-gilt effigy of the same saint, which had stood over the screen in the Great Hall.

In 1634 the Goldsmiths undertook what they hoped would be 'a quick, unobtrusive and inexpensive job of repair and reconstruction' of their Hall.[1] But when they got going, they found that the roof of the building was in imminent danger of collapse. Reluctantly, they accepted the advice of Inigo Jones, the King's Surveyor, who was at the time working nearby on St Paul's Cathedral. Jones advised that, instead of patching up their medieval premises, they should build themselves an all-new second Hall on a part of their land where previously their Clerk's house had stood. Jones also recommended the man for the job: his protégé Nicholas Stone (*c.* 1586–1647), chief mason to both James I and Charles I.

The second Hall, completed in 1636, was built of brick in the Palladian style in an awkward, irregular space that, according to the designer, had 'never a Right angle without side', but in which he managed (though he said so himself) to create 'al square Roomes Within side'.[2] As the Goldsmiths had feared, it cost them a fortune: in addition to the normal expenses of labour and building materials, their decision to follow Jones's advice required them to buy a licence for rebuilding; worse, their first consignment of stone was 'detained for the King's use', as the increasingly beleaguered and cash-strapped Charles I continued his fatal decline from cupidity to rapacity. The Company had to borrow heavily to purchase a replacement.

Thirty years later, the Hall was gutted by the Great Fire of 1666; only the walls were left standing. Its rebuilding, one of Edward Jerman's post-Fire undertakings, was completed in 1669. It is not known with any certainty the extent to which this was a new design or a re-creation of Stone's original, but its similarities to Sir Peter Killigrew's house in Blackfriars[3] and other Inigo Jones projects suggest the latter.

JEWELS · OR · FINE · GOLD
SURELY · THERE

Left: The Livery Hall, looking towards the Company's buffet of plate, which includes the Warwick Vase of 1820 by Philip Rundell and John Tapley (detail above).

Top: A bust of George IV by Sir Francis Chantrey is situated in front of a huge mirror on the north wall of the Livery Hall.

There was a further fire in the Assay Office in 1681, the damage caused by which resulted in some inconsistencies in the design of the façade on Foster Lane: an anomalous square-headed window and a missing dormer in the south-western corner.

Throughout the eighteenth century, the Goldsmiths were relatively frugal, balancing their books but neglecting their building: by the 1820s some parts of it were held up by scaffolding. Desperate times called for extreme measures; their Hall was demolished in 1829 and replaced with a third edifice, designed by Philip Hardwick (1792–1870), the Company Surveyor, who would later become famous for two great railway buildings: the Euston Arch (1837; demolished 1961) and Birmingham Curzon Street station (1838).

When the new Hall was formally opened in 1835, one commentator described it as 'marked by an air of palatial grandeur not exceeded by that of any other piece of interior architecture in the metropolis'.[4] Since then there has been plenty of ambitious construction in London, but little to challenge that apparently hyperbolic claim.

Goldsmiths' Hall narrowly escaped complete destruction when, on the night of 16–17 April 1941, a bomb exploded inside its south-western corner. The damage thus caused was restored by the mid-1950s. A further refurbishment of the interior and exterior of the whole building was completed in 1990.

Behind the Foster Lane entrance, the double-height Staircase Hall is sheathed in marble of ten different colours; the stones originated in Devon, Staffordshire, Belgium, mainland France, Corsica and Algiers. On pedestals here are marble statues by Samuel Nixon (1803–1854) of children representing the Four Seasons. The staircase – remodelled in 1871 and restored in 1954 – divides ten steps up; on the half-landing is an 1830 bust of William IV by Sir Francis Chantrey (1781–1841).

On the left-hand side of the first-floor landing, a gilded wooden figure of St Dunstan, made in 1744 for the Company's state barge, stands opposite a mahogany long-case clock made by B.L. Vulliamy to Hardwick's specifications. Above the huge oak doorways are the carved and painted arms of six of the Goldsmiths' major benefactors. On the west wall is a silk banner with the Company arms and, beneath it, a plinth bearing a bronze head of Elizabeth II by David Wynne (1926–2014).

On the eastern side of the first floor is the Livery Hall, with Corinthian columns of scagliola and a sumptuously decorated moulded ceiling from which are suspended six chandeliers; the main set of four are of English glass. The embrasure on the north wall was

The Court Room, seen from behind the Prime Warden's chair in the lower image. Philip Hardwick sought to replicate the ceiling of the second Hall.

designed to display the Company's plate. Above the arch of this opening are the arms of William IV; on either side of it, in front of huge mirrors, are busts of George III and George IV, again by Chantrey. At the south end of the room, the balustrade of a minstrels' gallery juts forward over fluted Ionic columns, between which huge mirrored doors lead to the servery.

In the north-western corner of the Hall, where Gresham Street adjoins Foster Lane, is the Court Room, which Hardwick undertook to make as close as possible to its predecessor. It is thought that the sumptuously adorned cornice, which is both gilded and silvered, is indeed from Jerman's Hall, and the marble chimney piece is a work of 1735 by Henry Cheere (1703–1781). Hardwick largely replicated Jerman's ceiling, with soffits displaying elaborate foliage (see fig. 42 on p. 254). At the north end of the room is a Roman stone altar of the second century AD, which was uncovered in 1830 during reconstruction. At first it was believed to be from a temple dedicated to the goddess Diana, but late twentieth-century scholarship showed that it was for votaries of the London Hunter-God.

The Drawing Room, badly damaged in the Blitz but reopened in time for the 1951 Festival of Britain, was redesigned by Fernand Billerey (1878–1951) in Louis XV style. A new fireplace was installed and seventeenth-century tapestries purchased to hang on either side of it. Some of the present furniture was retrieved from the rubble.

The Exhibition Room is another post-war redesign, this time by C.H. James (1893–1953). The panels on the walls are of English walnut; those on the doors are of Australian walnut. The inbuilt display cases contain selections from the Company's silver collection.

On the southern side of the Hall, the oak-panelled Court Luncheon Room is largely the work of James, with some additions by Donald Insall Associates, and the lower part of the fireplace is Hardwick's original.

NOTES

1 John Newman, 'Nicholas Stone's Goldsmiths' Hall: Design and Practice in the 1630s', *Architectural History*, vol. 14, 1971, p. 31.
2 Nicholas Stone, *The Note-Book and Account Book of Nicholas Stone*, ed. Walter Lewis Spiers, Oxford (Walpole Society) 1919, p. 137.
3 See Sir John Summerson, *Inigo Jones*, Harmondsworth (Penguin) 1966, p. 113.
4 Thomas Wright, *The History and Antiquities of London, Westminster, Southwark and Parts Adjacent*, vol. 5, London (George Virtue) 1837, p. 203.

Above: The first-floor landing, looking towards the Livery Hall. The arms above the doors are those of significant Company benefactors.

Left: An ormolu candelabrum of c. 1835 in the Drawing Room.

SKINNERS' HALL

THE WORSHIPFUL COMPANY OF SKINNERS
ORDER OF PRECEDENCE: 6TH OR 7TH
GRADE I LISTED; SCHEDULED ANCIENT MONUMENT

The Entrance Courtyard. The courtyard was rebuilt in a cloister style in the late 1770s and remodelled around 1900. The ceremonial entrance to the courtyard was made between Nos. 8 (the Company office entrance) and 9 (the Clerk's former abode), and was therefore given the precise location of No. 8½ Dowgate Hill.

It is thought that the wearing of furs as a fashion accessory was popularized in England by the Normans after the conquest of 1066. Dealers in animal pelts prospered and, perhaps during the reign of Henry III (1216–72) and certainly no later than 1295, Skinners gathered together, probably in Copped Hall on the east bank of the Walbrook. This river has since been covered over, but the land remains the site of the modern Skinners' Hall. The Company was granted its first Royal Charter by Edward III in 1327, the year of his accession.

Little is known of Copped Hall other than that it had a chapel, a large courtyard and, along its frontage, five shops with a residence above them.[1] John Stow adjudged it a 'faire house' in the paragraph following that in which he described Tallow Chandlers' Hall as a 'proper house'.[2] If this distinction meant anything, its significance was lost forever in the Great Fire, which destroyed the original buildings of both Companies. (Fortunately, the Skinners' plate and records escaped the inferno, having previously been removed to safety in Shoreditch.)

On 27 September 1666, three weeks after the fire was put out, the Skinners' Court gave instruction to start digging the burnt-out site for recoverables. Rebuilding began in 1668. By 10 April 1670, it was reported in the Court ledger that the Clerk's house was within a week of being finished. On 28 June of the same year, a meeting of the Court of Assistants was held in the Hall. In 1671 some of the property was let; in 1678 the bricklayer Joseph Lem (or Lemm; d. 1695) advanced his plan for construction on the land on which the Committee Room and the Library are now located.

Between the 1670s and the 1770s, the buildings were periodically further upgraded and modernized. The next major reconstruction phase was carried out in the 1730s under the direction of George Dance the Elder (1695–1768); this was followed in the 1770s by an extensive programme of works by Richard Jupp (1728–1799). The façade, the inner courtyard, the Outer Hall, the Court Room and the Cedar Drawing Room (now the Court Room) were all altered during this overall period.

The front range of the Hall seen today along Dowgate Hill was designed by Jupp. Its three storeys and attic are in English Palladian style. The rusticated ground storey of painted stone has two round-arched entrances on either side of three arched windows. Fronting the first and second floors, giant Ionic pilasters support a Coade stone (or Lithodipyra) frieze of lions and a three-bay pediment. The tympanum contains a modified version of the Company's coat of arms: the supporters of the heraldic shield, a lynx and a sable marten, conventionally rampant, are here couchant in order to fit the available space. No. 9 Dowgate Hill is a continuation of the frontage, but here the façade is of brick, with an arched doorway and a single window on the ground floor.

Behind the wrought-iron gates at the southern entrance (No. 8½), a vaulted passage with guilloche-pattern ribs issues on to the Inner Courtyard. On the western side of the yard, the external wall of the Banqueting Hall is of red brick with blue headers, arranged chequer-wise in Flemish bond; the doorway is flanked by pilasters bearing carved coneys (rabbits).

Skinners' Hall underwent substantial change in the nineteenth and twentieth centuries. Underlying causes included such issues as dry rot, deathwatch beetle, and wartime bomb and fire damage. In 1876 the Old Drawing Room ceiling was repainted and gilded. At the end of the nineteenth century, the garden was subsumed by a new kitchen and an entrance-hall extension. In the early twentieth century, ten panels painted by Sir Frank Brangwyn (1867–1956) were installed in the Banqueting Hall, with a further three added in the 1920s.

The stone cloister was added between 1902 and 1916 by W. Campbell-Jones after he had converted the former kitchens into the Outer Hall, which now has twentieth-century oak panelling in seventeenth-century style. Its plaster ceiling is in the style of a much older ceiling dating from 1670; Court entries reference nineteenth-century works in this part of the roof area.

By the 1930s, that plasterwork was lost due to structural failure of the supporting timber members. The existing plaster dates from approximately this period and was most likely obtained by squeeze-moulding the earlier work.

Substantial alterations to the fabric of the Hall were perpetrated by Second World War enemy action. Court records refer to 'The debris resulting from the incidents of the 19, 23 and 30 July 1944 (when Flying Bombs fell in Budge Row ...)'. Although Skinners' Hall survived the conflict largely intact, the partition by the staircase in the Court Room (now the Old Court Room) and the ceiling in the room above were destroyed. The Hall's recovery was quickly completed in 1948.

The Outer Hall is dual-level, a circular gallery having been added by J. Sampson ('Sam') Lloyd (1930–2009) of Green Lloyd Architects between 1984 and 1986.

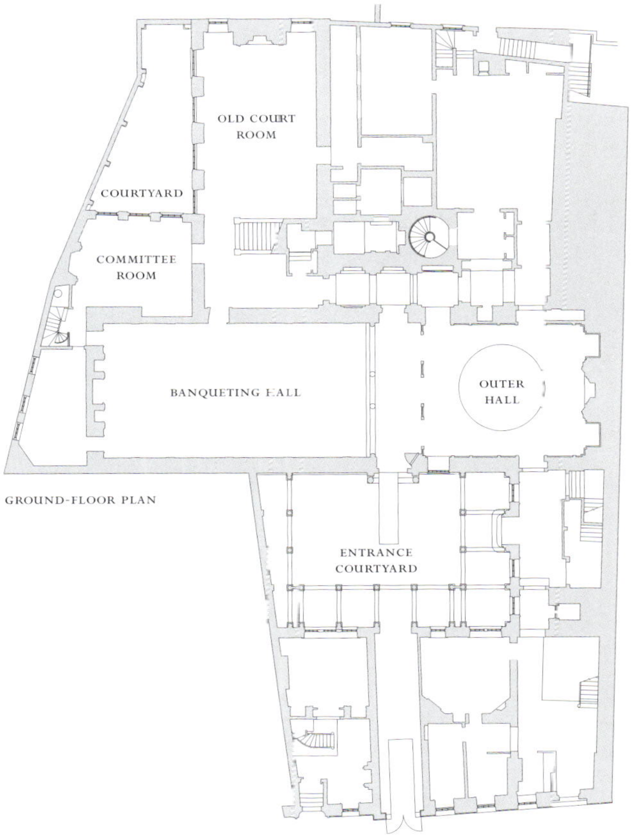

GROUND-FLOOR PLAN

The Old Court Room, with the main staircase behind. The table dates from the reign of George II and is believed to be one of the earliest mahogany artefacts made in England. It is reputed to be a gift from the East India Company, which for a time was allowed to use the Hall.

The Banqueting Hall features a series of panels by Sir Frank Brangwyn that illustrate important occasions in the history of the Company and the allegorical subjects Charity and Education, which are associated with present-day activities.

The Outer Hall. The circular gallery frames a chandelier that was reputably presented to James Harris, 1st Earl of Malmesbury, by Catherine the Great during his tenure as British ambassador to Russia.

Of much earlier date is the Bell, which was cast in 1190 and is believed to be one of the oldest creations of its kind in England (it was donated to the Company in 1927 by Albert A. Hughes, liveryman of the Company and Master Founder of the Whitechapel Bell Foundry).

Also of interest here are the glass chandelier – reputedly presented in the 1780s by Catherine the Great to the 1st Earl of Malmesbury, a Skinner and the British ambassador to Russia – and the four mirrors, which adorned the Skinners' barge until the Company disposed of the vessel in 1858.

The Inner Hall – the Banqueting Hall, the Hall proper – is entered through a screen. Structurally, this room remains much as it was when completed in 1670 after the Great Fire, but it is not without alteration, most notably the windows that were blocked off between 1847 and 1850 by George Moore. The panelling, modelled on the seventeenth-century work in the Chapel of Trinity College, Oxford, is by the interior designer J.D. Crace (1838–1919); Campbell-Jones added a skylight, which was lost in the interwar years. Brangwyn's paintings, installed 1902–1909, depict events connected with the history of the Skinners; three allegories were added in the early 1920s.

At the heart of the ground floor, to the west of the Banqueting Hall, is the Charity Corridor, which was installed between 1801 and 1803, it is thought by William Jupp the Younger (1770–1839). Between its arched openings are three painted gesso panels installed exactly 100 years after the structure's completion. These works by Robert Anning Bell (1863–1933) depict the principal concerns of the modern Skinners' Company: Charity, Education and Hospitality. A fourth panel, depicting Commerce, is believed to have been destroyed while it was being moved from the Hall for safekeeping in anticipation of the Blitz. The Corridor was extensively refurbished in 2010.

To the west of the Corridor, the Old Court Room has pedimented doorcases and egg-and-dart panelling that date from 1737 and are conventionally attributed to Dance the Elder.

To the south is the Committee Room, on the lower floor of the two-storey annexe built by Lem in 1678.

The main staircase – a magnificent open-well structure of three flights – dates from 1670. It has large square newels and intricately carved wooden balusters that have revealed even more of their original detail since 2014, in which year was completed a restoration project that also embellished the adjacent plasterwork with gold leaf.

On the first floor, the modern Court Room stands directly above the old one. Its former name, the Cedar Drawing Room, was inspired by the panelling made from Virginian cedar wood, reportedly imported as ships' ballast from Bermuda; this was installed in around 1670 by a joiner named Sheffield.

The design of the wooden doorcases – eared, with pediments on brackets – strikes Bradley and Pevsner

Opposite, top: The Court Room (formerly the Cedar Drawing Room) is panelled in pencil cedar from Virginia (the Company has past associations with the Virginia Company). It is said the wood was used as ships' ballast. Sadly, the original barrelled ceiling was lost to enemy action in 1944.

Opposite, bottom: The oak-panelled Committee Room was constructed by Joseph Lem as part of a small two-storey block in 1678.

Left: The view from the main staircase towards the Committee Room.

as more usually associated with exteriors than with interiors; nevertheless, they are not incongruous here, and they certainly attract the viewer's attention. So, too, does the thrusting modillion cornice. The doors at the far end of the room are blank. The simple plasterwork ceiling replaced its more flamboyant predecessor, which was destroyed by the Luftwaffe.

The first-floor Library is located directly above the Committee Room; its bookshelves are constructed of limed oak.

Outside the Court Room, a corridor connects with the Outer Hall gallery, from which an extension by J. Sampson Lloyd, completed in 1986, begins with a Venetian window that issues on to a roof garden above the new kitchens. This tranquil open area can alternatively be accessed via a chamfered square brick pavilion with a glazed octagonal lantern.

In 1987–88, excavations in the cellars of Skinners' Hall uncovered parts of the medieval revetment wall that held back the waters of the Walbrook. Since piles and transverse beams of the Roman waterfront have been identified beneath nearby Cannon Street railway station, it is thought possible that further digging may reveal even older relics here as well.

NOTES

1 See James Foster Wadmore, *Some Account of the Worshipful Company of Skinners of London, Being the Guild or Fraternity of Corpus Christi*, London (Blades, East & Blades) 1902, p. 128.

2 John Stow, 'Downegate warde', in *A Survey of London: Reprinted from the Text of 1603*, ed. C.L. Kingsford, Oxford (Clarendon Press) 1908, pp. 229–38; British History Online: http://www.british-history.ac.uk/no-series/survey-of-london-stow/1603/pp229-238 (accessed June 2018).

MERCHANT TAYLORS' HALL

THE WORSHIPFUL COMPANY OF MERCHANT TAYLORS
ORDER OF PRECEDENCE: 7TH OR 6TH
GRADE II* LISTED; SCHEDULED ANCIENT MONUMENT

The Eastern Entrance to the Hall, on Threadneedle Street, has Corinthian columns and a large armorial in the pediment. The door knocker (detail above) features the Company motto: Concordia parvae res crescunt *(With harmony small things grow).*

For almost a century and a half after the Norman Conquest of England, the distinction between the functions of the guild then known as the Taillours and those of the Drapers was clearly defined and jealously protected: the Taillours made and sold linen; the Drapers made and sold woollen goods; no functional change or overlap was permissible. In 1300 Edward I licensed the Taillours and Linen Armourers, and in 1327 his grandson, Edward III, granted them their first Royal Charter. Throughout the later Middle Ages they made quilted padding, surcoats and other such garments for knights to wear beneath their outer metal protection; the Company provided the same type of underwear for horses, as well as caparisons. In the meantime, the Taillours started importing wool for these purposes, thus annexing some of what had traditionally been Drapers' territory. In 1503, under Henry VII, the Taillours abandoned their original title and became the Merchant Taylors. Ordinances of 1662 suggest that by that year the Company had become a broad umbrella organization covering not only tailors but also milliners, butter-sellers, cruet-sellers, sailmakers and sundry other artisans and tradesmen.

In 1392 the Merchant Taylors formally acquired their first property: a Hall that fronted on to Threadneedle Street and which had a dining hall, a kitchen, a withdrawing room, a parlour and an ornate garden with (by the late sixteenth century) its own bowling alley. Detached from and to the east of the main buildings were the Company's almshouse, which was given to the Company in 1405, and its church, St Martin Outwich.

Some idea of the grandeur of the Merchant Taylors' first Hall may be gathered from the fact that, until the kitchens were built at Guildhall in the early sixteenth century, it was the venue for the annual Lord Mayor's Banquet. The original roof of the Great Hall was replaced in 1588 with one that was similar to the current roof of Middle Temple Hall.

The interiors of the building were obliterated in the Great Fire of London, but the stone walls withstood the inferno, and were thus used as the framework for the new Hall, which was probably built to designs by the prolific Edward Jerman. Among the post-1666 improvements were a new configuration of rooms on the western side of the building, a Grand Staircase at the northern end, and a larger Parlour to the south with a new Drawing Room above it and large brick cellars beneath. The embellishments included, in the Great Hall, an ornate wooden screen by Robert Hooke. This ambitious redevelopment was partially financed by the sale of much of the old garden.

Merchant Taylors' Hall thereafter remained largely unaltered until 1843–44, when the courtyard that had previously provided access from Threadneedle Street was covered over to become a corridor, now the Eastern Entrance. At the same time, the Western Entrance, off the same thoroughfare, was created to maintain the building's symmetry; this part was further modified in 1925–26 by Sir Reginald Blomfield (1856–1942).

In 1879 all rooms on the eastern and southern sides of the remaining garden were reconfigured by Edward I'Anson (1812–1888), who replaced previously tenanted property with a Library and a new Court Room slightly to the south of the old one. The upper storeys became offices on the first floor and domestic accommodation on the second; in the basement were service rooms. I'Anson's ranges are of Spinkwell stone in French Gothic style with steep roofs, dormers, crow-stepped gables and tall chimneys.

The Merchant Taylors' building was one of the first victims of the Blitz, which began on 7 September 1940.

Below: The double-aisled Cloisters, installed by Sir Herbert Baker in 1927, link the western and eastern sides of the Hall.

Right: The Grand Staircase is Sir Albert Richardson's post-war replacement for the one destroyed in the conflict.

Incendiary bombs destroyed the Great Hall and Hooke's screen, the Western Entrance and the Grand Staircase. The Parlour and the Drawing Room above it were also gutted, but the floor between them was constructed of fireproof material so remained intact and helped to prevent the contiguous walls from collapsing. The rooms to the east and south of the Garden – the Court Room, the Great Kitchen, the Library and the staff offices – were only slightly damaged.

After the Second World War, the architect who was first in charge of reconstruction, Sir Hubert Worthington (1886–1963), started on the Parlour, because its surviving ceiling made it the least blank canvas; completed in 1952, it is now a virtual facsimile of the pre-war structure.

Restoration of the Great Hall and the rest of the building was completed in 1959. The architect in charge, Sir Albert Richardson (1880–1964), was such a stickler for period accuracy that for many years he refused to have electricity in his own home, because otherwise, he contended, he would not fully understand how the people who constructed the buildings he was renovating

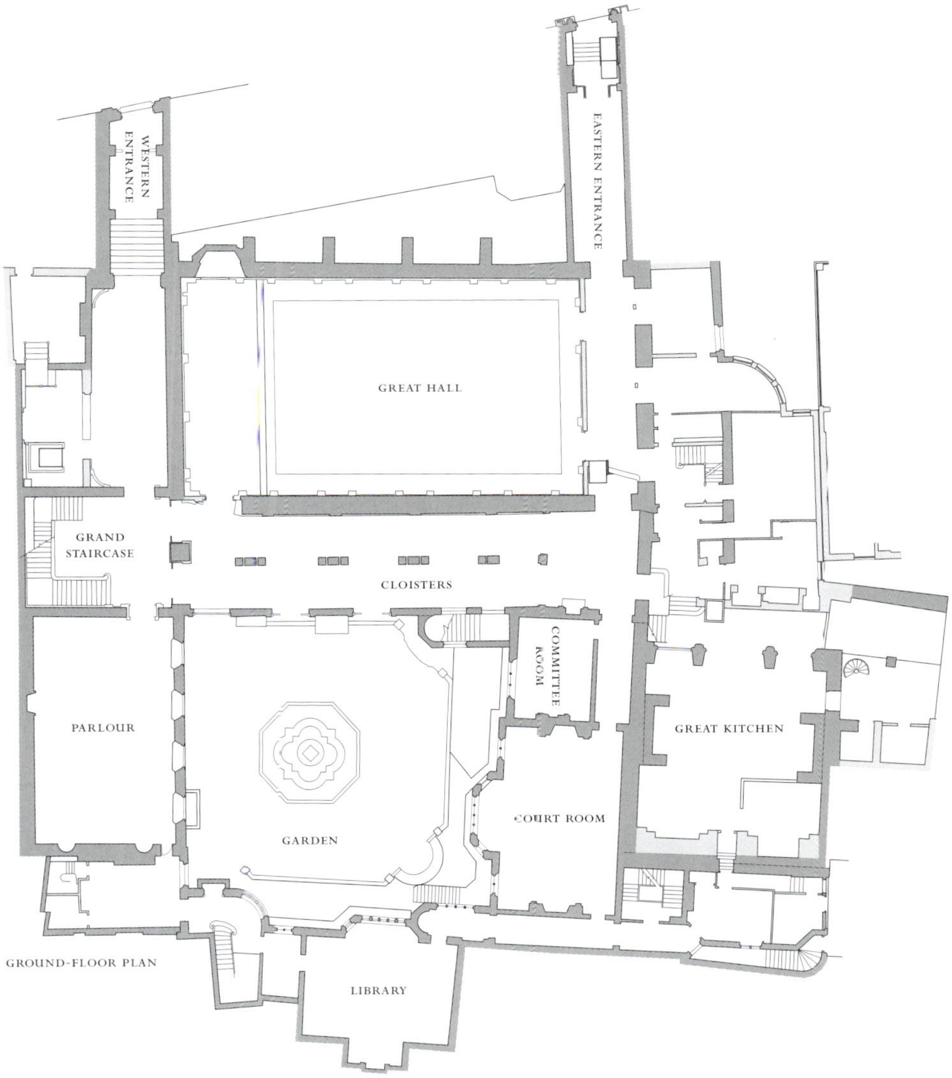

GROUND-FLOOR PLAN

1722
1966

The Great Hall has square-headed, stained-glass windows, five gilt bronze chandeliers and the only organ in a Livery Hall today. Banners bearing the Company's coat of arms hang at the west end of the gallery.

Right: The panelled Court Room, here laid for a private lunch, overlooks the Garden.

Far right: The top-lit King's Gallery overlooks the Great Hall.

Below: The Drawing Room suffered significant war damage, but has since been fully restored and decorated with beautiful Chinese wallpaper.

had lived. Partly as a consequence of Richardson's sense of history, Merchant Taylors' Hall today retains more of its original stonework than the premises of any other City Livery Company, and much of it remains visible. Beneath a trapdoor in the Great Hall are surviving fragments of earlier floors: beaten clay of the fourteenth century; red tiles of 1646 and Purbeck marble flagstones from the post-Fire Hall of 1675.

The lowest third of the walls of the Great Hall consists of mahogany panels topped by a gilt acanthus scroll cornice. Above these features is a wraparound gallery that is narrow on three sides but deep along the eastern flank, where sits the organ. The only such instrument in a City Livery Hall, this is a composite creation of 1963–66, rebuilt by Noel Mander (1912–2005) with a case by the Gothic Revivalist Stephen Dykes Bower (1903–1994); the pipework is by Renatus Harris (*c.* 1652–1724), originally for the instrument in St Dionis Backchurch, a Wren church in the City of London that was demolished in 1878.

Five gilt bronze chandeliers hang from the Great Hall roof, which is deeply coffered and made of cedar and lime, and has adjustable ventilation panels. The windows – shorter than those in the medieval building – contain stained glass by Francis H. Spear (1902–1979). Installed in 1963, this work was partially blown out by the IRA bomb in Bishopsgate in 1993 but later fully restored. Beside the dais in the north-western corner of the Hall, a selection of the Company silver is stored in a sixteenth-century oriel cupboard with an elaborate stone ceiling.

Along the southern side of the Great Hall are the Cloisters, designed by Sir Herbert Baker (1862–1946) and installed in 1927 while the architect was also working on India House in the Aldwych. Undamaged in the Blitz, they look out on to the oft-redesigned Garden. The features here now include two late eighteenth-century lead cisterns and a fountain of 1912, on top of which was mounted two years later a bronze statue by Gilbert Bayes (1872–1953) of the Infant St John the Baptist. In 2014, to mark the centenary of the outbreak of the First World War, the Company commissioned Old Merchant Taylor Martin Cook to carve a War Memorial, which was unveiled here in 2015. Above the roof of the Cloisters, the arch of the oriel of the old Great Hall is still visible in the masonry.

Left: The corridor linking the Court Room and the Library on the southern side of the Hall.

Below: The Western Entrance, with a statue of St John the Baptist, the Merchant Taylors' patron saint, donated by C.M. Clode, Master of the Company in 1873.

The Garden is flanked on its western side by the Parlour, on the south by the Library and on the east by the Court Room and the Committee Room.

The 1930s oak panels in the Parlour were originally intended for the Bank of England but never installed there. The corners of the plaster ceiling depict the royal arms at various stages of the Company's history: near the entrance are those used until 1340; on one side of the fireplace are those used from around 1400 until the accession of James I in 1603; on the other are the arms of William III (*r.* 1689–1702); opposite the entrance are the royal arms that have been used since the accession of Queen Victoria in 1837.

The Court Room is on the site of the former No. 3 White Lion Court, a property leased by the Company to tenants. According to a tale that may not be apocryphal, the acoustics here are such that people sitting in a certain spot beneath the shallow dome are audible to the Master, who appears to be sufficiently far away to be out of earshot. New members of the Court may consequently be seated there deliberately, so that their private views can be monitored by the Company's top brass.

Measuring 37 feet 6 inches (11.5 m) square, the aptly named Great Kitchen lies to the east of the Court Room, and is entered through arches in its north wall. It occupies the spot in which the Merchant Taylors have had their meals prepared since the late fourteenth century. Although the kitchen block was gutted in 1666, it was fully restored in the seventeenth century to the shape and layout created between 1425 and 1433 by John Goldyng and Thomas Mapilton. The pre-Fire stone corbels are still visible; the first post-Fire roof was removed by I'Anson in 1878 and replaced by offices.

The Crypt, beneath the Threadneedle Street end of the building, lost two of its bays to improver-vandals in 1853, but was partly restored in 1930 by Sir Charles Nicholson (1867–1949), who brought back into service the original doorway, long buried by masonry. Having survived the Blitz, this underground space remains otherwise much as it was in the late fourteenth century. The walls and roof are of chalk with Reigate stone dressings; the vault has hollow-chamfered ribs springing from moulded and sculpted corbels.

The Grand Staircase, between the ground floor and the first floor, is the same as the original destroyed in 1940 in almost every detail other than that its turn is clockwise rather than anticlockwise. Its finest features are the carvings on both sides of the panels beneath the handrail and the Adam-style lantern in the stairwell. The latter was retrieved from Paultons, a stately home in Hampshire demolished in 1963, and presented to the Merchant Taylors as a gift from the Salters' Company.

On the first floor there are two main rooms. The King's Gallery, at the west end of the Great Hall, is where the monarch dined away from his subjects, partly for security reasons and partly to reinforce the notion that the king was not like other men. The Drawing Room has two pairs of double doors at each end, but only one pair is real; the other is blank and merely for symmetry. The glass chandeliers date from the late eighteenth or early nineteenth century, from Ireland or Bristol. Of similar vintage but more exotic is the Chinese wallpaper, hand-painted with images of birds and flowers: so valuable is this that it is not stuck on to the wall but mounted on stretched fabric attached to wooden battens.

HABERDASHERS' HALL

THE WORSHIPFUL COMPANY OF HABERDASHERS
ORDER OF PRECEDENCE: 8TH

Behind these gates, a passage runs beneath Market View and debouches into the Hall's main courtyard.

Running east from Farringdon Street, West Smithfield starts off as a road but shortly turns into a circular space formed by the rotunda leading down to the basement of Smithfield Market. On the south-western side is the Haberdashers' latest Hall, which is entered through a passage beneath a residential and retail building, Market View. The story of how the Company came to be on this site is long and involved.

It is thought that the English word 'haberdasher' derives from the Anglo-Norman French term *hapertas*, which meant 'petty wares' and included certain grades of cloth. By the time the creation and sale of more fashionable clothing had become established in England, the trade had grown to encompass hat-makers, of whom there were two types: those who dealt in material imported from Milan became known first as 'millianers' and later as 'milliners'; those who traded hats of other types were known at first as 'hurrers' or 'cappers' and later generically as 'haberdashers'. The haberdashers then expanded further to deal not only in undergarments and headgear, but also in aglets (ornamental metal tags), ouches (clasps) and a host of other clothing adornments. One of these was a new device that was taking over from the thorns that had previously been used to fasten clothing: the pin. Pins made of metal were expensive at first, and hence became the medieval haberdashers' most profitable line of business.

Originally an offshoot of the Mercers' Company, the Haberdashers started out in the early Middles Ages as a fraternity that gathered in the old St Paul's Cathedral. Their control of London's clothing trade is at least as old as their earliest extant ordinances of 1371.

In 1448 Henry VI granted the 'Liegemen of the Mistery of Haberdashers' their first Royal Charter, which permitted them to own land and a Hall for their meetings. Membership of the Company was restricted to makers and sellers of beads, caps, gloves, pins, purses, ribbons and children's toys until 1502, in which year the Haberdashers joined forces with the Hatmakers' Fraternity under a Charter granted to them by Henry VII. The Haberdashers' current Royal Charter was awarded to them by Elizabeth I in 1578.

The Company's first building, acquired in 1458, was in Staining Lane, to the north of what was then Maiden Lane, which was linked in the nineteenth century with three other thoroughfares to form Gresham Street. Little is known about these original premises, other than that they occupied around half an acre (*c.* 2000 sq. m), since

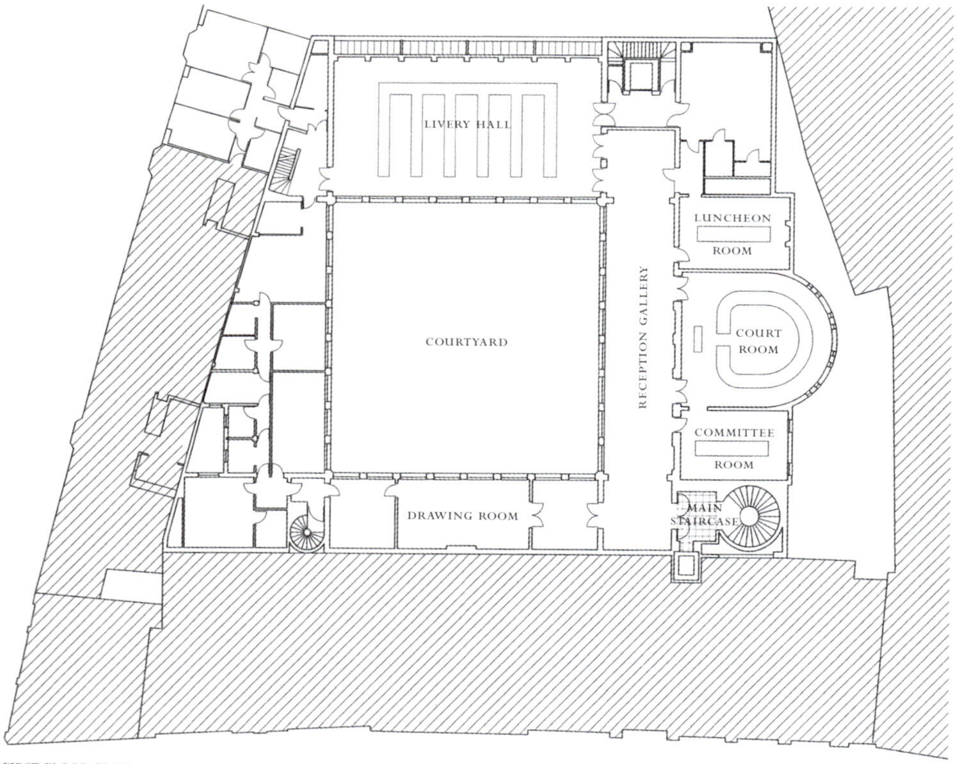

FIRST-FLOOR PLAN

William Pye's water feature (left) adorns the quadrangle, but does not dominate it. Surrounding the courtyard is a loggia, seen below through the glazed doors that lead to the main staircase.

both they and many of the records pertaining to them were destroyed in the Great Fire of London.

What is known in considerable detail, however, is the financial hit that the Livery Companies took throughout the seventeenth century as both the Stuart monarchy and the Commonwealth under Oliver Cromwell demanded that they finance England's foreign territorial ambitions: specifically, a plantation in Ulster and a colony in Virginia. Meanwhile, the trades that the Haberdashers were licensed to govern had become so diverse that the Company had diminishing effective control over their activities and correspondingly reduced revenues; nevertheless, the sums demanded were based on past performance, which is, in the well-worn warning phrase, no guide to future results. The Haberdashers made some of the biggest enforced loans; the overseas adventures failed, and the state repaid none of the monies.

The Haberdashers' second home, of which detailed records were made and painstakingly preserved, was one of the post-Fire Livery Halls designed by Edward Jerman. (At least, that's the conventional view; W.A.D. Englefield and Peter J.A. Lubbock raise the

possibility that the Hall may have been the work of Jerman's boss, Christopher Wren himself.[1]) The building was completed in 1668, with stonework produced under the supervision of the mason Thomas Cartwright, Snr. In his *Londiniana* series of volumes, published in 1829, the antiquarian Edward Wedlake Brayley praised this 'lofty and spacious' Hall, particularly its 12-foot (3.7-m) wainscots, the minstrels' gallery over a screen at one end, and 'several large glass chandeliers'.[2]

This Hall was again damaged by fire in 1836. The ensuing works by William Snooke, commenced in 1854 and completed ten years later, brought big alterations as well as repairs: the Chapel and other buildings in Staining Lane were demolished and rebuilt; the site of the Chapel was leased out and a new Chapel constructed with living rooms above it. The smaller buildings in Gresham Street were removed, and the land on which they stood leased out and covered by a warehouse. Otherwise the interiors were largely unchanged from their post-Fire condition.

And thus Haberdashers' Hall remained until 30 December 1940, when it was burnt off the face of the Earth in the firestorm created by the Luftwaffe during their bombing raid of the previous night. The initial post-war rebuild, designed by Major Arthur Ash, built by Sir Robert McAlpine & Sons and completed in 1956, made Haberdashers' Hall part of an office complex. Forty years later the Company moved out of the building, but retained the freehold; the vacated building was then redeveloped. The Haberdashers lodged in Bartholomew Close for the next six years, but meanwhile in 2000 work began on their next permanent residence. Designed by Michael Hopkins and Partners and constructed by Holloway White Allom, the Haberdashers' current Hall, their fourth, was opened for business in 2002.

The layout of the Hall is strikingly collegiate. From the Entrance Hall on the eastern side, on West Smithfield, a passageway with a porters' lodge on the left issues on to a loggia surrounding a quadrangle that is partly laid to grass. Also in this court is a paved area containing a water feature by William Pye. Three smooth laminar jets emerge from brass castings in the rock-strewn ground and congregate in a crucible at the top of the sculpture; from there, they tumble down a stepped series of containers. The jets symbolize the three types of freemen: those whose father was a freeman ('Patrimony'); those who have served apprenticeships in the Haberdashers' trade ('Servitude'); and benefactors of the Company ('Redemption'). The containers into

Left, top: The Reception Gallery runs along the northern side of the first floor.

Left and opposite: The oak-panelled Livery Hall as seen from the north, with the minstrels' gallery at the far end; and the Hall viewed from the gallery.

HABERDASHERS' HALL

Right: The Drawing Room is situated on the eastern side of the first floor.

Below: The statue of St Catherine of Alexandria, at the foot of the spiral staircase, is all that now remains of the Haberdashers' barge. The stairwell is illuminated by natural light.

Opposite, top: The Court Room has a curved north wall.

Opposite, bottom: The pine-panelled Luncheon Room flanks the west wall of the Court Room.

which the water falls represent the institutions supported by Haberdashers' charity.

The two-storey building that surrounds this centrepiece is faced with handmade bricks and lime mortar; its roof is made from hand-beaten lead panels. The southern and western sides of the ground floor are the Company offices, while on the north side is the Orangery, in which three cabinets contain vellum inscribed with the names of those who contributed to the second, third and present Halls.

The main spiral staircase, naturally illuminated by a roof lantern, has at its foot a carved-oak, gilded statue of St Catherine of Alexandria taken from the seventeenth-century barge that the Haberdashers had on the River Thames. (Catherine, who – according to tradition – was martyred on a wheel, is the Company's patron saint.)

Above the Orangery, running along the northern flank of the first floor, is the Reception Gallery with furniture by David Linley and doors on to three public spaces. The Committee Room is lit by two modern stained-glass windows; these are the work of Peter Sutton, a son of Norfolk who does most of his work in Norway.

The Court Room is horseshoe-shaped and has a handwoven Royal Wilton carpet that bears the Company arms. A partition between this and the Committee Room can be folded back to make a larger space, if required. To the west of the Court Room, the Luncheon Room has pine panelling dating from around 1730.

The north-western corner of the upper storey contains a servery and another staircase. Most of the western flank of the building is given over to the Livery Hall, 60 feet (18 m) long, 30 feet (9 m) wide and with a vaulted ceiling 30 feet (9 m) high. It is panelled in American oak and has wrought-iron stands (from two pre-1666 unrebuilt City churches) for the Sword and Mace of the City of London when the Lord Mayor is in attendance. On the walls are portraits of various Haberdashers who have held high office in the Company.

At the south end of the Livery Hall is a minstrels' gallery above a wine bin. Although the inward-facing southern side of Haberdashers' Hall is set at right angles to the eastern and western walls of the quadrangle, its outer flank broadens out from west to east in order to remain parallel to adjacent Hosier Lane. Thus, heading back east, the rooms gradually broaden out: the Beadle's flat, which comes first, is slightly narrower than the Master's flat. In the south-eastern corner of the building, another staircase leads back down to the ground-floor office area.

NOTES

1 W.A.D. Englefield, *The Halls of the Livery Companies of the City of London*, ed. Peter J.A. Lubbock, London 1981, p. 44.
2 Edward Wedlake Brayley, *Londiniana; or, Reminiscences of the British Metropolis*, London (Hurst, Chance & Co.) 1829, vol. 4, p. 151.

SALTERS' HALL

THE WORSHIPFUL COMPANY OF SALTERS
ORDER OF PRECEDENCE: 9TH
GRADE II LISTED

A view of Salters' Hall looking north, showing the modern entrance pavilion. The large coat of arms, made of glass fibre, identifies the Sir Basil Spence building as the Salters' headquarters.

The first fixed London headquarters of workers with salt and products that include that mineral were in Bread Street, which extends north–south between Cheapside and Cannon Street. This thoroughfare was named after the main goods produced by the bakers who formed the majority of those who plied their wares along it, but the presence among them of salters should not be regarded as an anomaly: the accounts of Edward I (*r.* 1272–1307) show payments of 'the wages of the salters' man, for salting fish all lent, to make into bread (*piscum in pane coquend*)';[1] this practice was widespread throughout the Middle Ages.

There were many disputes between the early salters and other tradesmen, and when these degenerated into something resembling turf wars, further intervention was required. Accordingly, in 1394 Richard II issued letters patent to all traders; those granted to the Salters licensed them to found the Fraternity and Guild of Corpus Christi in the church of All Hallows, Bread Street.

In 1455 Thomas Beamond bequeathed to the Fraternity some property in which its members had evidently been established for some time. The buildings – one already known as 'Saltershalle' and six houses – were then twice rebuilt: substantially after one fire in 1539, and partially after another in 1598. In the meantime, the Company had acquired a broad spectrum of members: not only salters, but also dealers in cochineal, flax, hemp, potash and, after the discovery of the New World, logwood (*Haematoxylum campechianum*) imported from the Central American tropics. The sixteenth century was a period of diversification for the Company: the use of salt as a food preservative drew it increasingly into the applications of chemistry in the comestibles industry, an involvement that has been maintained to the present day. In due course, therefore, the Company outgrew its original premises, and in 1641 bought Oxford House, a mansion with a large garden and warehouses on the corner of Cannon Street and St Swithin's Lane, a few hundred yards to the east of its original home.

The Great Fire of 1666 destroyed almost all of the Salters' buildings apart from a small vault in the north-eastern corner, but the whole place was rebuilt only two

The ground-floor reception area is light and spacious both horizontally and vertically.

years later by the Company's carpenter, John Wildgos (variantly rendered 'Wildgoose', 'Widgos' or 'Wildog'), who added a piazza and a loggia (see fig. 1 on p. 224).

This accommodation served its purpose for almost a century and a half, but in 1810 the Salters again deemed the building inadequate for their requirements, so they sold their Meeting House and Clerk's House by auction in order to fund another new structure on the remaining part of the site. The foundation stone was laid in 1823 and the building work – carried out mainly by Henry Carr, the Company Surveyor, with modifications by George Smith – was completed in 1827.

Salters' Hall was one of many buildings in the City of London hit during the notorious Luftwaffe attack on the night of 10–11 May 1941, at the height of the Blitz. Several of the incendiaries that landed on the roof were successfully dealt with by staff and ARP wardens, but one such device lodged in an unreachable place between the outer and inner casings of the dome of the Banqueting Hall. The ensuing fire raged out of control, and twenty-four hours later only the façade and a few small buildings to the north and east of the courtyard remained.

After the Second World War, the Salters were without a permanent base for more than thirty years. They worked from rented offices at No. 36 Portland Place in the West End and held their livery dinners in the public rooms of other companies, especially Ironmongers' Hall. In 1960 Sir Howard Robertson (1888–1963) designed a replacement in St Martin's Place, opposite the National Portrait Gallery, but his plans were never implemented. The Salters then acquired a site in Fore Street, adjacent to the Barbican, and in 1967 began the search for an architect to design a building that 'should be contemporary in style' but pay 'due regard to the traditional role of the Company'.[2]

In 1968 the competition for the best design was won by Sir Basil Spence (1907–1976), the designer of Coventry Cathedral, whose proposals were preferred to those of several rivals, including Ludwig Mies van der Rohe. Spence's plan was for a tall plinth comprising a ground-floor reception and four floors of offices beneath a cantilevered superstructure of three further storeys. Stair bays at each end of the plinth flank a row of concrete columns that divide the plinth into four bays.

Construction did not start until 1972. Owing to poor health, Spence was unable to see the project through: he died in 1976, just as the sixth Salters' Hall was being completed by the John S. Bonnington Partnership.

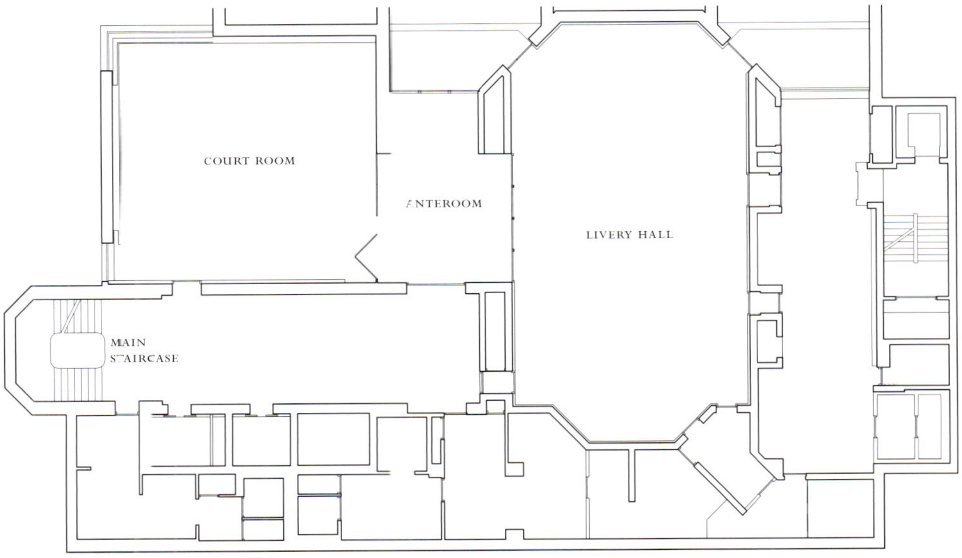

FIFTH-FLOOR PLAN

The ash-lined Livery Hall. The doors in the tall corner windows issue on to small verandas.

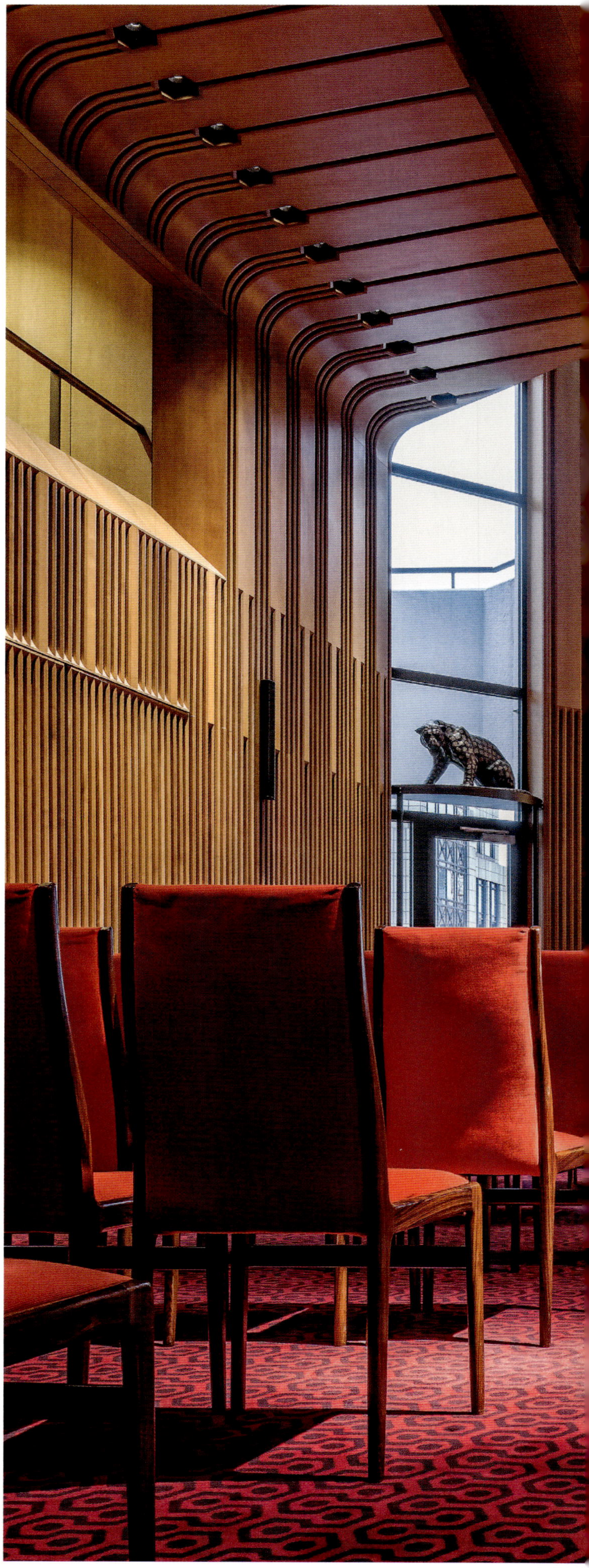

The result is a bold and innovative combination of Livery Hall and office space. It is an eight-storey rectangle (with two further levels below ground) made predominantly of concrete. The engineers were Oscar Faber & Partners, whose eponymous founder had died in 1956, but whose pioneering use of reinforced concrete here reaches an apotheosis. The Hall is broadly Brutalist in the manner of other major London buildings of the period, but in detail it displays greater adaptability than, and lacks the unblinking stare of, for example, Denys Lasdun's National Theatre, completed in the same year. The concrete in Spence's last work is attenuated by being variously ribbed, knapped and bush-hammered; the overall effect is further softened by aluminium curtain walls and smoke-coloured glass.

Within the context of the Worshipful Companies of the City of London, Spence's concept was radical, almost iconoclastic: he turned the building upside down. Flouting the then-conventional layout of Livery Halls, with Company rooms at the lower levels and rented-out offices above, Spence installed the Salters' ceremonial rooms on the cantilevered slab jutting out on the fifth floor, and topped off his design with unusual octagonal towers that are a twentieth-century take on the medieval castle.

The interiors are the work of David Hicks (1929–1998). Among this celebrated designer's notable contributions are the curved ash wall screens and the formal layout – with box hedging and areas of lawn – of the sunken public garden to the south of the building.

By 2011 Salters' Hall was badly in need of maintenance: the roof was leaking, and the air conditioning and boilers were decrepit. The Company commissioned de Metz Forbes Knight Architects (dMFK), not only to deal with these problems but also to refurbish the whole building and redesign the roof garden. This undertaking took until 2016 to complete, not least because, in addition to the urgent remedial

The Salters' Company

The Dining Room, on the sixth floor, hosts smaller events.

work, the architects extended the building 6 feet 6 inches (2 m) outwards on the northern and southern façades in order to increase by 2800 square feet (260 m^2) the rentable space between the first and fourth floors. They achieved this by clamping and bolting steel cantilever beams on to the edges of the existing concrete floor slabs, with a perpendicular beam connecting them back to the pre-existent columns.

To replace the garage block that formerly stood on the eastern side of the Hall, dMFK designed a new double-height glass-and-concrete entrance pavilion. In reorienting the building to the east (the previous main entrance faced Fore Street), the portcullis-like structure offers a grand sense of arrival, yet preserves views of old London Wall and maintains the public right of way into St Alphage Garden. Also repositioned on this side of the building are the wrought-iron gates of 1887, featuring birds and delicate foliage, that guarded Carr's Hall.

Inside, the entrance extension is attached to the east wall of the main building so as to leave Spence's concrete fluting visible above a tall screen of ash. The glazed roof provides views of the cantilevered upper levels. Beyond the screen, a travertine-lined lobby houses the lifts and a travertine staircase.

The lower ground floor, ground floor, and first, second, third and fourth floors are let out as offices. On the fifth floor, the Company's accommodation is entered via the 'Salt Lobby' – a vaulted corridor loosely modelled on a salt cave and lined on one side with antique silver salt cellars. The main cantilever staircase, with white travertine skirting, a smoked-glass balustrade and a silvered bronze handrail, is illuminated by a chandelier with lights made from crystals of rock salt. The Livery Suite features three main spaces. The Court Room has a low tray ceiling (formerly octagonal, now square) and is panelled mainly in coral rosewood. The travertine-lined Anteroom leads into the double-height Livery Hall, which is fully lined with fluted or reeded Canadian ash panels that curve over at the top in line with a shallow elliptical ceiling in which are concealed vents. In each corner of the Hall is a tall window, two of which issue on to verandas. At the western side of this level are the kitchen and the service rooms. On the sixth floor are two guest rooms and the Dining Room, with a gallery overlooking the Livery Hall. The top storey of the building houses the Salters' offices.

What was formerly the caretaker's flat in the basement is now additional offices overlooking the gardens. The latter were redesigned by Hicks to facilitate wheelchair access to the Hall; the fountain was funded by the family of Jock Russell, a Past Master of the Company and a prime mover of the refurbishments, who died suddenly in 2010 during the project's design phase.

NOTES

1 Quoted in William Herbert, *The History of the Twelve Great Livery Companies of London*, London (W. Herbert) 1837, vol. 2, p. 558.

2 Building Committee minutes of the Worshipful Company of Salters, 26 April 1968.

Below: The chandelier on the main staircase is made not of glass but, more appropriately, of rock salt crystals.

Above: The entrance to the Salters' silver vault and some of the Company's plate.

IRONMONGERS' HALL

THE WORSHIPFUL COMPANY OF IRONMONGERS
ORDER OF PRECEDENCE: 10TH

Neither the Tudor-Gothic entrance nor the neo-Tudor façade of Ironmongers' Hall is quite what it appears to be: both structures date from the early 20th century.

Iron has been mined and wrought in England since long before records began. The first written reference to dealers in the metal ('ferroners') in London is a complaint in 1300 to the Mayor, Elias Russell, that the irons on the cartwheels that were then being brought into town from the southern counties were 'much shorter than was anciently, to the great loss and scandal of the whole trade of ironmongers'.[1] It was partly in order to prevent such lowering of professional standards that the City guilds were originally formed.

The earliest record of an ironmonger is the grant of the Manor of Norwood to Mathew de la Wike by the Bishop of Rochester in 1241; the earliest record of the corporate body of Ironmongers is in 1364, when they contributed money to Edward III's campaign against France in the Hundred Years War. The Company's first Royal Charter was granted by Edward IV in 1463. This document required among other things that Ironmongers should be members of no other Company. Such a demand for exclusivity was unusual; many men (and latterly women) belonged and still belong to more than one and often to several Livery Companies.

At around this time many ironmongers worked in a lane that still bears their name off Cheapside. As the City became more crowded, however, the noise and smoke generated by their work made them unpopular with their increasingly numerous neighbours, and their desire to be closer to the main transport artery inspired their move to the riverside, in Thames Street. In 1457 they purchased a site in Fenchurch Street and completed their first Hall there in 1493. Later they gradually expanded their workshops, which, by the time various unspecified repairs to the Hall were completed in 1543, had spread as far as Leadenhall Street to the north.

In 1562 the Ironmongers considered new premises, but decided against a move, preferring to rebuild their existing Hall. The new structure, designed by Elias Jarman and built between 1578 and 1587, incorporated an extensive garden: *rus in urbe*, at least partly to offset some of the pollution caused by heavy metalworking.

Over the following century, however, the iron industry relocated to the Midlands and the North of England, where land and labour were cheaper and more plentiful. The Company in London therefore had to diversify because the trade had died out and members were no longer practising ironmongers. Members who prospered in other professions bequeathed their money for charitable purposes such as schools or almshouses, and they delegated the administration of both the capital investment and the charitable enterprise to their fellow members.

The Ironmongers' Hall escaped the Great Fire of London and was rebuilt again between 1748 and 1750 by Thomas Holden in the style of James Gibbs, architect of the Radcliffe Camera in Oxford, the Senate House in Cambridge and the churches of St Martin-in-the-Fields and St Mary le Strand. The Hall was then altered extensively during the nineteenth century.

On 7 July 1917 the Hall was damaged during the Germans' first fixed-wing air raid by Gotha IV bombers; a 110-lb (50-kg) bomb missed the building, but the explosion caused when it landed in the adjacent courtyard left a crater 8 feet (2.4 m) in diameter and 6 feet (1.8 m) deep. The blast knocked out all the Ironmongers' windows and doors facing the quadrangle, and sent fragments of York stone paving – some of them 2½ inches (6.4 cm) thick – into Clothworkers' Hall next door and as far as the church of All Hallows Staining.

The Banqueting Hall, the Parlour, the vestibules and the kitchen were all unaffected, and remained in use, but nevertheless after the First World War the Ironmongers decided to demolish what remained of the building and sell the freehold. Thus ended their 465 years in a single location.

In 1922 the Ironmongers purchased the site on which they are now based, land with an unusual history: in the early thirteenth century it was part of the Great Ditch used to drain a lake to the north of the City wall; in 1606 it was filled in, and in 1644 a house designed by Inigo Jones was built there for John Tufton, 2nd Earl of Thanet. This residence subsequently belonged to Anthony Ashley Cooper, 1st Earl of Shaftesbury, but the dampness of what had formerly been marshland was never entirely banished from the brickwork and so, regardless of the fact that the building was the brainchild of the man who is widely regarded as the greatest architect of the early seventeenth century, it was replaced in 1802 by tenement housing, which was in turn pulled down in 1910.

Left: A stained-glass window in the Banqueting Hall depicts the coats of arms of Company members who have been Lord Mayor of London.

Overleaf: The Banqueting Hall. The Waterford chandeliers date from 1803 and were brought from the Company's previous location in Fenchurch Street.

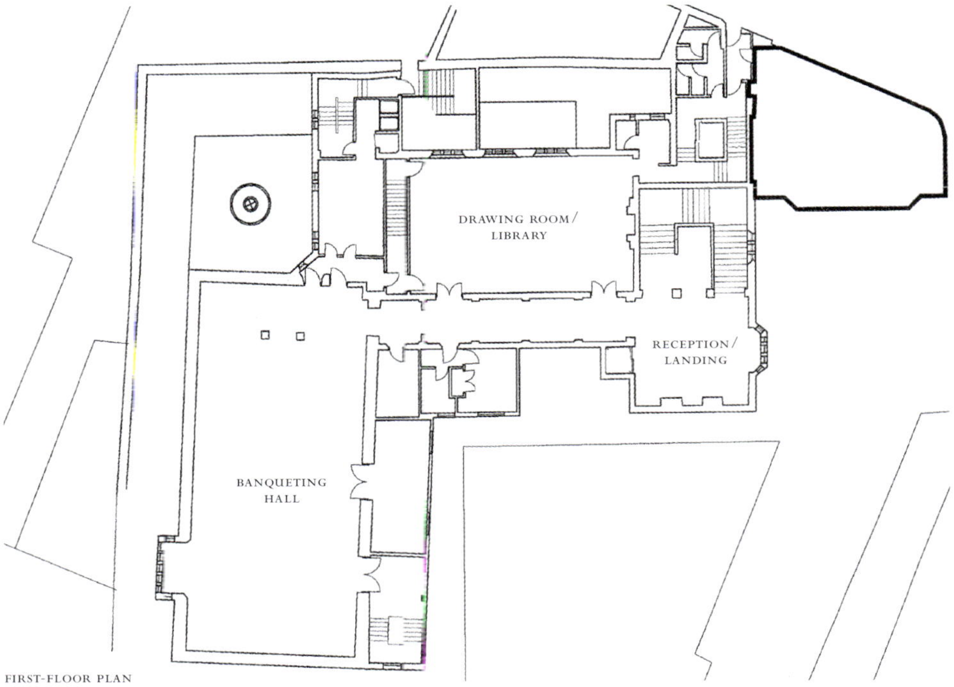

FIRST-FLOOR PLAN

The Ironmongers' current home was designed by their Surveyor, the architect Sydney Tatchell (1877–1965), and built by Holland, Hannen & Cubitts, the company whose previous achievements included the Cunard Building in Liverpool and in London the Prudential Assurance building in High Holborn, the Cenotaph in Whitehall and County Hall on the South Bank of the Thames. The completed Ironmongers' Hall was opened on 17 June 1925. The Tudor style was chosen partly because it seemed appropriate for the headquarters of an ancient guild, and partly also because it recalled what by this time was regarded as a (perhaps even the) golden age of craftsmanship.

In December 1940 a Luftwaffe fire-bomb raid destroyed all the surrounding buildings, but did no more than melt the Ironmongers' lead pipes and the glass in their windows. Everything else – structure, fixtures, fittings, records since 1555 – was untouched by the Nazi onslaught. According to one authority, this remarkable escape was attributable to the sprinklers that had been installed on the external walls of the building on Tatchell's advice.[2]

The Hall was threatened again after the conflict when the Corporation of London sought a compulsory purchase order in order to demolish it and replace it with the new Museum of London. But permission was not granted, and today the Hall is almost totally encircled by the megaliths that tried to devour it – the Museum (completed in 1976) and the High Walk. Its only opening to the outside world is on its western side through a passageway that links it with Aldersgate Street. And in this location is something of a paradox: Ironmongers' Hall is eminently missable by passers-by, and its footprint is almost invisible from the air, and yet anyone who ventures down the passageway and through its portals will find a building that more than makes up in quality and interest what it lacks in height beside its giant neighbours.

The neo-Tudor façade is of handmade red bricks at ground- and first-floor levels and half-timbered on the second floor. There are three dormer windows in the roof at the front and one at the rear. The building is L-shaped, with a cloister and a fountain on the outside of its corner.

The entrance is through a Tudor-Gothic stone porch with carvings by George Alexander (1881–1942); one of these depicts the Company arms, which feature two salamanders because of their supposed ability to survive fire, in the same way as iron. Beyond the entrance, the neo-Jacobean passageway is paved with rough flagstones and lined with oak panels.

The ceilings and friezes throughout the Hall are by George Jackson & Sons, the company owned by descendants of the eponymous Regency plasterwork master who executed commissions for Robert Adam. The decor is based on pre-existent works elsewhere: that in the entrance and corridors is inspired by Haddon Hall in Derbyshire; that in the Luncheon Room is

Above: The process of guests up and down the broad main staircase may be slowed as they stop to examine the portraits on the walls and the statues on the landings.

Above, right: The panelled Entrance Hall in Shaftesbury Place was built in 1923 in a Tudor style after the old Hall in Fenchurch Street was almost destroyed by German bombing in July 1917; the Elizabethan chest, seen in the lower image, still has the shrapnel damage it then sustained.

d'après Audley End, Essex, and Loseley Park, Surrey; the ceiling of the Court Room emulates one in Crewe Hall, Cheshire.

The oldest stained glass in Ironmongers' Hall is the work of Reginald Bell of the Clayton & Bell company, which was the most prolific and celebrated exponent of this art form throughout the late nineteenth century and the early part of the twentieth; post-war additions are by Michael Farrar Bell (1911–1993), an artist who moved into stained glass after achieving fame as a painter of pub signs.

On the half-landing of the broad staircase between the Entrance Hall and the first floor is *The Estridge* (ostrich), a wooden carving of 1629 to commemorate the appointment of James Cambell, a Past Master of the Ironmongers, as Lord Mayor of London. According to legend, ostriches could eat and digest iron; this accounts for the horseshoe in the bird's beak.

On the upper landing are two noteworthy statues. One is of the ancient Greek poet Sappho (1854), by the Neapolitan sculptor Tommaso Solari (1820–1889). The other, by John Francis Moore (*c.* 1745–1809), is a 1770 effigy of Alderman William Beckford, twice Lord Mayor of London (1762 and 1769). This is of particular interest for its similarities to and differences from a much larger and, in the view of many, more formal 1772 study of the same subject by the same sculptor at Guildhall.

On the first floor, the walls of the Drawing Room are lined with the largest William Morris bird-pattern textile wall covering in Britain. Among the paintings on the walls is a portrait of Izaak Walton (*c.* 1594–1683), author of *The Compleat Angler* (1653).

Adjacent to the Drawing Room, the double-height Banqueting Hall has an elliptical ceiling, a tall oriel window by the dais at one end and a deep minstrels' gallery at the other. The stained-glass windows have the coats of arms of the kings and queens who have granted Royal Charters to the Company and members of the Company who became Lord Mayor of London; the chandeliers of Waterford glass are taken from the previous Hall. The coats of arms of nearly all Past Masters of the Company are displayed in the panelling of the Hall.

NOTES

1 Quoted in William Herbert, *The History of the Twelve Great Livery Companies of London*, London (W. Herbert) 1837, vol. 2, p. 570.

2 A. Stuart Gray, *Edwardian Architecture: A Biographical Dictionary*, London (Wordsworth Editions) 1985.

Above: The Court Room is on the ground floor of the building. Some of the stained glass in these windows is taken from the Company's first, 15th-century Hall.

Left: On the upper landing of the Hall are displayed the likenesses of two distinguished members of the Company: John Francis Moore's marble statue of Alderman William Beckford, from 1770, and a 1784 portrait of Samuel, 1st Viscount Hood, by Thomas Gainsborough.

VINTNERS' HALL

THE WORSHIPFUL COMPANY OF VINTNERS
ORDER OF PRECEDENCE: 11TH
GRADE I LISTED; SCHEDULED ANCIENT MONUMENT

The front of Vintners' Hall, on Upper Thames Street, has two distinct parts: the east wing is linked to the windowless west wing by way of a colonnade over the central entrance corridor.

GROUND-FLOOR PLAN

Vintners' Hall stands on the corner of Upper Thames Street and Queen Street Place, the northern approach road to Southwark Bridge across the River Thames.

The Vintners were granted their first Royal Charter in 1363 by Edward III. In 1446 they acquired the site of their Hall through the bequest of Guy Shuldham. He was merely a trustee, and the Company had almost certainly been using the buildings, which included thirteen almshouses, for many years before that. Little is known about the pre-Fire Hall, but it probably adopted the standard medieval layout for a large house, with dining room, retiring room, service rooms and kitchen around a courtyard off Thames Street.

The Great Fire of 1666 destroyed all of the Hall. On the plus side, the Vintners had sufficient notice of the advancing flames to remove most of their portable valuables to safety (although many of their treasures were subsequently sold). Partially reopened in 1671 and completed four years later, the replacement Hall was much grander than its predecessor (see fig. 29 on p. 246).

The edges of the Vintners' land were subsequently reduced again, first by the construction of Southwark Bridge (1815–19), which necessitated the complete rebuilding of the east wing of the Hall, and then by the widening of Upper Thames Street (1822). Partly to make up for these losses of space, between 1908 and 1910 A.H. Kersey (1850–1938) filled in what remained of the courtyard to create the current Entrance Foyer. Kersey also oversaw a further reconstruction of the east wing on a site slightly further west, and refaced the west wing. The Portland stone frontage on Upper Thames Street is in Northern Renaissance style, with an arched main entrance beneath a colonnade that links the east and west wings. The east wing has four bays, with Ionic columns fronting the first and second floors. The façade of the west wing is intricately ornamented but windowless.

Within the gates to the Hall sit two ornate Coade stone swans (1801). In the Entrance Foyer is another Coade stone figure – that of a schoolboy (1840). This statue was removed from the debris of a school in nearby Brickhill Lane that was destroyed in the Blitz. Vintners' Hall, by contrast, came through the Second World War almost unscathed. Off to the left, leading down to basement cloakrooms, is an elliptical staircase designed by Saunders Boston Architects and installed in 1972. At the back of the Foyer is a carved memorial by Esmond

Right: The 17th-century main staircase, as seen from the first-floor landing.

Right, bottom: The elaborate doorcase within the Court Room, which still boasts its post-Fire oak panelling, carved by John Symes.

Burton (*c.* 1886–1964) to the fallen in the Great War. Further on is the Staircase Lobby, with a fireplace and panelling of the 1670s. The main staircase – four flights around a square well – was carved by a Mr Woodroffe and completed in 1673.

To the north of the Staircase Lobby, the Court Room, completed in 1671, is reputedly the oldest continuously used room in the City of London. Although this claim is unsubstantiated and not universally accepted, the room is certainly one of the prime candidates for that distinction. The floor-to-ceiling oak panelling, carved by John Symes, is as old as the room; so, too, are the coats of arms in the cornice. Among the eighteenth-century treasures here are the Master's chair and the long-case clock. The west wall had its windows closed up in 1717 as a fire precaution. The room was 'beautified' in 1804 by John Wright, a Past Master of the Company, whose portrait now hangs here along with paintings of, among others, Charles I, Charles II and Mary II. The original cross-beamed ceiling was replaced in 1908–1909. The windows are post-war replacements for those blown out by German flying bombs in 1944. In the basement directly beneath the Court Room is the Vintners' Red Wine Cellar.

Continuing south through the building, the next room is the Livery Hall, which is now reached through a door in the north-western corner. Inside the Hall, above this entrance, is a wooden plaque commemorating the feast in 1363 at which the Company entertained five kings: Edward III of England, David II of Scotland, Jean II of France, Valdemar III of Denmark and Peter I of Cyprus. At the east end, above the screen, is a minstrels' gallery with wrought-iron balusters.

To one side of the door is a carved wooden sword rest, presented by Past Master Sir Thomas Rawlinson in 1705, the year of his mayoralty. This is for the City Sword when the Lord Mayor dines in the Hall. The height of the sword rest on the wall accounts for the presence nearby of a small wooden platform, installed in 1956 in case the City Swordbearer should not be tall enough to reach it.

After it was found to contain deathwatch beetle, the ceiling was replaced in 1933 by a new cement-and-steel ceiling – with shields in the cornice – to a design by George Alexander Gale (later the Company Surveyor) based on that of the Old School Room at Winchester College. These materials saved the Hall from significant damage by incendiary bombs during the Blitz.

Right: A carved lion and unicorn sit atop the lower newels of the main staircase.

Far right and below: At the west end of the Livery Hall is a wooden screen with an alcove that houses some of the Company's fine pieces of plate. The royal arms sit within the broken pediment.

Opposite: The Livery Hall, looking towards the minstrels' gallery and the east screen, which dates from 1822. The ceiling was repainted in a new colour scheme in 2013.

VINTNERS' HALL

The chandeliers, by F. & C. (Follett and Clarkson) Osler of Birmingham, were installed in 1874. The collection of tastevins, arranged in alcoves in the east screen in such a way as to replicate the Company's coat of arms, was purchased in 2000.

Since the Second World War, the stained-glass windows in the Livery Hall have largely been replaced by clear glass, other than in the north-western corner, where there is an engraved window donated in the 1990s by Paul Wates of Wates City Ltd, to commemorate his firm's partnership with the Company in the construction of Vintners' Place, the office development that surrounds the Hall to the south and west.

Still in the Livery Hall, on the woodwork by Symes are carvings that depict grapes and other fruit and a woman whose demeanour appears increasingly disturbed in various images around the room that are plainly intended as a light-hearted but pointed warning against excessive ingestion of wine. At the west end of the Hall is an alcove framed by coupled Corinthian pilasters beneath a pediment broken by the royal arms. Within the alcove is a stand, constructed in 1842 and modified between 1934 and 1936, on which is displayed much of the Company's remaining plate. To the right of the stand, two surviving pre-Fire treasures are displayed in a glazed cabinet: a stoneware jug with gilt fittings presented to the Company in 1563, and a coconut cup hallmarked 1518–19.

At the southernmost extremity of the Vintners' building are the Gassiot Room and the Swan Room, both designed by Biscoe + Stanton Architects as part of the 1990s redevelopment of Company land. The Gassiot Room, named after another Past Master of the Company, has two fireplaces. One bears the date 1899, the year in which it was installed in the old Smoking Room; the other is dated 1992, the year in which that room was demolished to make room for Vintners' Place. Above the fireplaces are paintings that depict the Thames: one during the early nineteenth century, the other during Elizabeth II's Silver Jubilee in 1977. In other parts of the room hang one painting by Julian Barrow of the Vintners' Court in 2000, and another by Nick Botting of the Swan Feast of 2014. (This dinner takes place annually on the last Thursday of November; swans are no longer cooked, partly for ethical reasons, but mainly because, in spite of their reputation as a dish of exquisite luxury, they don't taste very good; turkey or chicken is now usually served.)

The Gassiot Room also houses a painting of an apple and grape harvest attributed to Lucas Achtschellinck (1626–1699) and a portrait of wine-treaders by a Flemish artist from the circle of Pieter Angillis (1685–1734). In a glass case at the east end of the room is a fine collection of antique bottles and decanters.

The Swan Room celebrates the Vintners' historic rights: they share ownership of the mute swans on the River Thames with the Crown and the Dyers' Company. Every year in July, Vintners officers travel up the river to count the adult cobs and pens and to ring the cygnets; this is one of the Company's most

Opposite, top: The entrance to the Court Room from the Staircase Lobby.

Opposite, bottom: The portraits in the Court Room include Sir Thomas Rawlinson, Master in 1687 and Lord Mayor of London in 1705 (left), and Charles II.

cherished traditions, a ritual known as Swan Upping. Two of the walls display artists' impressions of this event: a pastel by Patricia Ashmore and *Swan Uppers at Marsh Lock*, a watercolour by Bill Mundy. On the east wall are portraits of Richard Turk, Swan Marker for fifty-six years (1904–60), by James Dring; and of Bruce Todd, Swan Warden in 1964, by Aubrey Davidson-Houston.

Facing the French windows on the northern flank of the Swan Room are three false arches in which *trompe l'œil* paintings of 1996 by Colin Failes depict views from here across the Thames at different times in the Company's history. This wall runs parallel to the Thames and would be in sight of the river were it not for Vintners' Place, the office block built by the Company in 1992 and leased out to tenants. So perhaps a little disappointingly, Vintners' Hall has no riverside views from any of its windows; these paintings are the only available substitutes. Nevertheless, the Swan Room has an 'outdoor' feel, and is a favourite venue for wine-tastings.

The first-floor interiors of the Vintners' building look old, but none of them pre-dates 1899. Directly above the Court Room is the Drawing Room, which was decorated in its current neo-Jacobean style in 1899 and faithfully refurbished in 2017. The adjacent Annexe and Conservatory, designed by Biscoe + Stanton, were installed in 1989. The ironwork in the latter area is taken from the demolished Vintry House; the lead cistern bearing the Company's heraldic shield is dated 1701; the bronze swan, by Sally Arnup, was presented in 2002 by two Past Masters. Also at this upper level is the entrance to the minstrels' gallery in the Livery Hall.

Top: The Entrance Foyer, looking towards a 17th-century limewood carving of St Martin and the Beggar. St Martin of Tours is the patron saint of the Vintners.

Above: The Conservatory, created in 1989. The ironwork came from the 1920s Vintry House, demolished (save for its portal) when Vintners' Place was built.

CLOTHWORKERS' HALL

THE CLOTHWORKERS' COMPANY
ORDER OF PRECEDENCE: 12TH

Marble pilasters flank the walkway to the statue of Cedric the ram at the top of the stairs.

The Clothworkers' Company was formed through the merger of the Fullers (incorporated in 1480) and the Shearmen (incorporated in 1508), two offshoots of the Weavers' Company. Both guilds specialized in the treatment and finishing of cloth. The full original title of the organization was 'The Guild or Fraternity of the Assumption of the Blessed Virgin Mary of Clothworkers in the City of London'. The guild was granted its inaugural Royal Charter in 1528 by Henry VIII; one of the signatories to its ordinances, authorized in 1532, was Lord Chancellor Sir Thomas More.

The joint Company's first Hall was in Mincing Lane, where the Shearmen had been based since around 1472; the Fullers' furniture and ornaments were gradually moved into this building from their old Hall off Fenchurch Street.

Before long the Clothworkers had outgrown their premises, so in 1548 a new Hall was built on the site of the old one by the bricklayer Henry Davyson (or Davison) and the carpenter John Sampson; further extensions were added in 1594. A plan of 1612 by the cartographer Ralph Treswell (*c.* 1540–1616/17) shows the Livery Hall and the Parlour on undercrofts (fig. 25 on p. 26). Among the other rooms in the Hall were a plate chamber, a counting house and an armoury. The kitchen had a nearby knot garden in which were grown vegetables and herbs.

In 1633 surveyors discovered structural faults in the walls, so a complete rebuild was ordered and finished within the year. Little is known of the appearance and configuration of this building, however; it stood for only thirty-three years before it was razed in the Great Fire of London. It was one of the first buildings to catch fire and one of the last in which the flames were extinguished: indeed, it was still burning on the morning of Thursday 6 September 1666, a day after the conflagration was officially deemed to have ended, no doubt because of the oil stored in its cellar. This was the easternmost extremity of the conflagration: immediately beyond the Clothworkers' Hall is the churchyard of All Hallows Staining, an open space that provided a natural firebreak.

Perhaps surprisingly, the walls, though badly damaged, were salvageable, and as a result the replacement Hall, the Company's fourth, was completed very quickly, in 1668, and various additions subsequently made, including a new Court Room in 1725. In 1708, in his *New View of London*, the surveyor Edward Hatton described the post-Fire structure as a 'noble rich Building' and the Hall as follows:

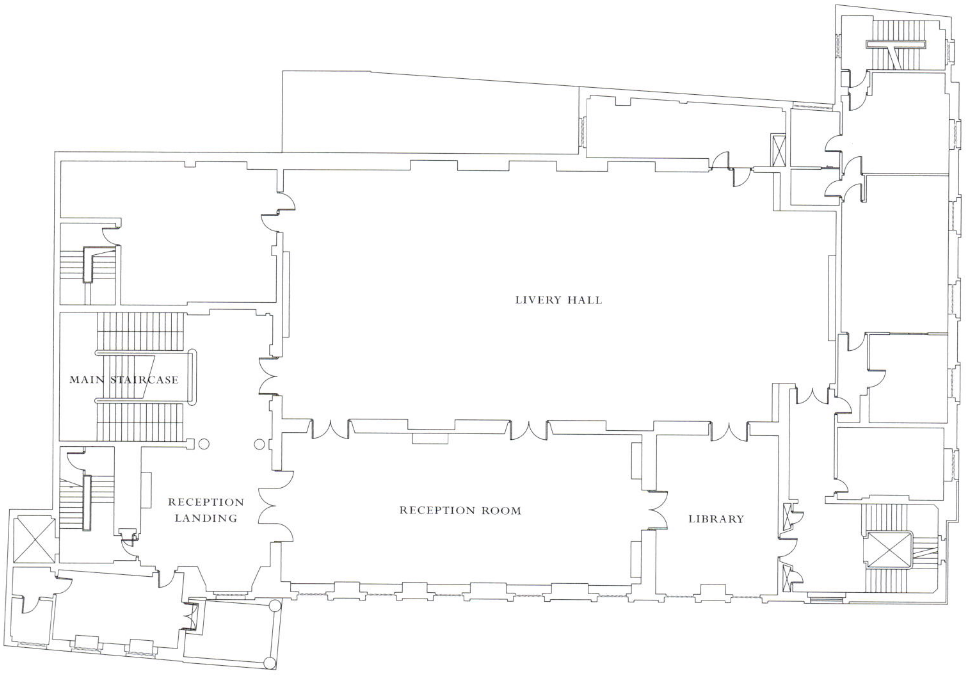

FIRST-FLOOR PLAN

... a lofty Room adorned with Wainscot to the Ceiling, where is curious Fret-work. The Screen at the S. end is of Oak adorned with 4 Pilasters, their Entablature and Compass Pediment of the Corinthian Order, enrich'd with their Arms, Palm-Branches, &c. The W. end is adorned with the Figures of K. James and K. Charles I, richly carved as big as the Life in their Robes with Regalia all gilt with Gold, where is a spacious Window of stained Glass ...[1]

This iteration of the Clothworkers' Hall was by all accounts externally glorious, but an enemy within it went unnoticed until the mid-nineteenth century, when dry rot was discovered to be so extensive that Samuel Angell, the Company Surveyor, saw no alternative but to pull the whole building down and start again. Which is exactly what happened between 1856 and the official opening of the fifth Clothworkers' Hall by Prince Albert in 1860. The new Hall – larger than its predecessor, because the garden was filled in to provide additional indoor space – was adjudged by contemporary commentators to be one of the finest examples of the Italian Renaissance revival style so popular in England during the reign of Queen Victoria; the entrance on Mincing Lane was particularly highly regarded.

During the Second World War, the Hall was one of many buildings in the City of London destroyed by a Luftwaffe air raid on the night of 10–11 May 1941. Above ground the devastation of the building was almost total, but the vaults in the basement withstood the flames, and five days later, when the heat had subsided sufficiently for people to open them up again, they found that the Company's archives and some of its artefacts and paintings were unscathed.

The Clothworkers' sixth Hall, their current home, was designed first by Henry Tanner (1876–1947) and then by Herbert Austen Hall (1881–1968) and built between 1955 and 1958. The façade is made of Portland stone on the ground floor and brick in the four storeys above. In these respects, it closely resembles its pre-war predecessor, but the main entrance from Dunster Court is a departure from tradition: the way in had always previously been from Mincing Lane.

The interiors were originally decorated and furnished in the spirit of utilitarian thrift that prevailed in the immediate post-war period; Bradley and Pevsner call them 'parsimonious'. In the more prosperous 1980s, however, the Company hired Donald Insall Associates to

Three Brussels tapestries, designed by Maximilian de Haese and woven in the workshop of Franz and Jacob van der Borght, 1771–75, tell the story of Cyrus, founder of the Persian Empire.

The Livery Hall. Among the many highlights here are Chris Ofili's celebrated woven triptych The Caged Bird's Song *(right) and the minstrels' gallery at the east end of the room (opposite).*

refurbish the public rooms in different styles from each of the periods through which the Clothworkers have plied their trade. The project architect was Nicholas Thompson.

The wrought-iron gates, taken from the Victorian Hall, lead into an Art Deco Entrance Hall, the main walkway through which is flanked by travertine marble pilasters. On the north- and south-end walls are 1986 *trompe l'œil* grisaille panels by John O'Connor that depict the four main stages of clothworking: fulling (cleaning and thickening the cloth by trampling it in water and treating it with fuller's earth), tentering (stretching cloth so that it retains its shape while drying), teaselling (nap-raising), and shearing (cutting off uneven fibres). Alongside the main passageway are glass cases in which are displayed artistic bookbindings and other treasures.

The main staircase has walls of travertine marble and a glazed dome. Around the perimeter of the latter is a plasterwork frieze depicting clothworking implements and addorsed letter Cs. A fixture on the half-landing incorporates carved ciphers of the two kings whose statues by John Bumpstead (*c.* 1679), to which Hatton refers above, were destroyed in the bombing raid.

Above: The Reception Room is convincingly Regency in appearance, but is in fact all of post-war construction.

Above, right: The present Library makes no attempt to rival the historic book collection destroyed in 1941, and now contains only a limited number of reference books relating to the history of London and its Livery Companies and guilds.

At the top of the stairs is Cedric, the gilded wooden ram carved by Jack Denny in 1968 to replace a similar creation that also fell victim to the Blitz. The Reception Landing is lit by a stained-glass window by Anthony Griffin commemorating Samuel Pepys, the famous diarist who was Master of the Company in 1677. This again is a modern replacement: the original glass was blown out in the war (fig. 34 on p. 30). (Pepys gave the Clothworkers three of their most treasured possessions: a rosewater dish, a ewer and a silver-gilt pierced and engraved loving cup.)

On the ground floor, the Drawing Room is decorated in a modern re-creation of the style of Thomas Chippendale. The marble fireplace with a carving of Apollo and the two mirrors are among the genuine eighteenth-century pieces brought in from elsewhere, but the firescreen is modern, embroidered with the Company's coat of arms by the Royal School of Needlework.

In the Court Room, lined with portraits of Past Masters, the marquetry bureau and the William Smith clock are both eighteenth century, but the decor is largely evocative of the Victorian era. The chandeliers (also in the Library) are especially remarkable: based on nineteenth-century colza-oil gasoliers, they have dishes of spectacle glass imported flat from Germany and cut in Britain; they are reputedly the largest of their kind in the country.

The Court Luncheon Room is also Victorian in style. It has hollow marble pilasters on its two longer walls and a false door at one end to enhance its symmetry. The 'lighthouse' chandelier appears to be Regency, but in fact postdates William IV.

The barrel-vaulted ceiling of the Reception Room, on the first floor, is a reproduction of the Victorian original destroyed in 1941, but the rest of the room is in eighteenth-century Adam and Sheraton styles. On the curved upper walls at each end of the room are plaster portrait medallions of Pepys and Thomas Massa Alsager (Master of the Company in 1836, *Times* journalist and, incidentally, the man into whose copy of Chapman's Homer John Keats first looked). The blue wall coverings, of silk and cotton damask, were made in Britain; the modern chandeliers are likewise largely British, but with droplets imported from Flanders. Among the paintings here are an Italian landscape of 1847 by Edward Lear and a portrait of Pepys by John Riley (1646–1691).

A small Library with a gilded and painted plasterwork ceiling lies adjacent to the Livery Hall, the magnificent focal point of the whole building. Strongly and deliberately redolent of the seventeenth century, the design of this great space is a tribute to Sir Christopher Wren, and the lime-wood wall panels of 1986 by

Left: The Court Room is lined with portraits of Past Masters. The canvas behind the Master's chair is a work attributed to the Dutch painter Richard van Bleeck of Sir Robert Beachcroft, Master in 1700 and Lord Mayor of London in 1711.

Below, left: The glass cases in the Art Deco Entrance Hall display ornate bookbindings and other artefacts made from cloth.

Below: Detail of one of the treasures of the Clothworkers' plate vault: the silver-gilt Waldo Cup of 1660 by Richard Blackwell II.

Anthony Harrington are unmistakably in the style of Grinling Gibbons. The five stained-glass windows here, bearing a range of coats of arms, were designed by Hugh Easton (1906–1965), who also created the Battle of Britain chapel window in Westminster Abbey. On the west wall hangs a newly commissioned tapestry designed by the Turner Prize-winning artist Chris Ofili and hand-woven by Dovecot Tapestry Studio in Edinburgh. *The Caged Bird's Song*, a triptych, measures 24 feet 7 inches (7.5 m) wide by 9 feet 2 inches (2.8 m) high, and depicts Ofili's vision of an island paradise. It took a team of five master weavers some two and a half years to weave, and was commissioned by the Company in 2013 in order to support the craft of hand-weaving.

In the bottom right-hand corner of the central window is a small but highly significant image of a moth – the creature that ensures there will always be work for clothmakers. A minstrels' gallery overlooks the east end of the Hall, and beneath it is the Master's chair, made from Australian black bean wood (*Castanospermum australe*) and carved with rams' heads and various tools of the clothmaking trade. This large and impressive piece of furniture was the gift of Sir Robert Menzies, Prime Minister of Australia (1939–41 and 1949–66).

NOTE

1 Edward Hatton, *A New View of London; or, An Ample Account of That City*, London (printed for John Nicholson *et al.*) 1708, vol. 2, p. 599.

DYERS' HALL

THE WORSHIPFUL COMPANY OF DYERS
ORDER OF PRECEDENCE: 13TH
GRADE II* LISTED; SCHEDULED ANCIENT MONUMENT

The Dyers' Company arms feature three bags of madder, the perennial plant from the roots of which the red dye alizarin may be obtained.

Henry VI granted the Dyers their first Royal Charter in 1471. There is evidence that the Company occupied a building in Anchor Lane in 1483, but the second Hall was in Thames Street (now Upper Thames Street); these premises were a gift in 1545 from Robert Tyrwhitt, Vice-Chamberlain to Henry VIII. Some years later, the Company acquired an additional property on the corner of Dowgate Hill and Elbow Lane (so named because it was dog-legged; now largely straightened out, it is renamed College Street). These buildings had been a college for priests until the Reformation, when they were seized by the Crown during the Dissolution of the monasteries. They were subsequently sold to two private individuals, William Green and Roger Higham, who passed them on to the Dyers.

In 1666 the Thames Street building was one of the first Livery Halls to be destroyed in the Great Fire of London. It was almost immediately rebuilt, only to be burnt to the ground again in 1681. After the latter disaster, the Dyers had to meet in rented accommodation because they had let out their Dowgate Hill property to the Skinners' Company, but they recovered partial possession in 1731. That was not the end of their accommodation difficulties, however: in 1768 the Court Room collapsed.[1] It was rebuilt by Richard Jupp (1728–1799) in less than two years; this work was remarkable for the speed with which it was executed, but not, as it turned out, for its structural soundness.

In 1831 the surveyor Charles Dyer (1794–1848) found that the Hall was settling dangerously. The rear wall was then shored up, but the problem got worse; further examination revealed that the structure had been built on top of rotten wooden sleepers on made ground. Until now, the Dyers' pragmatic philosophy had been make do and mend; after this revelation, there was nothing else for it but complete reconstruction of their home.

The fifth Dyers' Hall was commenced in 1839, partially opened in 1840 and completed in 1841. Its main entrance remained on College Street until 1857, when an extension designed by D.A. Cobbett was built on to Dowgate Hill.

In 1927 the Dyers considered returning to their former premises at what was by then No. 28 Upper Thames Street, but they eventually turned the part of Nos. 11–13 Dowgate Hill that had until then been a pub, The Bunch of Grapes, into offices for rent; they also added a third floor to the whole run of buildings.

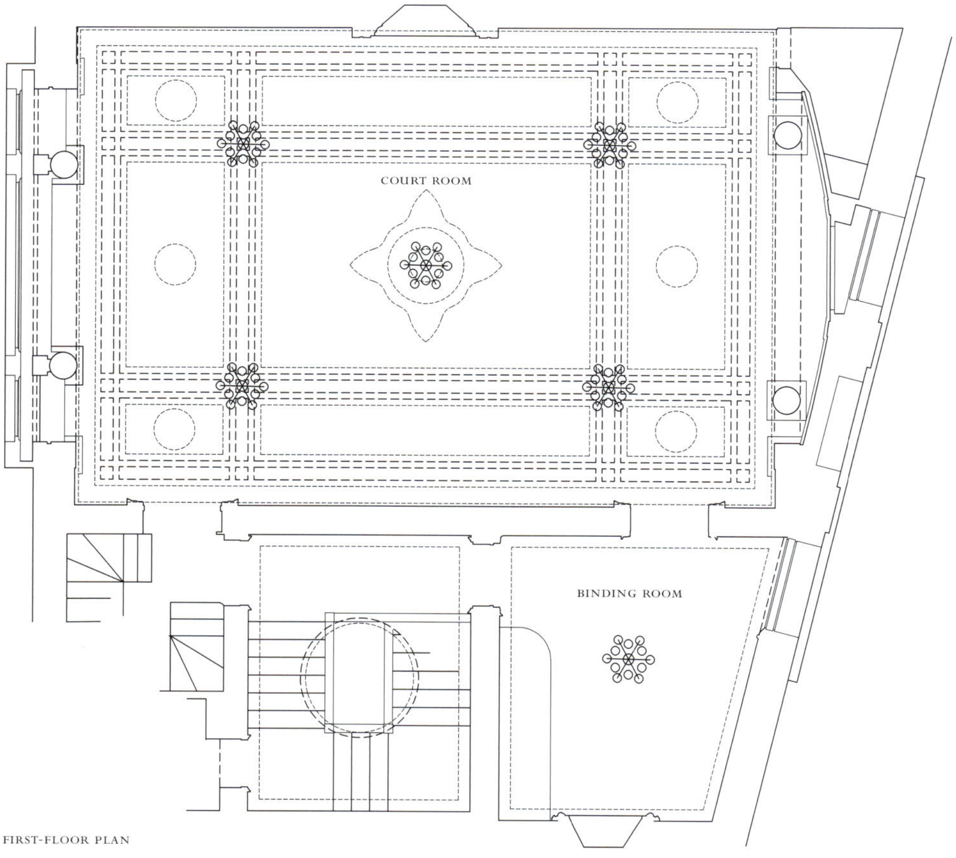

FIRST-FLOOR PLAN

A 1900s lantern brings natural light to the open well of the main staircase.

Dyers' Hall sustained little damage during the Second World War: although the building was hit by a German incendiary bomb, the ensuing blaze was quickly brought under control. The only major casualty was the glass in the main window of the Court Room, which was reinstated after the conflict.

Today Dyers' Hall has four storeys in addition to a semi-basement and dormers. The old entrance, on College Street, is now merely one of five windows, although it retains its outside steps. The ground floor of this southern façade is of stone; the upper storeys are red-painted brick.

The entrance to what is now the front of Dyers' Hall, facing east in Dowgate Hill, stands at the northern end of an arcaded ground-floor façade of stone. Between the five windows on both of the first and second floors the brickwork is punctuated by four Ionic pilasters. Above the three middle windows are a modillion cornice and a pediment with a lunette that fronts a set-back attic level.

Cobbett's Palladian-style wing lies beyond ornate wrought-iron gates surmounted by the Company's coat of arms. A groin-vaulted entrance with decorative tiles issues on to a long, glass-vaulted corridor. Along the walls of both are seven paintings of swans by Sir Peter Scott (1909–1989). A niche at the far end houses an early twentieth-century bronze sculpture of an angel and a fallen warrior by M.J.A. Mercié (1845–1916).

On the ground floor, the Committee Room has white-painted panels that may seem Regency but were created and installed by John Hatchard-Smith (1853–1936) and his son William (1887–1987) in the first decade of the twentieth century. Of around even date is the open-well, lantern-topped central staircase.

The most remarkable public space in Dyers' Hall is the first-floor Court Room. At each end are two Corinthian columns between two pilasters, all fashioned from yellow scagliola. The pairs are set further apart at the south end than at the north; there are three windows at the north end, with seventeenth-century armorial glass, and only one window along the southern flank. The chimney piece is dark marble. The mahogany wall panels were made in the late nineteenth century, but installed here only in 1965. The curtains are by Pop art pioneer Eduardo Paolozzi (1924–2005); the chocolate-brown colour scheme was applied in 1990 by H.T. ('Jim') Cadbury-Brown (1913–2009). A lavish rinceau frieze runs around the edge of the room, just below a nine-section twentieth-century ceiling.

NOTE

1 See John Norman Daynes, *A Short History of the Ancient Mistery of the Dyers of the City of London*, London (The Worshipful Company of Dyers/Witherbys of London), 1984, p. 37.

Below: The Anteroom, on the ground floor. The engraved-glass panel by Laurence Whistler was commissioned to mark the Company's quincentenary in 1971.

Above: The ground-floor entrance corridor features paintings of swans by the naturalist and broadcaster Sir Peter Scott.

Right: The white-painted panelling in the ground-floor Committee Room was installed in about 1910 by J. Hatchard-Smith & Son.

The Court Room. Note the difference between the spacing of the scagliola columns and pilasters at either end.

BREWERS' HALL

THE WORSHIPFUL COMPANY OF BREWERS
ORDER OF PRECEDENCE: 14TH

Right: The Hall's Portland stone façade is neither overawed nor diminished by the high-rise buildings that now surround it: compelling evidence that bigger is not necessarily more noticeable.

Below: Part of the Brewers' collection of Staffordshire pottery, The Dray Men *(c. 1820), by Obadiah Sherratt, depicts workers sharing a tankard of beer on an oval flower-strewn base in front of a gnarled bocage.*

The Brewers' Company was awarded its first Royal Charter by Henry VI in 1438, but the beer makers of England had been an association or fraternity for more than 250 years prior to that: the ur-administrative body, known as the Guild of Our Lady and St Thomas the Martyr, was in operation not long after the murder in 1170 of Thomas Becket, the Archbishop of Canterbury who is memorialized in part of its name.

A Brewers' Hall also pre-dates the Royal Charter; details are scanty, but it is known that such a building existed in 1403, in which year the records of the Dean and Chapter of St Paul's Cathedral refer to property of theirs in Addle Street that was leased to beer makers. The earliest record of a Brewers' Company Clerk (William Porlond) is dated 1418; his duties included letting the premises out to the Coopers, the Masons and other companies that had no Halls of their own and, on three occasions in 1422 and 1423, to 'footballpleyers' – early evidence of the apparently indissoluble chronic link between ale and soccer.

The Hall was destroyed in the Great Fire of London. To finance reconstruction, the Company levied from each of its members £5 or goods in kind to the equivalent value: one man offered 50,000 bricks. The Brewers raised additional funds by selling or pawning items of their silver and pictures that had not been lost in the inferno; they hoped to redeem the pawned valuables later, but as events transpired they could never afford to do so.

The new building was designed jointly by the Company Surveyor, Thomas Whiting (or Whiteing; see fig. 3 on p. 226), and a Mr Aldridge, and constructed by Captain John Caine in Aldermanbury Square, a short distance from the pre-Fire Hall. The wainscots were by John Symes (see fig. 36 on p. 251). Work started in 1670 and was completed three years later.

This Hall remained in largely uneventful use until the night of 29–30 December 1940, when it was all but obliterated during the Luftwaffe's single most devastating air raid on London. Although the Company's records had been moved to a bank vault in Lombard Street as a precaution at around the time of the outbreak of the Second World War, neither the building nor any of its remaining contents survived the firestorm apart from some small pieces of leaded windowpanes, which are now treasured relics of those terrible events.

After the conflict, the Brewers quickly decided to rebuild their Hall, but it took them until 1958 to

The circular Lobby at the top of the main staircase. The shelves were designed for books but now hold distinguished-label beer bottles. To quote A.E. Housman, 'malt does more than Milton can'.

obtain the requisite Building Licence, which the City of London eventually granted to them only in return for surrendering part of their freehold property to the Corporation. Completed in July 1960, the new Hall was designed by Sir Hubert Worthington (1886–1963). A pupil of Sir Edwin Lutyens, Worthington was also the architect of the Commonwealth war cemetery at El Alamein.

The exterior of the modern three-storey Brewers' Hall is of Portland stone. Its aspect has been adjudged severe by some, but it gives an air of venerable authority to an area in which upstart commercial high-rises now predominate. Severe or not, the contrast with the interior could hardly be greater: the panelling around the ground-floor entrance and the oak staircase are elegant and warmly inviting.

The street-level rooms are let to tenants. The Company's three reception rooms are on the first floor, just as they were in the Stuart Hall. From the top of the service stairs at the eastern end of the building, the first room is the Livery Hall, which is 1 inch less than 44 feet (13.4 m) long and the same amount short of 23 feet (7 m) wide. It is panelled in English oak and has four wall-to-ceiling windows along its southern flank. Also worthy of note are the fine plasterwork ceiling with hops-and-barley motif; the chandeliers; and, along the sides of the room, the hand-carved architraves and the coats of arms of the City of London, St Thomas Becket and the Company's principal benefactors. The shelves beneath the pediment are used on ceremonial occasions to display the Company's silver.

At the east end of the Livery Hall, within the broken pediment, are the Company arms; at the other end, the arms of Charles II stand above the door to the Court Room, which has the same panelling and is the same width as the Livery Hall, although it is somewhat shorter: 27 feet 10 inches (8.5 m) from end to end. The marble fireplace here has a Carrara panel sculpted by Sir Charles Wheeler (1892–1974), who also created the inscribed keystone outside the front entrance.

At the western end of the first floor is the Committee Room, 11 feet 10 inches (3.6 m) long and only 17 feet 8 inches (5.4 m) across: the width here is reduced in order to accommodate a circular Lobby, which issues on to a landing at the top of the main staircase. On the northern flank of the building, behind these public rooms, are the kitchen and cloakrooms. The top floor of the Hall houses the Company offices.

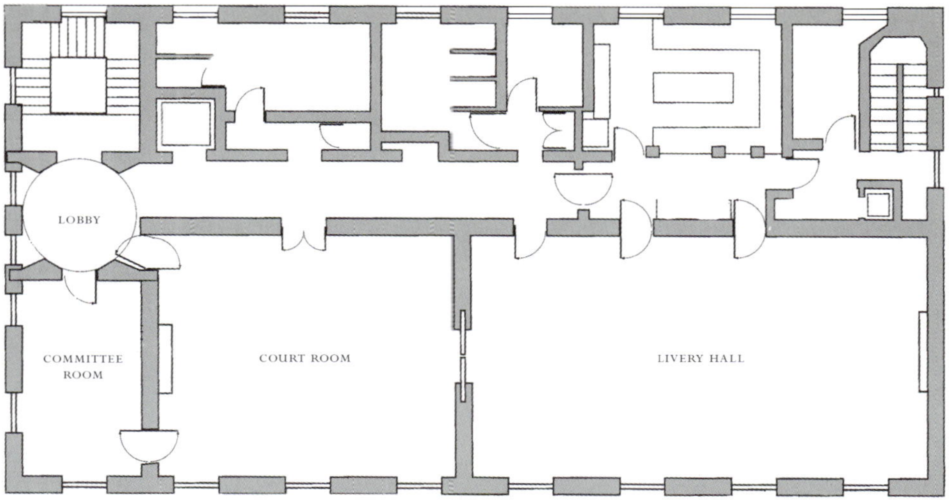

FIRST-FLOOR PLAN

The Livery Hall. The doors on the left issue on to a corridor, on the far side of which are the amenities and service area.

The wooden staircase has a warmth that contrasts markedly with the austerity of the exterior, yet there is no dissonance; each complements the other.

LEATHERSELLERS' HALL

THE WORSHIPFUL COMPANY OF LEATHERSELLERS
ORDER OF PRECEDENCE: 15TH

Visitors enter the present Hall through elaborate wrought-iron gates made in 1878 for the fifth Hall, flanked by bronze statues of the Company's heraldic beasts made in 2000 for the sixth Hall.

This is the seventh of the Leathersellers' Halls. The first was on London Wall; all the others have been in St Helen's Place, on a site that was the dorter (dormitory) for nuns of a Benedictine priory until the Company took it over in 1543 after Henry VIII's Dissolution of the monasteries (see fig. 27 on p. 27).

Designed by Eric Parry Architects and officially opened in 2017, the current iteration presents a somewhat misleading face to the outside world. The approach to it is strongly redolent of the interwar years: from Bishopsgate, the visitor passes beneath a great archway built in the 1920s through Hudson Bay House (now Hasilwood House) to gain entry to St Helen's Place. The façade of the Hall itself, by Henry Saul, erected in 1923, is wholly consistent with the other grand frontages in the lane; this and the gates, survivors of the fifth Hall, hand-wrought in 1878 by J. Starkie Gardner, give scant indication of the interiors, which, while maintaining the ancient traditions of the Company, are in other ways an unabashed celebration of modernity.

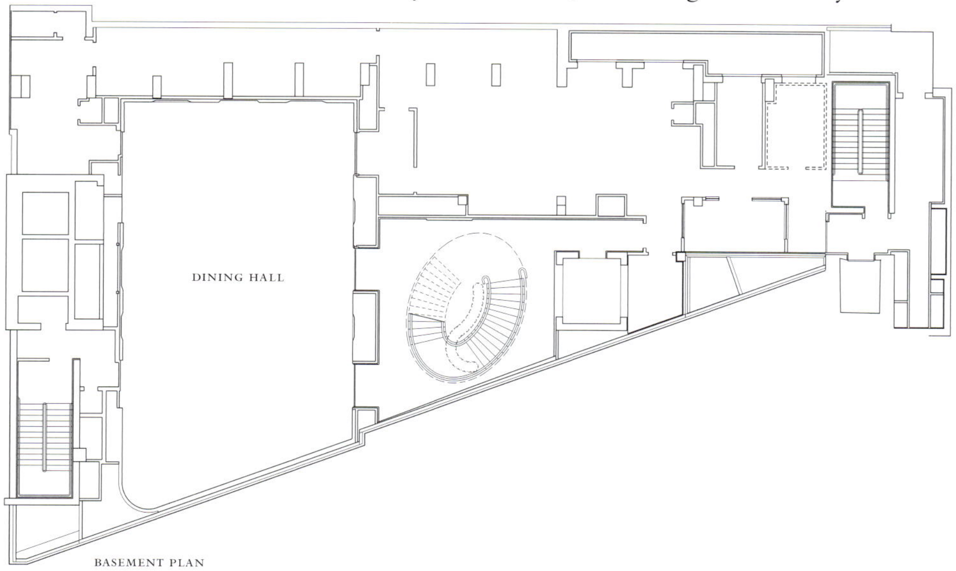

BASEMENT PLAN

The first intimations of things to come flank the entrance: two bronze statues of the ram and the roebuck, the Leathersellers' heraldic beasts, carved by Mark Coreth to commemorate the Millennium; there is nothing medieval or Victorian about their design.

The lobby has a grey granite floor inscribed with a version of the Company's coat of arms. This area is dominated by a mirror surmounting a cast-iron fireplace with glass display cases on either side. Here, too, is an inscription that records the official opening of the Hall by the Earl of Wessex on 16 May 2017.

The Court Room measures 39 feet by 23 feet (12 m by 7 m). It has double-height walls of American walnut. On the floor, a border of dark oak timber surrounds a 1950s Axminster carpet woven for the previous Hall. The coved ceiling with recessed lighting is also made of timber around a central panel of plaster, from which nineteenth-century chandeliers hang over a great table of European walnut by Luke Hughes and Company. The wall hangings here include a portrait of Henry VI and the original Royal Charter that the king granted to the Company in 1444.

In the south-facing Reception Room is a blue-and-white drawn-glass sculpture by Dale Chihuly, with a carpet specially designed by Parry to complement it: in the architect's words, the latter 'takes [the sculpture's] colour and tonality … and its geometry from medieval paving schemes, thus combining time and origin references'.[1] The circular table, made of glass and bronze, bears a Latin inscription from the foundation Charter. The large window looks directly on to the north wall of St Helen Bishopsgate, where there is a stained-glass window depicting William Shakespeare, a one-time resident of the parish. The external wall of the Hall is clad in intricately detailed ceramic tiles.

In the hallway outside the Reception Room is a large stained-glass window depicting Henry VI. The work of Leonard Walker, this was originally installed in the Company's fifth Hall in 1937, but dismantled and removed into store shortly afterwards in response to

Right: A spiral staircase leads down two floors to the subterranean Dining Hall. The purple carpet alludes to the famous Leatherseller Sir William Perkin, who in 1856 created the world's first synthetic dye.

Right, bottom: Outside the Dining Hall, a stained-glass window from the old Hall commemorates the Company's 550th anniversary in 1994. Each year a new name is painted on the panels alongside, bringing the long list of Masters up to date.

wise counsellors who anticipated war with Germany. This was indeed prophetic: the building in which the window had stood was destroyed in 1941 during the Blitz. After the Second World War, the stained glass was put back into the sixth Hall, where it was badly damaged by the IRA bombing of the Baltic Exchange in 1992, but it has since been restored to its original glory.

Among the other highlights of the hallway are the scagliola pilasters on the walls and ceiling. Made from plaster that has been pigmented to resemble marble, they were taken from the sixth Hall and reinstalled here in a way intended to reimagine the Company's long heritage in an arrestingly contemporary manner. Also worth contemplation is the skylight, deliberately positioned to provide a prospect of Foster + Partners' Gherkin at No. 30 St Mary Axe, a magnificent tower that dominated the nearby skyline when it was completed in 2004, but which is now being overshadowed by more recent structures that are starting to dwarf its 590 feet (180 m).

The adjacent corridor of the Hall has walls lined with green and maroon leather; the walkway leads into the Library, the walls of which are hung with two paintings by Gillis Mostaert (1528–1598) of Antwerp, showing various stages of leather production.

Beneath the Walker window is a leather-lined spiral staircase that leads down to the Dining Room, one of the most striking features of which is the 130-foot-long (40 m) tapestry by Victoria Crowe that runs around three walls, above American walnut panels extending from floor level to a height of 10 feet 2 inches (3.1 m). The tapestry depicts the history of leather production and the Leathersellers' Company; the face of the tanner scraping flesh from animal hide is the same as that of *The Flesher*, the statue by Etienne Millner, commissioned for Elizabeth II's Diamond Jubilee in 2012, that stands outside the main entrance.

The Dining Hall is a tour de force that highlights both the problems of the whole site – triangular and tightly constricted – and the architect's bravura solution to them. Although the room is beneath ground level, it is designed in such a way that the church wall above remains in view on the south side; the other three flanks of the Dining Hall are illuminated by clerestories.

NOTE

1 Eric Parry, 'Architects' View', *Leathersellers' Review 2015–16*, p. 15; http://www.leathersellers.co.uk/wp-content/uploads/2017/01/ReviewFinal2015-16.pdf (accessed June 2018).

Below: The basement-level vestibule.

Below, right: The green-and-maroon leather panels, decorated with leaf motifs associated with tanning, are reminders of the Company's original raison d'être.

Bottom: A key feature of the Dining Hall is the richly coloured tapestry, designed by Victoria Crowe and woven by Dovecot Tapestry Studio in Edinburgh.

Top: The walnut panelling and table in the Court Room contrast with the colourful Axminster carpet from the 1950s. The Royal Charter of 1444 has place of honour at the far end.

Left: The focal point of the Reception Room is a striking blue-and-white glass sculpture by the American artist Dale Chihuly.

Above: The Reception Room has a floor-to-ceiling view of the north wall of St Helen Bishopsgate, which contains a stained-glass window of Shakespeare, a resident of this parish in the 1590s.

PEWTERERS' HALL

THE WORSHIPFUL COMPANY OF PEWTERERS
ORDER OF PRECEDENCE: 16TH

Right: The Master's chair, made of walnut in a late 17th-century style with a central hide panel headed by a pierced and carved crest depicting two putti holding aloft a plate and flanked by foliate scrolls, the side rails headed by turbaned men's heads above acanthus carved scroll supports and open foliate scrolls and buds.

Right, bottom: One of a pair of Queen Anne porringers, made by John Quick of London, c. 1710.

For the greater part of the Middle Ages, pewter – an alloy of, originally, one part lead and between three and nine parts tin – was the material most widely used to make dinner plates and drinking vessels. Those who made and sold it were granted their first Royal Charter by Edward IV in 1473. (This document was unusual in that it bestowed on them trade rights throughout the kingdom; most early Charters gave the recipient companies jurisdiction only in London.)

By the following year the Pewterers had made No. 15 Lime Street – where it seems they were informally established already – their first permanent residence. This was an extensive property with, in addition to a capacious main hall, six adjoining tenements and a garden containing a bowling alley, an arbour, a vine and rose trees. Rebuilt in 1496 by Simon Birlyngham, a carpenter, the place remained the focal point of the Pewterers' activities until its destruction in the Great Fire of London in 1666.

The second Pewterers' Hall, on the same site, was designed by John Wildgos and a Mr Tayler. It is sometimes claimed that Christopher Wren also contributed to the design and construction, but the supporting evidence for this seems rather slighter than the enduring desire to link the great architect's name to almost every London edifice of the late seventeenth century.[1] The new building was completed in 1670. Among its most frequently praised interior features were its elaborate plasterwork and panelling and its beautiful brass chandeliers.

In the eighteenth century pewter lost much of its market share to products made from china and glass; the Company correspondingly fell on hard times. The Hall became surplus to requirements, and after 1801 was no longer used for dinners; Pewterers' events were held in one of the Company's smaller adjacent houses in Lime Street. Then one day in 1883 a cook turned on the gas in the kitchen, failed to light it, and omitted to turn it off; the Beadle came in and, unaware of any danger, lit a match and thereby caused a non-fatal but devastating explosion. The Pewterers abandoned the building, making no attempt to repair the damage; the Hall fell into further disrepair and was eventually demolished in 1932. (They still own the site, on which offices now stand.) The oak panelling and the plaster ceiling in the Master's Parlour were saved, however, and installed at the Geffrye Museum in Kingsland Road. This was removed from the museum in 2006 and placed in storage. Also preserved is the second Hall's 1668 Portland stone gate, which was removed to University College London under the guidance of the architect Sir Albert Richardson (1880–1964) and now forms the rear entrance to that foundation's Faculty of Life Sciences' Medawar Building in Gower Street.

After 1883 the Pewterers' Company had no permanent home until 1961, in which year its present Hall was completed on land purchased in 1958 off London Wall. Designed by D.E. Nye & Partners and two years in construction by Holloway Brothers, whose other works included the Old Bailey (1902–1907), this three-storey building overlooks on its eastern side the churchyard of St Mary Staining (destroyed in the Great Fire), which is now a garden, still owned by the Church, but serviced by the City of London Corporation.

The south-facing frontage on Oat Lane has three ground-floor windows, with the main entrance between the first and second windows on the left. The interiors are a captivating blend of old and new. In the ground-floor Livery Hall, the high ceiling, tall sash windows and, above all, the slight but readily perceptible outward curve on the east wall are all neo-Georgian; in the also slightly convex Court Room on the first floor, the panelling dates from the seventeenth century, brought over from the second Hall. The Hall underwent a major programme of internal refurbishment by Dolby & Taylor in 2011–13.

The Court Room is also remarkable for the large oval compartment in the centre of its ceiling: Bradley and Pevsner describe this feature as 'not well done and harshly coloured'; viewers of the image overleaf may form a more favourable opinion of it.

The landing between the ground floor and the first floor is lit and enlivened by a 1974 armorial stained-glass window by Brian Thomas (1912–1989), whose depictions of six acts of mercy from St Matthew's Gospel had been installed in 1958 in Westminster Abbey.

The top floor of Pewterers' Hall has a tiled hipped roof that was increased in height in 1996 by Lloyd Leroy Architects. This level now houses the Company's offices: no part of the building is rented out to tenants.

NOTE

1 See Charles Welch, *History of the Worshipful Company of Pewterers of the City of London Based upon Their Own Records*, London (Blades, East & Blades) 1902, vol. 2, p. viii.

The work of W.J. Englefield, this pewter inkwell, ornamented in relief, was presented to the Company by Clements Collins, Master in 1906.

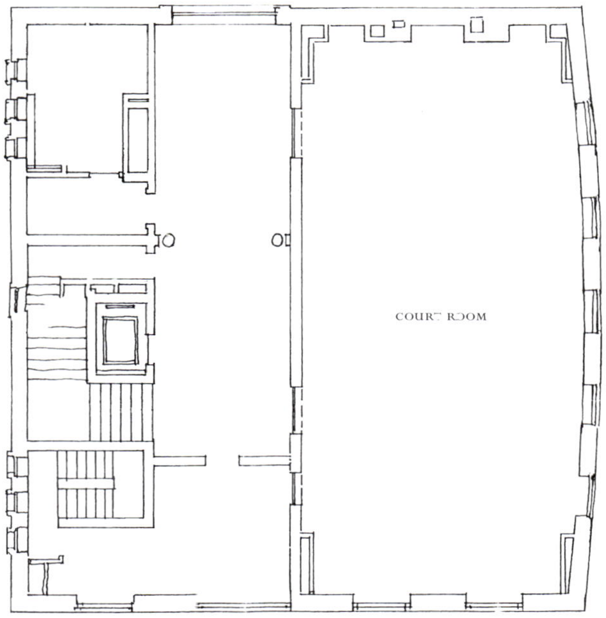

FIRST-FLOOR PLAN

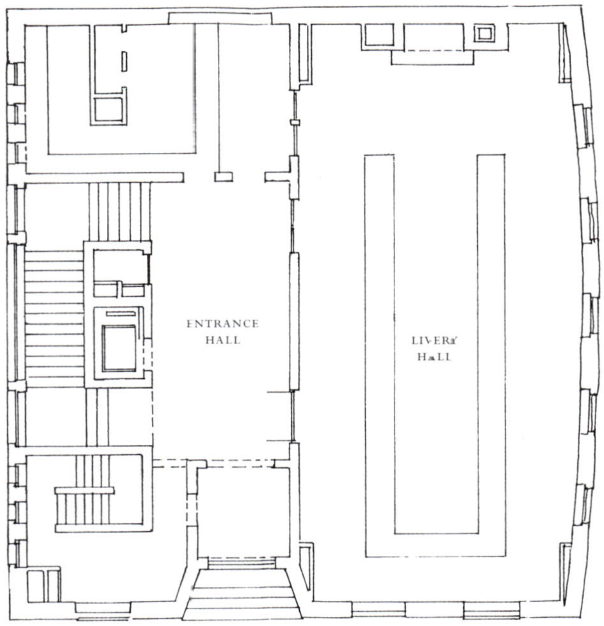

GROUND-FLOOR PLAN

Right and opposite, top left: The Court Room features panelling taken from the second Hall, which was completed in 1670 with, it is sometimes claimed, contributions from Christopher Wren. The elaborate chandeliers are also from the previous Hall.

Bottom: The Livery Hall, with pewter chandeliers by Albert Bartram. The room was redecorated in 2012 by Dolby & Taylor, using such traditional techniques as hand-gilding. The bespoke carpet incorporates the Company's arms.

Below: A selection of gill measures, including a bulbous gill measure, probably by James Dixon, c. 1820–30.

BARBER-SURGEONS' HALL

THE WORSHIPFUL COMPANY OF BARBERS
ORDER OF PRECEDENCE: 17TH

Right: The 'mildly Neo-Georgian' frontage of the Hall on Monkwell Square.

Below: The current arms of the Barbers' Company were officially granted in 1569, during the reign of Elizabeth I.

The Barbers have owned this site near the Barbican for approaching 600 years. Although their tenure has often been fraught with difficulties (not the least of which have been financial), they retain the freehold, having resisted periodic temptations to cut their losses and sell.

In the early Middle Ages, monks practised medicine, but in 1163 Pope Alexander III banned the clergy from letting blood. Since this was regarded in the twelfth century as an essential medical treatment, someone had to take it on, and barbers – who, of course, habitually used razors – were the outstanding candidates to fill the unexpected vacancy.

For hundreds of years thereafter, barbers were also surgeons, and surgeons were also barbers. In 1540 the interventionist Crown demanded that the Company of Barbers and the Surgeons' Fellowship, previously allied but separate, be united into a single guild, the Worshipful Company of Barbers and Surgeons of London, which thereafter took charge of both businesses. The new dispensation sought to demarcate the territory: surgeons were forbidden to cut hair; barbers were no longer allowed to cut people up. Although practitioners of both vocations shared the objectives of maintaining professional standards and banishing charlatans, these were about the only matters on which they acted in concert.

What was never a happy alliance grew increasingly strained as surgery became more of a science while hairdressing remained a trade. Meanwhile, another crisis befell the Company: the original Hall was almost completely destroyed in the Great Fire of London; all that remained of it was the anatomy theatre, designed by Inigo Jones and built in the 1630s (see fig. 14 on p. 236). This was incorporated into the post-Fire rebuild, but demolished in 1784 to make way for housing.

After the reconstruction of the Hall, a split in the Company became inevitable, and this was eventually recognized and confirmed by a 1745 Act of Parliament. Thereafter, the Surgeons went their own way.

Under the terms of this separation, the Barbers kept many of the joint Company's accumulated treasures and, most importantly, the Hall. These were major assets, but as the status of hairdressing declined, so too did the Barbers' liquid cash; the buildings fell into disrepair because the Company could not afford to maintain them. By the middle of the nineteenth century, they were dilapidated indeed.

And then came the Second World War. On the night of 29 December 1940, during the Blitz, the whole structure – forever known as Barber-Surgeons' Hall, but now in the sole ownership of the Worshipful Company of Barbers – was destroyed by fire. This might have been the end for the Barbers' permanent residency, but thanks to careful planning the Hall rose again from the ashes.

The current Barbers' building, their third, dates from the 1960s. It was designed by Kenneth K. Cross (a Past Master of the Company) and Laurence King & Partners, and constructed by Dove Brothers of Islington. Bradley and Pevsner fairly describe the façade as 'mildly Neo-Georgian'.

To the right of the Entrance Hall, on the west side of Monkwell Square, are the Charter Room and the Court Room. The former contains a small library: the current paucity of volumes is a consequence of the Company's decision to sell its collection not long after the split with the Surgeons (in 1749 they raised £13 from the sale). The modern Barbers are now working to re-create the old inventory; by the end of 2017 the earliest book they had re-acquired was a copy of Claudius Galen's *Opera* (1529). The Court Room contains a stained-glass panel from the pre-Fire Hall.

To the left of the Entrance Hall is an L-shaped Reception Room, which is basically an oblong but from which a section has been partitioned off to accommodate a staircase and a lift. Further along the southern side of the building are the kitchens.

The main attraction is directly opposite the entrance: the Great Hall, a double-height room with a large bow window in the middle of its western flank. On either side of the doorway are eighteenth-century Chinese-style painted and gilt leather screens.

The Hall interior is lined with Japanese oak panelling and dominated by the greatest of the Company's art treasures: a painting by Hans Holbein the Younger (1497/98–1543) of Henry VIII and the Barber-Surgeons. This masterpiece commemorates the 1540 Act of Parliament that united the two previously separate organizations. In it, the king is crowned and seated, wearing ermine-lined state robes and the insignia of the Order of the Garter, and holding the Sword of State. With his left hand he passes a document to Thomas Vicary, his Serjeant-Surgeon, who would later become Master of the Company. To the left are the monarch's physicians and his apothecary. The figures on the upper row are later additions by one or more other hands.

Above the Holbein are the carved arms of the Company that stood above the main entrance in 1940 and survived that year's conflagration. The bevelled gilt wall mirrors date from around 1730.

On the ceiling of the Hall are carved relief mouldings of red roses and fleams (spring-loaded blades that made surgical incisions). The latter, while clearly appropriate to this setting, are not to everyone's taste.

In the grounds, within the remains of bastion 13 of the Roman City Wall, is a Physic Garden containing a wide range of plants, not only those used in traditional medicine and dentistry (some of whose supposed beneficial properties are now discredited), but also several used in modern pharmaceuticals. To the left of the bastion are two trees planted in 2002: a yellow magnolia to mark the Golden Jubilee of Elizabeth II, and a winter-flowering cherry in memory of Queen Elizabeth The Queen Mother, who died in March of that same year.

The first floor of Barber-Surgeons' Hall houses a servery, Company offices and the Master's Lodge. The rooms on the second, third and fourth floors are let out; also on the fourth floor, at the top of the building, is the Beadle's flat.

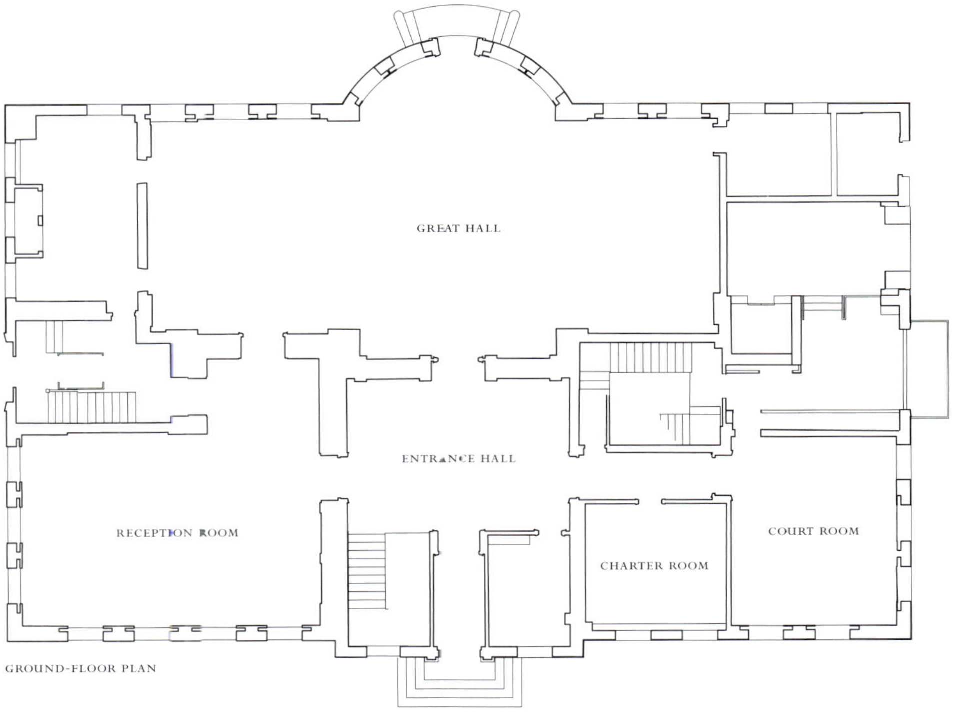

GROUND-FLOOR PLAN

A stained-glass window in the Court Room depicts the Company's arms. It was originally installed in the Barbers' first Hall in 1660.

Right: Portraits on the wall of the Reception Room: from left to right, Inigo Jones; Lady Hopton; her husband, Sir Ralph Hopton, a Royalist soldier in the Civil War; Sir John Frederick, Master of the Company in 1654 and 1658 and Lord Mayor of London in 1661.

Below and opposite, bottom: The Great Hall is panelled in Japanese oak. Note in particular the group portrait by Holbein (below) and the large bow window in the middle of the western side.

Left: The doorway to the Great Hall, on either side of which are painted and gilt leather screens in Chinese style no later than 1711.

CUTLERS' HALL

THE WORSHIPFUL COMPANY OF CUTLERS
ORDER OF PRECEDENCE: 18TH
GRADE II LISTED

Top: The façade on Warwick Lane boasts a finely carved terracotta frieze by the sculptor Benjamin Creswick. It depicts cutlers working at their craft.

Above: Detail of the hammer posts in the Livery Hall, featuring carved elephant heads. The elephant motif is found throughout the Hall.

The Company's earliest premises, known as the 'House of the Cutlers' and first recorded in the late thirteenth century, were on or near the site of the current Mercers' Hall in Ironmonger Lane. However, by the time the Cutlers were granted their first Royal Charter – by Henry V in 1416 – they had moved to a building in Horseshoe Bridge Street (now Cloak Lane), which they then purchased in 1451. This was by all accounts a spacious place, with a Great Hall, several chambers and parlours, a counting house, a store house and a garden with grape vines; later a Yeomanry Hall was added.

The Cutlers were wealthy, and in 1661 they decided to rebuild their Hall in its entirety. Work was completed in June 1666, but just three months later the entire structure was burnt down in the Great Fire of London. Reconstruction was swift: the Cutlers were back in action on the same site in 1670. There they remained until 1882, when they lost most of their land to a compulsory purchase order that cleared the way for the section of the present District Underground line between Cannon Street and Mansion House stations.

The Cutlers then moved to a site in Warwick Lane that from 1674 to 1825 had been the headquarters of the Royal College of Physicians and was at that time being used as a foundry. Designed by the Company Surveyor, Thomas Tayler Smith (1834–1910), the new Hall was opened in 1888.

The exterior of the two-storey building is of red brick and sandstone. At the northern end of the façade, on the ground floor only, is a small bow window. Between the latter and the main entrance, the terracotta frieze showing cutlers at work is by the sculptor Benjamin Creswick (1853–1946), a pupil of John Ruskin. On the upper floor, the Livery Hall has three pairs of windows, each window divided by one mullion and two transoms.

The hallway interior has dark neo-Jacobean oak wall panels. Straight ahead is a cloakroom with tippable shelves that were originally for visitors' top hats but are now used mainly for their laptops. On the left is a stained-glass window by Powell & Sons (1903). To the right is the Stair Hall, with columns resting on carved elephants. (Elephants are prominent in Cutlers' iconography because, historically, blade handles were made of ivory taken from their tusks; today the Company is active in the conservation of these creatures.) Facing the street on the ground floor is the Court Room, which, according to demand, may be transformed into two separate spaces through the use of sliding doors. Here and throughout the building, the wrought-iron candelabra are worthy of special note. On the western side of the Hall are the Beadle's office and stairs down to offices and the kitchens.

In a glass bell-jar on a table on the ground floor at the foot of the main stairs is a sculpture of a tree, the leaves of which are made from tiny penknife blades – 1851 of them, in reference to the year of the Great Exhibition, for which it was made by apprentice cutlers. On the wall nearby is a 1569 oak carving of the Company's coat of arms – one of the few of the Cutlers' possessions that survived the Great Fire. The stained-glass windows lighting the stairs were rescued from the Cloak Lane Hall. Displayed on the landing are several fine examples of the sword-maker's art.

On the first floor, the Livery Hall has a steeply pitched hammer-beam roof with pairs of carved elephant heads at the springing points, arched braces and a plaster ceiling. Along the north-end wall is a minstrels' gallery; across the south end is draped the huge Barge Banner used for the Lord Mayor's Procession in 1763, when the incoming holder of the office, William Bridgen, was a Cutler. Behind the Master's chair, a wooden canopy surmounted by the royal arms of the House of Stuart is a work of no later than 1688.

The tusks in the Stair Hall (below) are a reminder of an age when knife handles were made of ivory and elephants were not an endangered species. The dark oak panelling is offset by the stained glass, the light-coloured ceilings and the sheer height of the space.

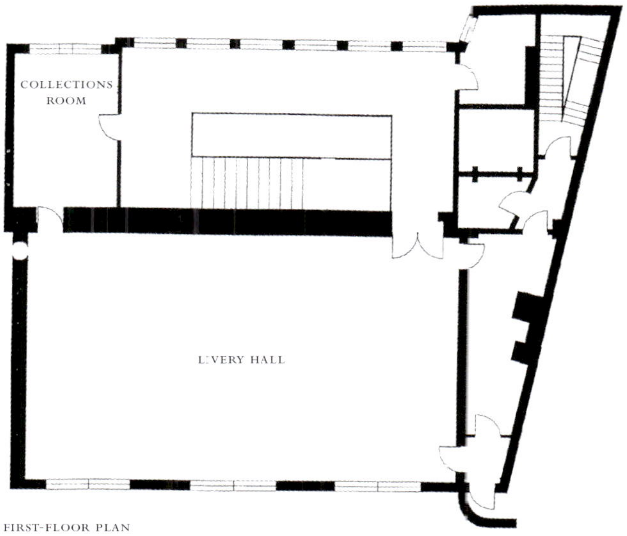

FIRST-FLOOR PLAN

The north wall is of particular interest. Cutlers' Hall survived the worst night of the Blitz unscathed: photographs taken the next day, 30 December 1940, show that it and St Paul's were just about the only buildings left standing in this area of the City. (The Cathedral had been missed deliberately, because it gave German pilots a landmark by which to orient themselves; the Cutlers' escape, however, was merely fortuitous.) The Company was less lucky on 10 May 1941, when a bomb demolished the next-door building in Newgate Street. The proximate wall of the Cutlers' Dining Room went with it, but the rest of the Hall was largely unaffected. By 1951 the damage had been repaired and the building was back in full operation.

Next to the Livery Hall is the Collections Room, formerly the Smoking Room. Some of the nineteenth-century stained-glass windows here extol the health-giving properties of tobacco: *autre temps* ... The room now houses some of the Company's cutlery, a collection that contains cutting instruments and eating utensils from prehistory to the present day, and livery medals from a variety of Companies.

Left: A portrait of Margaret Craythorne, a Company benefactor in the 16th century, is displayed in the Court Room. The wrought-iron chandelier is contemporary with the Hall.

Below: At the far end of the Court Room are portraits of Sir Robert Carden and Henry Winchester, Company members who served as Lord Mayor of London in 1857 and 1834, respectively.

Bottom and opposite: The Livery Hall, with its Victorian hammer-beam roof. A minstrels' gallery dominates one end, while the large 18th-century Barge Banner hangs at the other.

CUTLERS' HALL

BAKERS' HALL

THE WORSHIPFUL COMPANY OF BAKERS
ORDER OF PRECEDENCE: 19TH

The entrance to Bakers' Hall, on Harp Lane. Completed in 1963, this was the first of the post-war Modernist Livery Halls.

Harp Lane is so small and tightly surrounded by thoroughfares of great pith and moment that it may be difficult for any creature with eyesight inferior to that of a young sea eagle to locate it on the A–Z Map. But it is well worth seeking out because Bakers' Hall, which stands on its eastern pavement, is a modest Modernist beauty.

Established in 1155 – within a year of the coronation of Henry II – the Bakers are the second oldest guild: only the Weavers pre-date them. From the thirteenth century they held court four times a year; the only other trades that had the right to govern themselves in the Middle Ages were the Weavers and the Fishmongers. The Bakers remained self-regulating until 1815, at the end of the Napoleonic Wars.

For hundreds of years there were fiercely maintained distinctions and rivalry between bakers of white bread and bakers of brown bread: no one was allowed to produce both types. Then as now, brown bread was more nutritious than white bread, but white bread was more popular. Consequently, the White Bakers were more prosperous, and when they rented premises in Dowgate in 1486 they had sufficient economic power to compel the Brown Bakers to join them.

The White Bakers went from strength to strength at the end of the fifteenth century, so it was they who were first able to afford their own property: in 1506 they purchased from one of their number, Richard Roper, premises in Sigrymes Lane, subsequently renamed Hart Lane and now Harp Lane.

This was or became a grand building, with great gates on yellow posts leading into a courtyard around which was more-than-adequate accommodation for all the liverymen, as well as almshouses. The dark-red-panelled main assembly room had a gilt chimney piece and windows emblazoned with the Bakers' arms – a heraldic design featuring waves and anchors in reference to the Company's patron, St Clement, the third pope, who was martyred by being thrown into the sea with a weight tied around his neck. (The White Bakers' shield has always had two anchors vertically, whereas the old Brown Bakers' shield had a single horizontal anchor.) The early saint was also commemorated here in the Clement Parlour, a summer lounge with an enormous glass window. The garden of the Bakers' first Hall stretched down to the River Thames; it had a house, grape vines, a herb garden and a bowling alley.

In 1509 the White Bakers were incorporated by a Royal Charter granted to them by Henry VII. This did nothing to help their relations with the rival bread makers, and indeed the animosity between the Whites and the Browns became so intense that in 1528 they were ordered to separate. The brown-bread bakers sought their own Charter in 1544, but their application was turned down. In 1569, when the Whites were granted a new Charter by Elizabeth I, they forced the Browns to rejoin them. The two factions' subsequent split was gradual; they just drifted apart. In 1614 the Brown Bakers were finally awarded their own Charter, but within a generation the two Companies – though unwilling to coexist – found it impractical any longer to remain apart, so they petitioned the Crown for a reunion, which was officially ratified in 1645.

Then the unified Bakers' Hall was razed in the Great Fire of 1666; only the silver plate and the Charters were saved. The second Hall was completed in 1673, but in 1715 it went the way of its predecessor, engulfed in flames. Construction of the third Hall began in 1719 and was completed in 1722. It had oak and pine panelling, and each stair was made from a solid balk of

Right: The phoenix wallpaper in the Charter Gallery is believed to have been screen-printed by hand at the Sanderson wallpaper factory in about 1960. On the far wall is the futuristic cityscape by Ricardo Cinalli, acquired in 2017.

Right, bottom: A bust of Winston Churchill sits at the bottom of the stairs leading into the Charter Gallery. It was presented to the Company in 1971 by Liveryman Alan Mears, a nephew of the sculptor, Bryant Baker.

wood. Various embellishments added by the Victorians were frowned upon in the early 1930s and removed, but all this effort was for naught: the Hall was almost completely obliterated during the Blitz on the night of 29 December 1940.

Work started on the current Bakers' Hall, their fourth, in 1961, and was completed in 1963. Designed by Trehearne & Norman, Preston & Partners in collaboration with W. Newcombe-Wright, a liveryman, it is a small, square podium-set block, with offices for rent above the Company's premises. Its footprint is smaller than that of any of its predecessors, because a compulsory purchase order forced the Bakers to give up part of their land for the construction of a main road in Byward Street. The exterior was reclad in brown brick between 1984 and 1986 by the Whinney Mackay-Lewis Partnership.

The Entrance Hall is partly illuminated by a stained-glass window bearing the Company's arms of 1525. On the walls of the stairs to the basement are eight marble panels with lead inlays depicting the history of the Company. Designed by Joseph Clarke of Clarke & Shoppee, these were installed in 1882 in the street range leading to the eighteenth-century Hall. These artefacts were among the few of the Bakers' possessions to have survived the Second World War.

Also on the ground floor is the Charter Gallery, with its wall covering of stylized gold phoenixes on a dark background. Here are displayed the Company's silverware and art. A 2017 addition to the latter collection was a futuristic cityscape vision by Ricardo Cinalli. Just off here is the Print Room, which is now used for small meetings. Beyond it is the Livery Hall, with panels of Brazilian mahogany, the carved arms of George II and – most strikingly – three stained-glass windows by John Piper (1903–1992) depicting the three fires that determined the course of the Bakers' history: in 1666, 1715 and 1940. The Bakers' Company commissioned Piper shortly after his window in the Baptistery of Coventry Cathedral was unveiled to the public. These works were highly controversial at the time, and some critics believed that the Company was making a mistake; but what seemed radical in the 1960s seems classical today, and the works are the crowning glory of the Hall.

In the basement are the kitchens, the wine cellars and the Court Room. The last has resplendent light oak and ash panelling by John W. Tompkins.

The Court Room, where the Master Baker, Wardens and Assistants meet formally four times a year. The bar (right) is topped by unicorn finials (detail above). The view from the Wardens' bench is pictured above, right.

Above: The Livery Hall set for a luncheon attended by the Lord Mayor of London.

Right: The Livery Hall's outstanding feature, the stained-glass windows by John Piper, commissioned to commemorate the three Halls that previously occupied the site and were all destroyed by fire.

WAX CHANDLERS' HALL

THE WORSHIPFUL COMPANY OF WAX CHANDLERS
ORDER OF PRECEDENCE: 20TH

Right: The rusticated ground floor of Wax Chandlers' Hall escaped destruction during a bombing raid in 1940 and was incorporated into Seely & Paget's new Hall, completed in 1958.

Right, bottom: The coffered hallway; the entrance to the Court Room is just visible on the left.

Wax chandlers made candles from beeswax. Beeswax was more expensive than animal fat, and so while tallow chandlers produced workaday lighting, wax chandlers provided candles for the rich and powerful and, especially, for the Church. In fact, before the emergence of the Wax Chandlers' Company, many medieval parish priests had kept their own beehives for this very purpose.

The Company developed gradually and may have existed as early as during the reign of Richard I (1189–99). By 1330 it was sufficiently well established to have been required to contribute to Edward III's war chest.

Most of London's chandlers were among the 40 per cent of the population of England who succumbed to the Black Death (1348–50), but the trade quickly regenerated thereafter, taking on many new apprentices to service the increased demand for funerary ornamentation. (Indeed, the business thrived until the Reformation, when Thomas Cromwell restricted the use of candles in churches because it smacked to him of popery.)

In 1358 the trade was regulated after a scandal involving an Italian-born tradesman who had been accused of peddling 'false torch' – candles that purported to be all-beeswax but which had been adulterated with tallow and other cheaper components.

Richard III granted the Company its first Royal Charter in 1484; a year later it was awarded its own coat of arms. In 1501 a group of six Wax Chandlers took over The Cock on the Hoop, a brewhouse on a thoroughfare that was then named Maiden Lane. By 1525 they had converted it for their own commercial purposes. In 1609 an Act of Parliament confirmed the freehold rights of the Company to these premises and the land on which they stood.

The buildings were destroyed in the Great Fire, but a new Hall, designed by the prolific Edward Jerman, was completed on the same site by 1670. It was replaced in 1792–93 with a Hall that incorporated warehouse facilities, all designed by Richard Wooding.

Then in 1845 the Corporation of London widened Maiden Lane, Cateaton Street, St Anne's Lane and Lad Lane, amalgamated them and named the thoroughfare thereby created Gresham Street, after the founder of the Royal Exchange. The Wax Chandlers opposed the new street plan, successfully at first, but in 1849 a new Act of Parliament forced them to give way to vehicular traffic, and their Hall was demolished.

A chair and a long-case clock in the Master's Room are inlaid with marquetry. The chair seat is embroidered with the Company arms and the motto 'Truth is the light'.

The compensation that the Company received enabled it to rebuild its Hall on what was basically the same site minus the strip shaved off by the widened street. Completed in 1853, the resulting Italianate structure was the last work of Charles Fowler (1792–1867), designer of, among other important buildings, Covent Garden Market.

The basement and ground floor of the fourth Hall were the only parts of the building that survived the German air raid on the night of 29 December 1940. Post-war austerity slowed reconstruction. The current building was commenced only in 1954 and not completed until 1958. Its superstructure is the design of John Seely, 2nd Baron Mottistone, of Seely & Paget Architects.

The modern Wax Chandlers' Hall retains much of the external character of its predecessor: an entrance canopy and wall facings of granite beneath two storeys of brick and a mansard roof clad in copper. The east wall of the building was refaced in 2003 by Foster + Partners. Bradley and Pevsner describe the middle section of the north front as 'curiously attenuated', but the mix of materials makes an eye-catching contrast, whereas a homogeneous granite façade might have been oppressive and an all-brick frontage banal.

On entering the building, the Parlour on the left of the ground floor is used as a small meeting room; behind it are cloakrooms and toilets. The Court Room, on the right, overlooks Gutter Lane, which runs along the western flank of the building. These interiors were refurbished in 2007.

The first floor is rented out as offices. On the second floor, the Livery Hall is wider on its western side than on its eastern; it tapers, slightly but noticeably. This small legacy of the road-widening scheme gives the room a strikingly offbeat quality. The Hall can seat approximately 70 for formal dining or around 100 for buffet-style meals. The servery is on the eastern flank and the Master's Room on the western side. This level has a mezzanine on which a minstrels' gallery stands above the entrance to the Hall.

The top floor contains the Company offices and two flats, one for the Master, the other for the Beadle.

The basement is of particular interest, not only for its separate wine stores, one for red, the other for white. (There are also the kitchens, a pantry and two other rooms below ground.) The damage caused here by an electrical fire in 2017 necessitated additional refurbishment, during which were uncovered nineteenth-century brick arches behind what had previously been a post-war suspended ceiling. The door of the fire exit from the underground level on to Gutter Lane is of fibreglass made to look like the granite skirtings that surround the rest of the street-level exterior: that it is not entirely convincing is part of its charm.

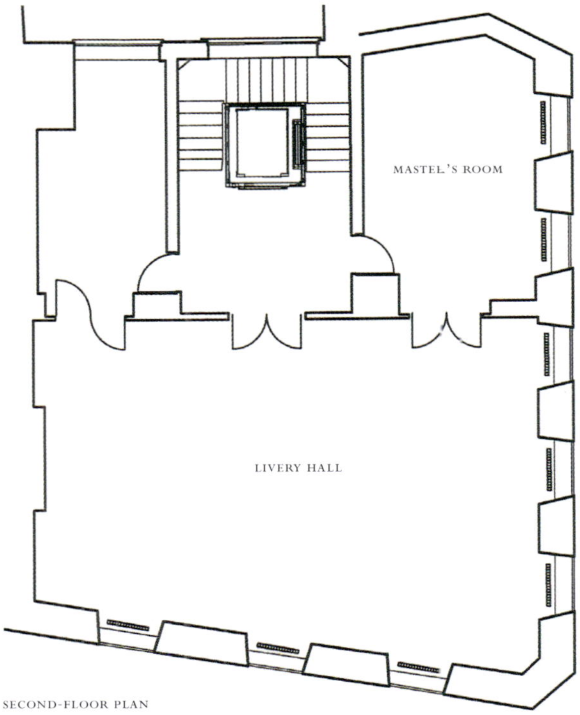

SECOND-FLOOR PLAN

Top and right: The Livery Hall, showing the minstrels' gallery above the main doorway, and the view from the doorway towards the windows on Gutter Lane.

Above: The Master's Room, which adjoins the Livery Hall on the second floor.

The Court Room was refurbished in 2007 to update the classic interior in a contemporary style and to create a sense of openness and space.

TALLOW CHANDLERS' HALL

THE WORSHIPFUL COMPANY OF TALLOW CHANDLERS
ORDER OF PRECEDENCE: 21ST
GRADE II* LISTED; SCHEDULED ANCIENT MONUMENT

The entrance to the oak-wainscoted Parlour, which is now the venue for small lunches and dinners for up to 30 people.

That tallow chandlery – the fashioning of candles and soap from animal fat – was once big business is reflected in the modern name of one of the City of London's major thoroughfares: Cannon Street is a corruption of the medieval 'Candelwrichstrete' and then of 'Candlewick Street', from what was historically the main local trade.

By the end of the seventeenth century, oil was supplanting wax as lighting fuel, and the development of paraffin wax in the mid-1800s rendered the industry moribund for more than a century. More recently, however, it has experienced something of a revival through the burgeoning market in edible oils.

Tallow Chandlers' Hall lies just off Cannon Street. It is built on the foundations of a Roman building that is believed by some to have once been the palace of the provincial governor of Britannia. The Company bought it in 1476. It was burnt to the ground on the first day of the Great Fire of London, 2 September 1666. Reconstruction was completed in 1675 to a design by Captain John Caine (twice Master Tyler and Bricklayer) that copied Thomas Whiting's Brewers' Hall.

Since then the buildings have been extensively refurbished, although most of the alterations have been made willingly rather than perforce; they escaped the worst consequences of the Blitz. Both this Hall and the adjoining Skinners' Hall were hit by a 500-lb (227-kg) bomb in 1941, but damage to the Tallow Chandlers was relatively slight and their premises remained open throughout the conflict. By the standards that obtained in the City during the Second World War, this Company got off lightly.

Today the entrance through heavy iron gates on the west side of Dowgate Hill leads into a passageway that opens on to an intimate courtyard of York stone. The Livery Company's ceremonial rooms are on the western and northern sides of the square (straight ahead and to the right as one approaches); the rooms on the southern and eastern sides, currently offices, were converted from warehousing by Joseph & Pearson in 1883–84.

Directly beneath the Banqueting Hall, on the western side of the courtyard, is a rusticated ground-floor loggia with Tuscan columns supporting semicircular arches; this screens the kitchens. Straight ahead is the Entrance Hall, the interior of which was repanelled in oak in 1962 to mark the 500th anniversary of the Company receiving its Charter from Edward IV. (The guild is much older, however; there is evidence that it was well established by 1300.)

The stairwell has a domed roof lantern. On the staircase is a painting of the coat of arms of the Stuarts; this was installed at the time of the post-Fire reconstruction to honour the reigning monarch, Charles II. On the first-floor landing are seventeenth-century leather panels, originally room dividers, which depict the life of the period.

On the left at the top of the stairs, the Parlour has oak wainscoting donated after the Great Fire by Sir Joseph Sheldon (see fig. 25 on p. 244), whose coat of arms is depicted in festooned cartouches on the doorcase pediments. The carved ceiling has a large central oval between two bands of three rectangular panels.

The Banqueting Hall has an unusually broad entrance doorcase surrounded by Corinthian columns supporting a broken pediment. The interior walls have oak panelling (1674–75), with circular windows along the sides, above the cornice. At the dais end of the Hall, the prominence of the Master's chair is emphasized by, behind it, half-pilasters and brackets that bear another pediment, this one broken by the royal coat of arms.

The magnificent square-well staircase, panelled in oak in 1962, is illuminated by a domed roof lantern.

Directly below this feature is a 1930s curved niche with display shelves.

On the east wall are five stained-glass windows of 1903 depicting the patron saints of England, Ireland, Scotland and Wales (St George, St Patrick, St Andrew and St David) and Edward VII. Along the west wall are four paintings donated in 1826 by Roger Monk, who was then Master of the Company. One is a portrait of the benefactor himself. Another is of the marriage of Henry VII to Elizabeth of York, daughter of Edward IV. The other two paintings were originally taken to be of William III and Mary II, but were later shown to be portraits of James II and Mary of Modena. The oriel window is illuminated by the coats of arms of other Worshipful Companies; this is the only Livery Hall that displays such ecumenism.

During the Second World War the Banqueting Hall ceiling suffered more than any other part of the Company's buildings, but it has since been fully restored to its pristine state of 1868, when a plaster ceiling replaced a Gothic-style hammer-beam roof.

Above the Parlour on the second floor, the Court Room, the oldest extant in the City, is largely unchanged since it served its original purpose as a forum in which disputes between tallow chandlers were tried and settled. The room retains the Master's dais and, uniquely among the Livery Halls, fixed benches and the sliding bar at which petitioners had to halt until summoned forward by the presiding Master. The plainness of the flat nineteenth-century ceiling serves to highlight the beauty of the oak wall panels. The painting above the fireplace here depicts the Company's valuables being rescued from the Great Fire by the Master and the Clerk.

Among the displays on the stairs are several candlesticks from various royal celebrations, including the coronations of Queen Anne in 1702 and Elizabeth II in 1953, and from the marriage of Charles, Prince of Wales, to Lady Diana Spencer in 1981. Also here, overlooking a flight above the second floor, is the oil painting *After a Court Meeting*, which features the hidden mouse that became the trademark of the artist, Terence Cuneo (1907–1996). The top (fourth) floor contains the Beadle's flat, the Clerk's flat and a small Library.

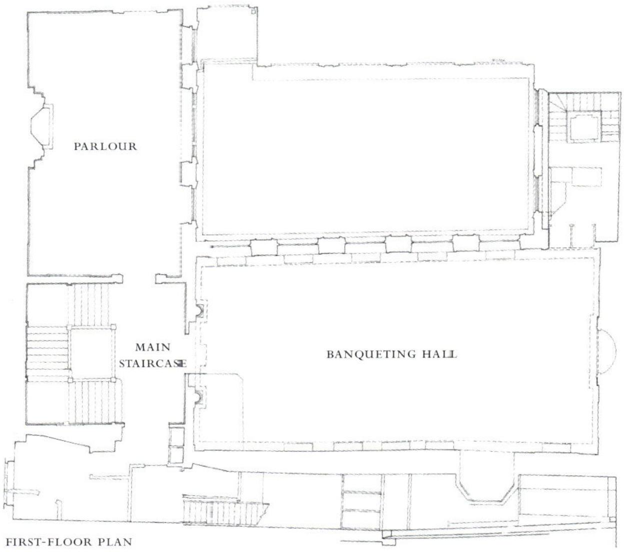

FIRST-FLOOR PLAN

Below: The first-floor landing, with the entrance to the Parlour on the left and the Banqueting Hall to the right. The 17th-century leather panels behind glass on the walls were originally screens used to divide the Hall.

Below, right: The oriel window in the Banqueting Hall, with stained glass depicting the arms of 19 Companies that did not have their own premises and used the Tallow Chandlers' Hall. Its centrepiece is the coat of arms of Edward IV, the king who granted the Company its first Royal Charter in 1462.

Right: The Court Room. There is a retractable wooden bar between the two oak panels in the foreground.

Opposite: The two ends of the Banqueting Hall. Its fine original wainscoting was installed by John Symes in 1674–75.

ARMOURERS' HALL

THE WORSHIPFUL COMPANY OF ARMOURERS AND BRASIERS
ORDER OF PRECEDENCE: 22ND
GRADE II* LISTED; SCHEDULED ANCIENT MONUMENT

Part of the present Hall stands on the site of an inn (The Dragon) and a row of five shops that were acquired by the English Crown through the expulsion of the Jews by Edward I in 1290. These premises were occupied by the Armourers in 1346, and then purchased by them in 1428, a quarter of a century before the Company was granted its first Royal Charter by Henry VI. The buildings narrowly escaped the Great Fire; the blaze was finally brought under control only a few yards away from their threshold. At the end of 1666 the Armourers' premises comprised a counting house, a parlour, a buttery, a larder, a kitchen with three chimneys, a Hall, a beer cellar, a lumber room, a posting room, a court room, a drawing room and, of course, an armoury.

As armour became redundant in warfare, the Company diversified its activities into brass work; this change of emphasis was codified in 1708, when Queen Anne granted a new Charter to what was henceforth the Armourers and Brasiers' Company. To cope with the consequent growth in business, the Company then expanded its premises, almost doubling them in size through the acquisition of two adjacent buildings on London Wall, one in 1750, the other in 1777. But upkeep was relentlessly expensive, and the property was soon costing more every year to maintain than it was believed at the time to be worth. Faced with a stark choice between cutting their losses and investing in the future, the Armourers and Brasiers decided first on a facelift: the dilapidated fifteenth-century façade was reworked in 1796 by William Cresswell. Then in 1835 the Company commissioned its own Surveyor, Joseph Henry Good (1775–1857), a pupil of Sir John Soane, to rebuild the Hall; this work was completed in 1841.

Over the next thirty years, many leading practitioners of the brass trade moved to Birmingham, where overheads were cheaper than in London. This might have brought an end to the Armourers and Brasiers, but the Company again responded positively to changing market conditions, and increased its broader involvement with all forms of metallurgy.

Unlike so many other Livery Company buildings, those of the Armourers and Brasiers emerged from the Blitz largely unscathed, apart from the glass in a few of their windows.

Good's frontage is of plain brick with, on the ground floor, six windows and the main entrance; on the upper storey there are seven windows. Between

Above: Stained-glass windows sit beneath the Gothic barrel-vaulted ceiling of the Livery Hall. 'Make all sure' is the motto of the Armourers.

Right: Detail of the brass finger-plate on the Drawing Room door.

The walls of the main staircase display armour and weaponry from the Middle Ages.

the second and third windows on each side and on both sides of the door are four Roman Doric pilasters. On top of the door, protruding over Coleman Street, is a lamp mounted on cast-iron brackets. Emblems of armour are set in each of the metopes (inset panels) on the frieze of the entablature, directly above the pilasters. The roof-level centrepiece is a carved coat of arms with two armoured figures as supporters and a demi-man of arms as the crest. There are two Company mottoes: 'Make all sure' is the Armourers' alone; 'We are one' (as seen on the centrepiece) is that of the Armourers and Brasiers combined.

The Entrance Hall fronts on to an Imperial-style top-lit staircase with iron balusters. At a mezzanine landing it splits into two and turns back on itself to the first floor, where the four main rooms are ranged south to north.

On the left-hand (southern) side is the Livery Hall, most of which remains as it was at the time of its Gothicization, a refurbishment completed in 1873. The walls are attractively stratified: from the floor up, within reach are various liverymen's coats of arms set on oaken panels. Above head height are numerous wall-mounted suits of armour. Above them is a tier of quarter-circle coving and, higher still, timber coving that, at the short ends of the Hall, displays the Company mottoes. Above the coving is a tier of stained glass, which, at the short ends, takes the form of Venetian windows: a large, arched central panel flanked by shorter oblong panels. Venetian windows were first popularized by the Italian Mannerist architect Sebastiano Serlio (1475–1554), who was himself inspired by Roman triumphal arches. The Hall is topped by a barrel-vaulted ceiling, from which are suspended three George II brass chandeliers.

To the right of the Livery Hall, turning north, are the Court Room and the Library, which are again largely unaltered since Victorian times; among their finest features are the doorcases, fireplaces and coved ceilings.

The north side of the building is officially named the Drawing Room, but is popularly known as the Gold Room for its walls of Dutch metal, an alloy of copper and zinc used to imitate gold leaf. These were installed in the 1980s. Among the paintings here are portraits of Sir Henry Lee and his mistress, Anne Vavasour; Lee was Elizabeth I's Champion, and his third suit of field armour is also displayed here.

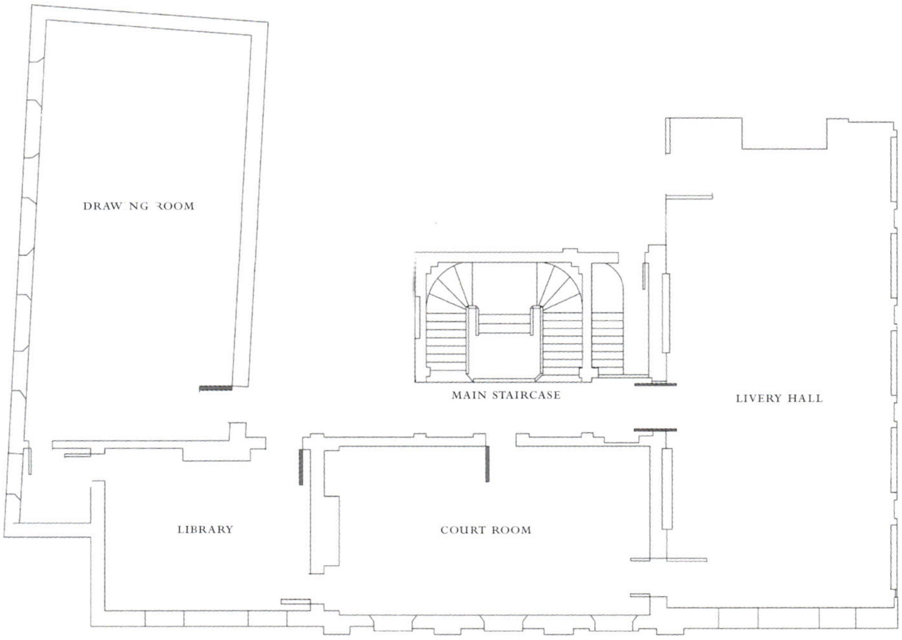

FIRST-FLOOR PLAN

Top: Officially the Drawing Room, this is commonly known as the Gold Room, after the colour of its walls.

Above: The Court Room has a Regency dining table and late 18th-century mahogany chairs. The clock above the door was made for the Armourers in 1767.

Right: The corridor leading to the Livery Hall. On the right-hand wall is a 1710 painting of the Company's new coat of arms.

Further examples from the Company's extensive collection of armour are mounted on the walls of the Livery Hall, above the panelling. The brass chandeliers have been in constant use since the mid-18th century.

GIRDLERS' HALL

THE WORSHIPFUL COMPANY OF GIRDLERS
ORDER OF PRECEDENCE: 23RD

Right: The main façade of Girdlers' Hall from the eastern lawn; Bradley and Pevsner describe it as 'villa-like'.

Below: Detail of the Master's chair, presented to the Company by the Rt Hon. Sir William Jordan, PC, KCMG, Girdler and High Commissioner for New Zealand in the United Kingdom from 1936 to 1951.

Girdlers' Hall is surrounded on three sides by high modern buildings: City Tower (21 storeys) to the west; Standard Chartered Bank (10 storeys) to the south; Legal & General (9 storeys) to the north. Yet it is not overshadowed or obscured from view by its imposing neighbours. This is partly because of the green spaces in front of and behind it, and also partly because of its own strong architectural character.

With four great pillars supporting a pediment that surrounds a centre-mounted half-moon window, the main entrance, facing Coleman Street, resembles a Regency villa, but the building was completed in 1961 to a design by Cedric Ripley of Waterhouse & Ripley Architects. Twenty-one years previously, the Hall had been destroyed during the Blitz; that was the second Girdlers' Hall, completed in 1681 after the first had been consumed by the Great Fire of 1666.

The date on which the Girdlers formed an administrative body to regulate practitioners of their trade is unknown, but in 1327 Edward III granted them letters patent that empowered them to regulate their trade and restrain unsanctioned girdle-makers and their products. They established their first Hall on land bequeathed to them by Andrew Hunt (or Hunte) in 1431; their second Hall occupied substantially the same site, and the present building is in much the same position.

In 1449 Henry VI granted a Royal Charter to 'The Master and Guardians of the Mystery of Girdlers in the City of London'. Five years later the Girdlers were granted arms: their shield depicts three gridirons or girdle-irons; these are strips of metal that are placed over a flame and used to cook food, and hence nothing to do with what the Company actually made – waist belts. The play on words (griddle/girdle) was largely inspired by the Company's spiritual home, the church of St Lawrence Jewry-next-Guildhall – St Lawrence, the Company's patron saint, having reputedly been martyred by being roasted on a gridiron.

Between the Second World War and the completion of the new Hall, the Girdlers were of no fixed abode: they lodged at various times with the Clothworkers, the Innholders and the Armourers and Brasiers.

When the current Girdlers' Hall was opened, it had only two floors above ground (there is also a basement containing kitchens and a wine cellar); the third storey was added in 2008, beneath a new mansard roof. Here at the top of the building are the Master's flat and Company offices that form a square around the heart of the upper structure: a delightful open courtyard. As part of the 2007–2008 redevelopment, the woodwork on the ground and first floors was refurbished.

Many of the furnishings and fittings throughout the building were donated by liverymen and well-wishers. In addition, a significant number were acquired from all over the world by Malcolm Henry Sherrard (1910–1998), Master of the Company at the time of the reopening; one of the highlights is the Chinese wallpaper in the Court Dining Room, sourced in Paris.

The Court Room, on the ground floor, is panelled with Nigerian walnut. Hanging on the wall over the new staircase are photographs of girdles and stoles used at the coronations of George V in 1911 and George VI in 1937. (The sword belt worn by the monarch is the only girdle that the Girdlers now produce; their interests have long since diversified into property and charitable enterprises.)

At the west end of the double-height Great Hall are two full-length oblong windows, a glass door and three round windows just under the ceiling. There are further windows along the northern flank. The entrance is at the east end, and the southern flank has a minstrels' gallery,

The spiral staircase in the south-eastern corner of the reception area.

which is larger than most structures of its type – it is often used for meetings – and, most unusually, oriented along the side of the dining area, rather than at one end.

On the wall beneath the gallery is the most famous and widely admired of the Company's priceless artefacts: the Girdlers' (or Bell) Carpet, which was used originally as a tablecloth on the Court Room table; indeed, it was explicitly commissioned for that purpose, and today bears marks and stains from such usage. Woven in Lahore and donated to the Company by Robert Bell, Master in 1611 and 1634, the work comprises 224 hand-tied knots of wool per square inch and at least seven different dyes, all of which are derived from vegetable matter other than the black, which is made from iron filings.

Remarkably, the carpet survived the two great catastrophes of the Girdlers' history. The Hall was one of the last buildings to be consumed by the 1666 conflagration; consequently, the liverymen had three days' notice of the advancing flames and sufficient time to get the precious item to the safety of the Clerk's home in Hoxton. (The table that it covered was not so fortunate.)

In the autumn of 1940, the Master of the Company, Lionel Vincent Straker, had the carpet moved for safety into the vaults of a City bank. This was both prescient and well timed; only a few weeks later the Hall was obliterated in the firestorm resulting from the enemy action that targeted the City on 29 December 1940.

The lawn at the front of the Girdlers' Hall is maintained by the City of London Corporation; the multiple Gardeners' Company Award-winning garden at the rear of the building is one of the Company's proudest possessions. Its north wall is made from bricks reclaimed from the debris of the second Hall. At right angles to this structure is another low wall, which is all that remains of the Victorian drawing room and kitchen extension of 1877. This now creates a dual-level garden, landscaped in 2009 under the direction of the Company's then Gardener, Sue Madden. It features a beautiful lead cistern, a small fountain with a cherub made of lead, mature camellias, a fig tree, a mulberry tree and Japanese maples; a west wall was added in 1968.

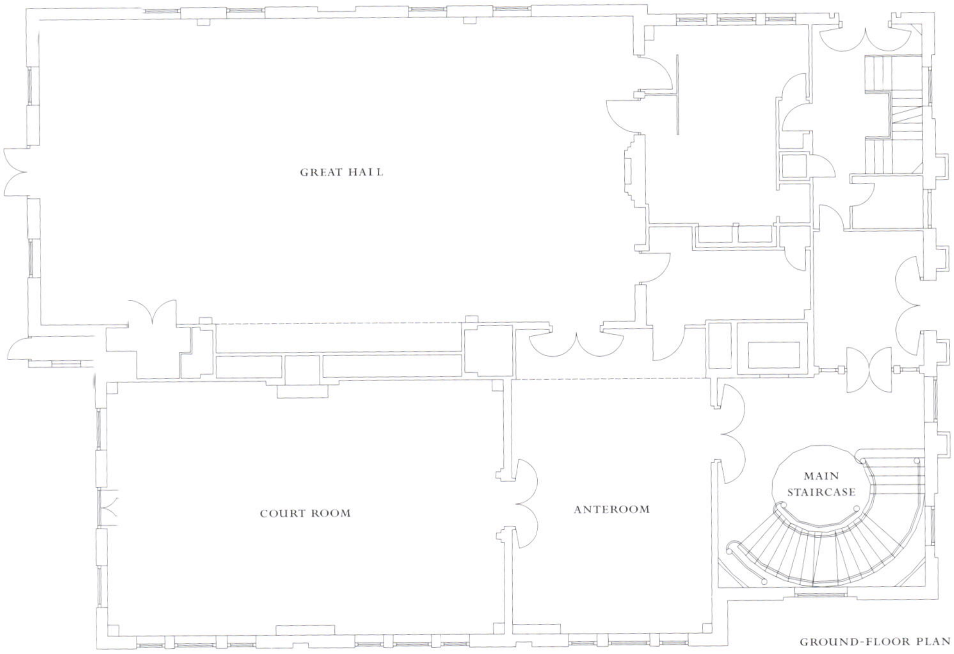

GROUND-FLOOR PLAN

The Great Hall. On the south wall (below) is one of the Girdlers' most precious and historic treasures: the celebrated artefact that was made as a carpet, used as a tablecloth and has now become a wall hanging to prevent more damage than it has already sustained.

The Court Room, with a George II gold-and-black eagle console table (above) and a fire grate bearing the Company's arms (right). Dating from about 1830, the grate was found on a dump during the renovations of the Company's almshouses in 1973. It had originally been in a bedroom, but had never been used.

BUTCHERS' HALL

THE WORSHIPFUL COMPANY OF BUTCHERS
ORDER OF PRECEDENCE: 24TH

Right: The 1960 exterior of Butchers' Hall is a replica of the late 19th-century façade destroyed by enemy action in the Second World War.

Below: Above the main entrance is the Company's coat of arms, which bears the Latin motto Omnia subiecisti sub pedibus, oves et boves *(Thou [God] hast put everything under the feet [of Man], [all] sheep and oxen).*

The earliest reference to a butchers' trade association in London is dated AD 975, during the reign of Edward the Martyr. The earliest record of a guild of these skilled tradesmen is in 1179, under Henry II.

Between the thirteenth and the fifteenth century, the Butchers occupied several different locations in the English capital. During the reign of King John (1199–1216) they resided in Eastcheap. In 1282 they moved in with a branch of the Fishmongers to a building on the site of what became the Mansion House. They later shared premises, first with the Brewers and then with the Carpenters.

In 1548 the Butchers moved from Monkwell Street (now Monkwell Square) to Butchers' Lane (formerly Stinking Lane; now King Edward Street) into what had been the parsonage of St Nicholas Shambles, a medieval church until its demolition in the previous year as part of the Dissolution of the monasteries.

The Butchers rented this property from St Bartholomew's Hospital on a lease that was due to expire in 1671. Unfortunately, the whole building was destroyed in the Great Fire five years before the end of the term. The immediate effect on the Butchers' finances was parlous, but they eventually raised sufficient money for a new Hall built on land that they had owned since 1620 in Scalding Yard on the east side of Pudding Lane (where the Great Fire had broken out).

The Company remained here from 1677 until 1884, when it was forced out by a compulsory purchase order that cleared the way for the section of the present District Underground line between Monument and Tower Hill stations. The Butchers then moved to Bartholomew Close, which was closer both to their pre-Fire premises and to Smithfield Market, the heart of the British meat trade. Designed by the Scottish architect Alexander Marshall Peebles (1840–1891), their new building was lavish and extensive. The ground floor featured the Clerk's offices, a committee room, a waiting hall and a cloakroom. On the first floor, atop a wide stone staircase, were the Court Room and the Drawing Room; on the floor above them was the Banqueting Hall.

The building was hit by a bomb dropped from a Zeppelin during the First World War. The explosion blew out all the stained-glass windows, but these were replaced without undue expense or difficulty. In April 1941, during the second global conflict, another bomb hit the Hall and caused more serious damage, but this was as nothing compared to the disaster of 31 July 1944, when a German V-1 ('doodlebug') – possibly the last ever to be fired before the end of the war – exploded on the roof. No one was killed – the Beadle and his family, in residence at the time, escaped with minor injuries and shock – but the building was obliterated.

A post-war appeal slowly raised sufficient funds for reconstruction: the foundation stone of the new Hall was laid on 2 April 1959; the building was ceremonially reopened on 4 May 1960.

The rebuilt exterior of the Butchers' Hall resembles as closely as possible its pre-war predecessor: stone-faced neo-Georgian, this time by Howard Kelly & Partners. The basic configuration of the windows – six on each of the five floors – is rendered asymmetrical by the main entrance, which occupies the third space from the right-hand (northern) flank of the building. The double-height second floor has large round-headed windows with animal heads carved in the keystones.

Inside the Entrance Hall is the glass Borthwick Screen, which is engraved with images of voluptuous women representing the Four Seasons; each section is linked by swallows in flight and intercalated by flocks of sheep and herds of cattle. This is the work of the

New Zealand-born artist John Hutton (1906–1978). Alongside it is a stained-glass window created by Mel Howse to mark the quatercentenary of the Butchers' Company in 2005 (the Company was granted its Charter of Incorporation by James I in 1605).

The Court Suite on the first floor comprises two adjacent rooms that can be separated or joined as required. The panels throughout are made from the wood of the Australian black bean (*Castanospermum australe*). The white marble fireplace was originally in Henham Hall, a Suffolk mansion designed by James Wyatt (1746–1813) and demolished in 1953.

The wall panels in the pilastered, double-height Great Hall on the second floor are of Southland beech (*Nothofagus menziesii*) from New Zealand; the floor is of Canadian maple (*Acer saccharum*). The large Vestey Tapestry – a gift of Ronald Vestey, of the meat-production company of the same name – occupies almost an entire end wall. Completed and installed here in 1964, it was made in Aubusson, in the Limousin region of France, to a vibrant design by the painter, engraver and upholsterer Lucien Fleury (1928–2004).

There is also a lower ground floor, in which the Taurus Suite is used frequently but not exclusively for masonic functions.

Owing to the major redevelopment in Bartholomew Close – driven by the sale of redundant hospital buildings to a developer – Butchers' Hall shut at the end of 2014 and then became the site office for the contractor rebuilding the close. This continued until early January 2018, when the Hall was handed back to the Company and major refurbishment began to bring the building into the twenty-first century. The plan is for the top floor (which was added as recently as 1996) to be demolished and then rebuilt in order to support a roof garden and a pavilion for Company offices. The rear of the Hall will be removed and will extend into a light well, giving some 20 per cent extra space. Three new lift shafts will be added, a mezzanine floor will be extended to provide an additional dining and meeting space, and the kitchen will move to the lower ground floor. The front door will be moved across the façade in order to improve the Hall's ergonomics, and major refurbishment will take place throughout the building. Two floors will be available as Grade A office space, and the latest audiovisual and lighting equipment will be integrated into the Hall.

Above: The Borthwick Screen of engraved glass in the Entrance Hall was presented to the Company by the family of that name to commemorate those of its members who worked in the meat industry.

Left: The Vestey Tapestry in the Great Hall measures 25 feet (7.6 m) across and 12 feet (3.7 m) from top to bottom.

The Great Hall – with a detail of its Adamesque plaster ceiling (top) – is shown laid out for a formal dinner.

SADDLERS' HALL

THE WORSHIPFUL COMPANY OF SADDLERS
ORDER OF PRECEDENCE: 25TH

Right: The main entrance to Saddlers' Hall is via a little courtyard on the western side of the building. The entrance court is overlooked by the Great Hall.

Below: In the Great Hall is a roundel with the Company arms – a chevron between three saddles on the shield, with a horse at the crest and two horse supporters – and the motto 'Hold fast, sit sure'.

Rival companies make light-hearted fun of the street address,[1] but this Hall has much to commend it. Not the least of its merits is as a symbol of triumph over adversity and the indomitability of the human spirit.

This is the fourth Saddlers' Hall. Details of the first are sketchy; all that is known is that William de Lincolne, a Saddler who died in 1394, left the Mystery of the Saddlers of London £6 13*s*. 4*d*. on condition that they build a common hall within three years of his death. The earliest documentary evidence for the existence of such a building is in the City's records for 1427, when the Lord Mayor and Aldermen fined one John Lever 40 shillings for making a vow with one John Charringworth 'in the hall of the Saddlers'.

The Guild of Saddlers itself is even older, the exact date of its origin lost in medieval mist: according to some authorities, it was granted its first Charter by Edward I in 1272, the year of his accession; however, the oldest surviving royal grant to the Saddlers was made by Edward III on 1 December 1363. A subsequent Charter, granted by Richard II on 20 March 1395 to the Saddlers of London, confirmed the corporate nature of their fraternity and gave them the right to acquire and hold property.

The original Hall, built at the western end of Cheapside, was probably completed by the start of the fifteenth century and in any case no later than 1427. The whole edifice and much of its contents were destroyed in the Great Fire of 1666.

The Company's second Hall was opened in 1671. It was by all accounts a grand building: among its modern conveniences was a new type of water supply; what had formerly been drawn from an on-site pump was now obtained from an extension of the New River, an artificial waterway completed in 1613 between the wetland plain near Hertford and Ware and close to Sadler's Wells in Clerkenwell, London.

The Hall was damaged by fire in 1815, then fully restored with funds provided by a payout from the Company's insurance policy with Royal Exchange. In March 1821 another fire broke out in No. 140 Cheapside – which was owned by the Company and leased to a manufacturing chemist – and spread to the newly refurbished Hall. It caused severe damage to both the building and its contents, and as a consequence the Hall had to be completely rebuilt. The new building was designed by Jesse Gibson, the architect who had made a name for himself through his innovative reconstruction along neoclassical lines of the church of St Peter le Poer in Broad Street (1792). Gibson's work for the Saddlers was completed in 1823.

In 1864 the Company purchased an adjacent property, the Sun Tavern at No. 2 Foster Lane (west of and parallel to Gutter Lane). This enabled the addition of a side entrance from Foster Lane, along the south wall of the church of St Vedast, thereby allowing separate access to the Company's offices and kitchens. In the following year the adjoining premises were refronted to make them appear a single entity.

Saddlers' Hall was one of many buildings destroyed on the night of 29–30 December 1940, when German aircraft dropped more than 24,000 bombs and 100,000 incendiary devices on the City. This was one of the worst nights of the Blitz, and caused what became known to some as the 'Second Great Fire of London'.

In order to take control of the post-war shape of the devastated Square Mile, the Corporation of London acquired significant tracts of land under compulsory purchase orders, including much of the Saddlers' medieval freehold. The fourth Saddlers' Hall was built

The Tunnel Room, with its barrel vault and Tuscan columns, is modelled on the cinema room of the ocean liner RMS Queen Mary.

on Nos. 40–44 Gutter Lane (the Company already owned No. 44, but in order to have sufficient land for its proposed new Hall, added Nos. 40–43, which it acquired from the Goldsmiths' Company in an exchange of land). The new building was designed by L. (Leo) Sylvester Sullivan (1878–1964); the foundation stone was laid by Travers Humphreys, the distinguished barrister and judge. Work began in 1955 and was completed three years later.

The main entrance, formerly on Cheapside, is now on the western side of the building (the eastern façade is on Gutter Lane). This makes no practical difference to accessibility, however, because roadways around all four sides of the premises provide easy (though restricted) vehicular access through portes cochères on the northern and southern flanks. When first opened, the building had seven storeys; a tiled eighth floor, designed by Denis Poulton, was added in 1970. The Saddlers lease out all but the basement, ground floor, first floor and part of the second floor to tenants.

The basement is given over to amenities. On the first floor, three linked rooms run alongside Gutter Lane: these are, from north to south, the Livery Room, the Court Room and the Wardens' Room. These are all neoclassical in style and furnished and decorated with some of the period furniture and paintings that survived the fire disasters. On display in these rooms and the Tunnel Room (see below) is the Company's extensive and valuable collection of ancient and modern saddlery.

Along the southern side of the Hall runs the Tunnel Room, so named for its long, thin shape. Barrel-vaulted with Tuscan columns, it is modelled on the first-class cinema room of RMS *Queen Mary*, the transatlantic liner that was the pride of the Cunard line between the two world wars and which is now preserved as a tourist attraction in Long Beach, California.

The western flank of the building is dominated by the Great Hall. Its most striking external feature is a small entrance court, landscaped by James Welch in 1989. On the south wall of the courtyard is a carved pediment of 1877 that stood over the Foster Lane entrance to the third Hall. The interior of the double-height Great Hall is beautifully lit by five tall round-arched windows, some of the panes of which have stained-glass coats of arms. The ceiling is Adamesque. At the south end is a minstrels' gallery. Beyond the north end is a servery directly beneath the Company's kitchens.

NOTE

1 Unwarrantedly: the name Gutter Lane has nothing to do with gutters. Its origins lie in one of two English personal names: either Guthrum (d. *c.* AD 890), king of the English Danelaw; or Goderun, a woman recorded as a tenant in the Domesday Book of 1086. In a rent roll of 1441, the thoroughfare is referred to as 'Goturlane'.

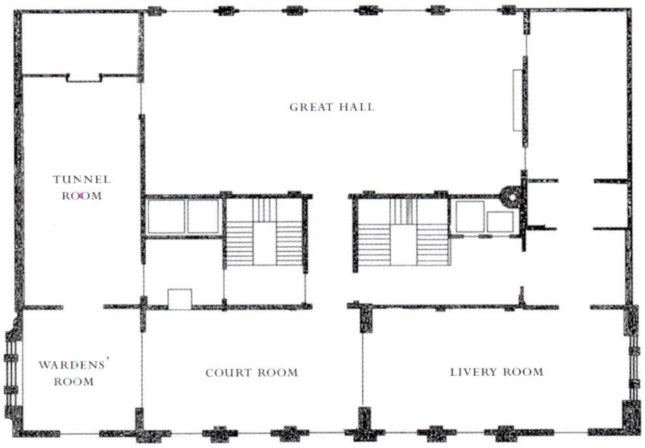

FIRST-FLOOR PLAN

Right: The Court Room, looking towards the Wardens' Room.

Far right: The bronze sculpture Bust II *by George Bingham, bought by the Company in 2014, sits in the window on the southern side of the Wardens' Room.*

Below and opposite: The Great Hall, with its Adamesque ceiling rose and minstrels' gallery at the south end.

SADDLERS' HALL

CARPENTERS' HALL

THE WORSHIPFUL COMPANY OF CARPENTERS
ORDER OF PRECEDENCE: 26TH
GRADE II LISTED

Right: The Caesar Augustus Panel, in the Reception Room, is a high-relief wood carving by Master Carver Shane Raven, completed in 2005 in natural lime wood.

Below: The Court Room is panelled in burr oak and burr walnut veneer with a dado rail and doors made of Australian walnut.

The current Carpenters' Hall is the Company's third. The first was built on land leased in 1429 from the Hospital of St Mary without Bishopsgate (aka St Mary Spital). The five cottages that stood there when the Carpenters arrived were demolished and replaced by 1457 with a meeting room and four new dwellings. In 1520, seven years before the lease was due to expire, the site was purchased by Thomas Smart, Master of the Company, who left it to the Carpenters in his will.

Thereafter the property was expanded: a new Parlour in 1579 and a new wing on the Court Room block by John Wildgos in 1664 (see fig. 9 on p. 230). In the meantime, grape vines and a bowling alley were added to a well-stocked and elaborately tended garden. It was this open space around the Hall that saved the building from the Great Fire of London by stopping the advance of the flames. The Company suffered financially in the aftermath, however, losing much of its business as burnt-out wooden buildings throughout the capital were replaced by structures of brick and stone.

By 1849 the Carpenters' building had been given a street address: No. 68 London Wall. In October of that year a fire in the nearby wool merchants' at No. 65 spread, destroying many of the windows and one wall of the Hall, and badly damaging the staircase and the roof. This disaster was one of the main inspirations for the construction of a new Hall. Another was the coincidental desire of the neighbouring Drapers to redevelop their

own premises. Together the two companies sought and were granted permission to build a new road running north–south between London Wall and Throgmorton Street. The thoroughfare thereby created, Throgmorton Avenue, was (and remains) private, and thus the owners had a much freer hand with building developments than they might have had on a public highway.

The Carpenters commissioned one of their liverymen, the architect William Willmer Pocock (1813–1899), to design a new Italianate building that incorporated various fixtures and fittings from their old premises. These included the panels of 1579 and the oak chimney pieces of 1664, which were installed in the new Court Room, and in other parts of the building two Tudor oak corbels carved in the shape of angels, three wall paintings and the window glass that had survived the 1849 conflagration. Work on the Carpenters' second Hall began in 1876 and was completed in 1880.

In the late 1930s, as armed conflict between Britain and Germany became inevitable, the Carpenters were one of the Livery Companies that moved their portable treasures to safety in case the worst came to the worst, which for them it did on the night of 10–11 May 1941, when their Hall was burnt out by a gas explosion on London Wall caused by a Luftwaffe incendiary bomb. The walls remained, however, and the brick vaulting in the underground strongrooms withstood both the initial blast and the ensuing showers of rubble; as a

The stained-glass windows in the Banqueting Hall were designed by Alfred Fisher and made in 1988; they depict tools of the craft around the Company's coat of arms.

consequence, most of the Company's archives, furniture, paintings and plate survived the Second World War.

The third Hall, designed by Herbert Austen Hall (1881–1968), was opened in May 1960, four years after the foundation stone had been laid. This was no straightforward reconstruction job: although the insides of the old building had been obliterated by the Nazis, the external walls remained standing and could not be removed because of a preservation order. Consequently, it was decided to insert a steel-framed structure within the existing shell.

Another difficulty was that after the war the Corporation of London had compulsorily acquired a strip of the Carpenters' land for a road-widening scheme along London Wall. To compensate for this loss, the Company built an arcade at street level along the southern side of London Wall and a bridge over the northern end of Throgmorton Avenue, thus creating enough room on the first floor for a Banqueting Hall of the desired size.

The other innovations on the post-war exterior were additional windows on the second floor and two more upper storeys for offices, which were set back and largely concealed behind a balustrade.

Today the ceremonial entrance to Carpenters' Hall is beneath the bridge just off the northern end of Throgmorton Avenue, the junction of which with London Wall is guarded by heavy wrought-iron gates. The main doors are made of teak and surmounted by panels carved with images of the fruits of the trees from which they were obtained.

Throughout the interior, as might be expected, the woodwork is a major feature. The panelling of the Entrance Hall is mainly oak veneer, but there is also some teak. The walls of the Court Room are panelled in burr oak and burr walnut veneer; the dado rail and doors are Australian walnut. Also here are three carved panels of 1579 from the old Hall.

The staircase panels are partly teak; the steps are oak and the handrail along the wrought-iron balustrading is mahogany.

On the first floor, the L-shaped Reception Room is also partially panelled in mahogany. On the south wall, opposite the windows, is a carved lime-wood panel depicting the breastplate of the Roman Emperor Augustus. The west wall is dominated by a portrait of Queen Juliana of The Netherlands.

The interior of the Banqueting Hall was designed by Clifford Wearden (1920–1999), whose work is

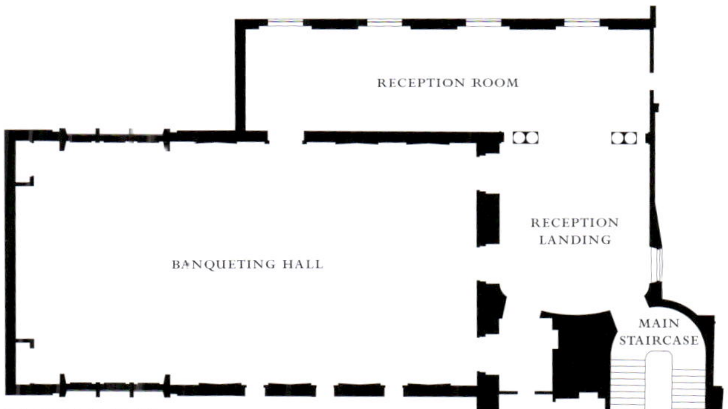

FIRST-FLOOR PLAN

plainly influenced by that of Sir Basil Spence. The light in the room comes from Alfred Fisher's two stained-glass windows on the bridge over Throgmorton Avenue. Around the windows, the walls are panelled in alternating plain and decorative surfaces made of crown elm and utile mahogany. The west wall bears a Tree of Life, a 1966 carving by Sir Charles Wheeler (1892–1974). At the darker, eastern end of the room is a minstrels' gallery. Beneath the dark-blue upper ceiling is a suspended ceiling of octagonal pieces of cedar. The floor comprises strips of Zimbabwean teak.

The Reception Room, with walls partially panelled in mahogany, specially designed Georgian-style cut-glass chandeliers, 18th-century Chippendale-style mirrors, a portrait by Sierk Schröder of Honorary Liveryman Queen Juliana of The Netherlands (top) and windows with modern stained-glass panels of coats of arms of members of the Court (above).

The Banqueting Hall, designed by Clifford Wearden, has side walls panelled in crown elm and utile mahogany, an octagonal-pattern cedar ceiling and a Zimbabwean teak strip floor. The teak Tree of Life was carved by Sir Charles Wheeler in 1966; he also designed the Tree's vari-wood marquetry background and the display case for the plate.

PAINTERS' HALL

THE WORSHIPFUL COMPANY OF PAINTER-STAINERS
ORDER OF PRECEDENCE: 28TH
SCHEDULED ANCIENT MONUMENT

Right: The main staircase, viewed from the Entrance Hall, includes carved walnut heraldic leopards.

Below: The Livery Hall, on the first floor, features A Ship at Anchor *by Peter Monamy (1681–1749).*

In the Middle Ages these were two separate guilds: the Painters, who worked on solid surfaces, and the Stainers, who decorated fabrics. The two professions worked separately, although there was some overlap, which resulted in rivalry between them. Faced with an influx of foreign artists to the court of Henry VII, the two guilds merged in 1502 to form the Painter-Stainers' Company, which received its Royal Charter from Elizabeth I in 1581.

The present Painters' Hall is the Company's third on this site, which occupies sloping ground around 100 yards (90 m) north of the bank of the Thames to the west of Southwark Bridge. The first Hall was burnt to the ground in 1666; the second was razed on 11 May 1941, the day after a Luftwaffe night raid caused a fire in adjacent buildings that spread out of control because of the lack of accessible water to douse it; the hydrants had been destroyed in the attack, and the river was at low tide during the crucial period. The Dining Room and Court Room were completely obliterated, along with their contents, but the Painted Chamber and adjoining offices, although damaged, survived. The latter was good news in the short term,

but subsequently it would limit the amount of war damage compensation that the Company received, thus delaying rebuilding for many years.

Reconstruction by D.E. Harrington – following the broad outline of the seventeenth-century Hall, while reinstating some minor modifications introduced during the First World War – eventually began in 1959 and was completed in 1961, the same year as Sir Charles Wheeler (1892–1974) finished his bronze sculpture of St Luke and the Virgin Mary, which now stands on the landing of the dog-leg oak staircase. (Although Luke is best known as an Apostle, there is an ancient tradition that he was also a painter and that he painted the Virgin Mary from life. One of the most important dates in the Painters' Company calendar is 18 October, the saint's feast day.)

Near the entrance on the wall are carved wooden drops and garlanded capitals from the 1675 doorway, which survive because they happened to be off-site during the Blitz.

The modern Hall includes a number of paintings by past liverymen, along with examples of false marble (scagliola) columns and false grained walls (in the Painted Chamber, on the first floor), techniques developed by the Company in the nineteenth century. Among the other striking works of art on the ground floor, in the Court Room, is a Carrara marble bust of Thomas Evans, Master in 1666, by Edward Pearce, Master in 1693. Also notable are the two seventeenth-century group portraits of senior officers of the Company (see fig. 15 on p. 20). That on the left features John Taylor, whose own work includes the only extant portrait of William Shakespeare painted during the playwright's lifetime. Known as the 'Chandos portrait', this was the first work acquired by the National Portrait Gallery when it was founded in 1856.

The Painters' Company has a long and distinguished history of promoting the fine and decorative arts. It sponsors aspiring artists, and the walls of the Court Dining Room, adjacent to the Court Room, are hung with colourful selections of modern paintings. Sliding doors between these two rooms make the whole space highly versatile and adaptable for groups of up to 150 people.

The magnificence of the Livery Hall on the first floor exceeds even that of the other rooms. Entering from the main staircase (there is also a lift) through the east doors, the visitor first passes beneath a minstrels' gallery, which is oddly positioned to the side of the room and (perhaps consequently) seldom used, but is nevertheless attractive and quirky.

Then, to the right, the full splendour of the Hall is revealed: it is 70 feet (21.3 m) long from east to west and 50 feet (15.2 m) across at its widest point, although it narrows laterally in two stages to make the focus the north wall, in which the stained-glass windows display the arms of prominent liverymen, including all those who have been Lord Mayor of London. The other walls are lined with royal portraits from the late seventeenth century to the present day and other historical paintings. Crystal chandeliers hang from the double-height ceiling. The kitchens are situated in the north-western corner.

The Painted Chamber, on the first floor, where painted panels dating from the early 18th century hang on walls painted to appear as wooden panelling.

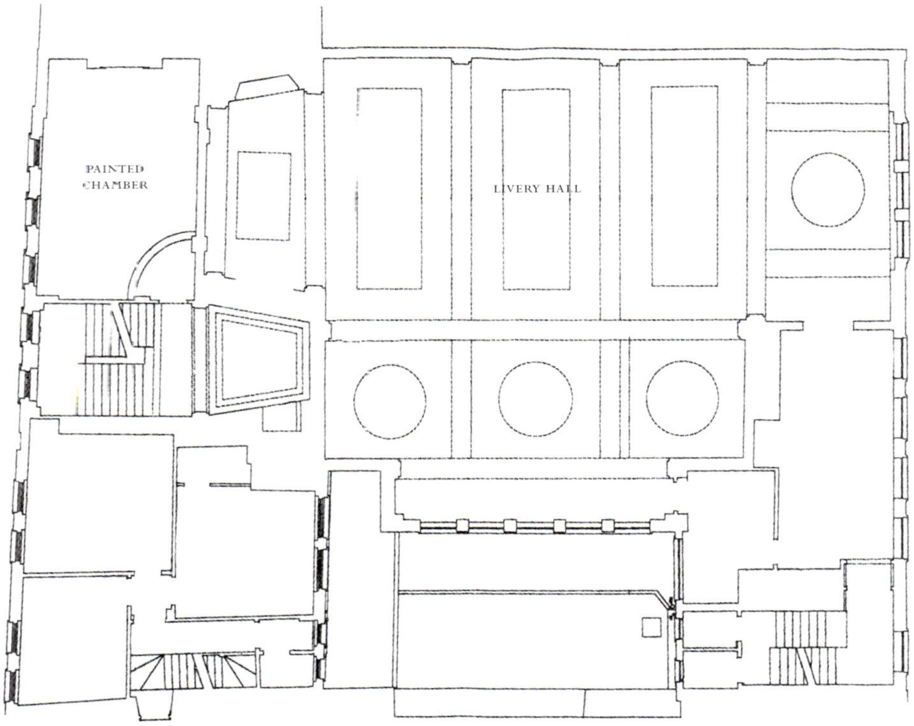

FIRST-FLOOR PLAN

Below: A marble bust of Past Master Thomas Evans by Edward Pearce takes pride of place on the west wall of the Court Room.

Right: The south wall of the Court Room.

Right, bottom: The Court Room (at left) and the Court Dining Room (right), as viewed from the Entrance Hall.

The Livery Hall. The east wall (left) features Landscape at Sunset *by Robert Aggas (d. 1679), seen at the right of the image. The west window (below) displays the coats of arms of Elizabeth II, the Prince of Wales and the City of London, and the north window (bottom) those of 12 Lord Mayors who were liverymen of the Painter-Stainers' Company.*

INNHOLDERS' HALL

THE WORSHIPFUL COMPANY OF INNHOLDERS
ORDER OF PRECEDENCE: 32ND
GRADE II* LISTED; SCHEDULED ANCIENT MONUMENT

People who ran inns offering overnight accommodation to wayfarers were originally known as 'hostellers and haymongers', and this was the original name of the guild, of which the first recorded mention was in 1327. 'Haymongers' was dropped from the title in 1446. The term 'hosteller' fell into disfavour in the fifteenth century, probably because it was being confused with 'ostler' (the hosteller's servant), and so in 1473 the Court of Aldermen approved the change of name to 'Innholders'. In 1514 Henry VIII granted them their first Royal Charter and they became the Worshipful Company of Innholders.

The Company has been in its current location, on the thoroughfare formerly known as Elbow Lane, since at least 1522, in which year an Innholders' Hall appears in a property valuation. The antiquarian author John Stow refers to the building in *A Survey of London* (1598).

In the seventeenth century, the Master of the Innholders was *ex officio* personally liable for the Company's valuables, as he technically still is to this day. In 1665 that year's holder of the office, Robert Briscoe, in accordance with the normal practice of the time, removed the Company's plate to his own inn, The Ram in Smithfield; this turned out to be a lucky intervention, since the Great Fire of the following year consumed Elbow Lane but stopped 200 yards (183 m) short of where the valuables had been stored for safety.

The main façade of Innholders' Hall faces College Street. The entrance is now through No. 30, but the 17th-century carved door of No. 29 has been preserved (below).

Innholders' Hall was rebuilt between 1667 and 1670 by Joseph Lem (d. 1695), a bricklayer and liveryman of the Wax Chandlers' Company, and a carpenter, 'Mr Darby'. Lem, who also served on the Court of the Tylers' and Bricklayers' Company, subsequently worked on Vintners' Hall (1671–75), the 1678 additions to Skinners' Hall and the west range of Merchant Taylors' Hall (1681–83).

In the late eighteenth century and throughout the greater part of the nineteenth, the Company's principal domestic concern was with the upkeep of its buildings. Throughout this period, minor repairs were no more than cosmetic, and did little to tackle the premises' deeper structural malaise. By 1882 drastic intervention was needed; the Company's architect, J. Douglass Mathews (1838–1923), began a programme of works that would completely rebuild the Hall and divide it into two: No. 29 College Street would remain the Company's headquarters; No. 30, next door on the east side, would be leased at rack rent, under the terms of which any tenant would have to pay the owner the whole value of the property every year.

Completed in 1886, Mathews's exteriors of Nos. 29 and 30 were demonstrably Victorian, but retained the Georgian-style windows: large, with double-hung sashes. The post-Fire doorcase was demolished, but the original coat of arms and the shaped pediment above it were restored (see fig. 31 on p. 248). The old door was also stripped and reused. Inside, in the double-height Great (Banqueting) Hall, most of the original oak panels and the 1681 minstrels' gallery were preserved, but the room required a new ceiling and windows. A new Court Room was installed on the first floor. Reconstruction of the Old (or Lower) Court Room on the north-western corner of the building was particularly difficult: the oak panels here had to be removed pending the rebuilding of three of the walls; the timbers above the plaster ceiling also needed replacing. The basement was refitted with a new kitchen, a wine cellar and serving areas.

The exterior of the Hall was damaged by shrapnel from grenades dropped from a Zeppelin during the First World War, the scars of which can still be seen around the old front door.

In 1937 the ceiling of the Court Room showed signs of collapse. Prompt intervention was required. Jefferiss Mathews, the architect grandson of J. Douglass Mathews, took charge of the works, which he later described thus:

The central pane of glass in the main window of the Great Hall is engraved with the Company's coat of arms.

> We took up the floor of the room above and found that the laths had been ruined by furniture beetle, and that the key of the plaster was also rotten. It was confirmed that the ceiling had been for years unsupported ... We first shored up the ceiling from underneath with a number of timbers, and between the timbers and the ceiling we inserted felt pads.[1]

Having done this, Mathews further safeguarded the ceiling by making a lattice of laths of the same dimensions as the floor above. He suspended this structure from the beams on copper wires, which he secured at the bottom with pennies that had holes drilled through them. The lattice and upper side of the ceiling plaster were bonded to each other with a mixture of adhesive and newspaper.

These works not only made good the historic decay but also served the building well in the cataclysm that was to come. As Britain prepared for war with Nazi Germany, Jefferiss Mathews was again called in to make Innkeepers' Hall as secure as possible against enemy air raids. Among his safety measures, he covered the windows and doors with vertical wooden slats that would divert the force of any blast upwards or downwards, away from the interior of the building. Most innovative, however, was his strategy for protecting the ceiling of the Old Court Room: for this, he made a shallow tray of the same size as the ceiling, filled the container with sand, then jacked it up and fixed it in place with supports below; the mineral grains moulded themselves to the shape of the plasterwork, and cushioned it to at least some extent against the force of any explosion.

These were wise precautions: on the night of 10–11 May 1941, the Hall was hit during the Luftwaffe attack that also destroyed the Chamber of the House of Commons. Although the Innholders' building was not directly hit, the Great Hall was wrecked, its west wall shattered and its ceiling caved in, leaving it open to the sky; the domed glass roof above the pantry at the east end had completely melted. However, thanks to its protective covering, the ceiling of the Old Court Room was undamaged.

After the Second World War, the Corporation of London tried to acquire Innholders' Hall through compulsory purchase, but was prevented from doing so by the designation in 1950 of No. 29 College Street as a listed building – a status it would not have been awarded if the Old Court Room ceiling had been destroyed. The Hall was subsequently designated as a scheduled ancient monument. Reconstruction, overseen again by Jefferiss Mathews and completed in 1950, largely preserved the seventeenth-century layout.

In 1984 the lease on No. 30 College Street expired, and the Innholders decided to redevelop their property more radically than ever. Leaving only the Old Court Room and the Court Room unaltered, they gutted the eastern end of the Hall. The original front door of No. 29 was preserved but the doorway blocked; the new entrance was through the front door of No. 30. In the Great Hall, the minstrels' gallery was moved from the north-eastern corner to the east end. The whole building now comprises a basement with kitchen; ground-floor reception rooms (including the Great Hall and the Old Court Room); the Court Room and the Master's flat on the first floor; the Beadle's flat and four bedrooms on the second floor; the Clerk's offices at the top. The reception area has two parallel rows of columns where formerly stood the wall between the two houses.

This project, directed by J. Sampson Lloyd (1930–2009) of Green Lloyd Architects, was started in 1989 and completed the following year. The current layout has enabled the Innholders to provide modern facilities in No. 30 while maintaining the historic part of their Hall, No. 29, much as it has been since the reign of Charles II.

Subsequent work to comply with disabled access regulations (as far as is possible in a building of this age) was carried out by Robson Warren Architects under the direction of Albena Robson, who, back in 1989–90, had been one of Sam Lloyd's junior associates.

NOTE

1 Quoted in Stephen Coote, *The Innholders: A History of the Worshipful Company of Innholders*, Circencester (Collectors' Books) 2013, pp. 212–13.

The Great Hall retains some of its 17th-century oak panelling. A minstrels' gallery sits at its east end (right). The Master's chair (above) features the Company's coat of arms.

The rich plaster ceiling of the Old (or Lower) Court Room, with a central oval frame, dates back to 1670.

FOUNDERS' HALL

THE WORSHIPFUL COMPANY OF FOUNDERS
ORDER OF PRECEDENCE: 33RD

Above: The main entrance is set in a lively façade that alternately protrudes and recedes both horizontally and vertically.

Above, right: The plaque on the floor at the foot of the stairs to the Livery Hall is a copy of a medal that the Founders' Company had made. It shows the casting of a piece of one of the sphinxes that adorn the base of Cleopatra's Needle by the Thames. The sphinxes were cast at Young's Pimlico foundry in 1881.

Right: The exterior is further enlivened by decorations such as this bas-relief of the Founders' arms: a laver-pot (ewer) between two taper candlesticks.

The earliest record of an English guild of founders – casters of metal, principally brass and brass alloys, into pots, pans, candlesticks and similar articles – is its official enrolment at Guildhall in 1365. Although metal-casting was almost certainly practised in London for several centuries before that, this is the year in which the Founders claim to have been established, and hence the rationale for their sexcentenary celebrations in 1965. In 1614 they were granted their first Royal Charter by James I.

The Founders were itinerant until 1531, when they purchased two houses and a garden in Lothbury and there set up their own first Hall. The site is still called Founders' Court. This was a lavish structure, with parlours, a kitchen, a buttery, a basement and at least one upper storey, but none of it survived the Great Fire of London.

A new Hall – a brick building with a frontage of stone – was completed in 1672. The Founders struggled hard to finance this work, and their straitened circumstances were influential in their subsequent approach to revenue-raising: they rented their premises so much that they began to pine for a building of which they had sole use. To this end, in 1845 they demolished the buildings around the Hall in Founders' Court and replaced them with an additional Hall by J.B. Gardiner. They leased the old Hall to the Electric Telegraph Company and in 1853 the same company also leased the new building.

In 1854 the Founders purchased a new headquarters at No. 13 St Swithin's Lane. In 1876 they pulled down this

Above, left: The porthole windows in the basement look out on to the church of St Bartholomew the Great, the oldest remaining parts of which date from the 12th century.

Above: The stairway to the basement is lit through glass panels on the Cloth Fair frontage.

building and replaced it with one designed by George Aitchison (1825–1910). The Company had its Court Room here, together with offices for the Clerk and the Beadle and a weights office, where it checked for short measure, but again it let the greater part of the premises as offices and shops.

The Founders' Hall was more fortunate in the Blitz than many surrounding buildings: it was damaged a little by fire on 11 May 1941, but was otherwise largely untouched by the Second World War.

In 1964 the Founders sold the freehold of the Lothbury property to private bankers Brown Shipley. With the funds thus raised they rebuilt and modernized their building on St Swithin's Lane to include a new Parlour, kitchens, cellarage and offices for the Master, Clerk and Beadle. But still they had insufficient room for full livery dinners, which had to be held elsewhere, at the Mansion House and in the Halls of other Companies.

In the 1980s the Founders sold St Swithin's Lane and moved to Cloth Fair, their current location, into newly built premises designed by J. Sampson Lloyd (1930–2009) of Green Lloyd, architects whose other commissions included the Courtauld Institute. The co-founder of this practice, William Curtis Green (1875–1960), had been a significant figure in the Arts and Crafts Movement, and there is evidence of that heritage in the exterior of this building, which the architect and architectural commentator Roderick Gradidge described as 'lively yet courteous street architecture'.[1]

The main entrance to the five-storey structure stands at the northern end of a stock-brick façade enlivened by pantiled gabled bays, alternately proud and recessed, and, at the lower levels, by metal-framed glazing over cast-aluminium spandrel panels. The Hall faces the church of St Bartholomew the Great. The rear elevation, on Kinghorn Street, is less striking, but the circular windows at the upper levels are noteworthy.

The main room at street level is the Parlour. In a display case in one corner of this room is the last of twelve castings of a bronze statuette by Charles Sargeant Jagger (1885–1934) of Edward, Prince of Wales (later briefly Edward VIII), playing tennis.

From the reception area, a staircase lit by a timber-framed bay leads down to a basement, where the lobby features stained glass transferred from the previous Hall. Entered through an aisle formed by Doric columns, the Livery Hall has nineteenth-century panels. Natural light is drawn from a row of porthole windows that look out on to a sunken courtyard area beneath a garden that extends to the wall of the church. As currently presented, this room is an object lesson in the effective use of full-height mirrors to create a sense of space. Throughout the interiors, the Arts and Crafts theme recurs in furniture in the style of Charles Rennie Mackintosh (1868–1928).

NOTE

1 Quoted in Jasmine Kilburn-Toppin, 'Cast to Endure: A Short History of the Founders' Company', pamphlet, 2014.

Left: A maquette of Soldier Reading a Letter *by Charles Sargeant Jagger is at the north end of the Livery Hall. The finished piece is on Platform 1 at Paddington railway station.*

Below: The Gold Wall on the east side of the Livery Hall is hung with the shields of more than sixty Past Masters of the Company.

Right: The Parlour, on the ground floor, is used for pre-dinner receptions, small events and meetings. In the far corner is a Jagger statuette of Edward VIII, then Prince of Wales.

Below: The entrance lobby to the Livery Hall features windows brought from the previous Hall; they show the armorial bearings of several Past Masters.

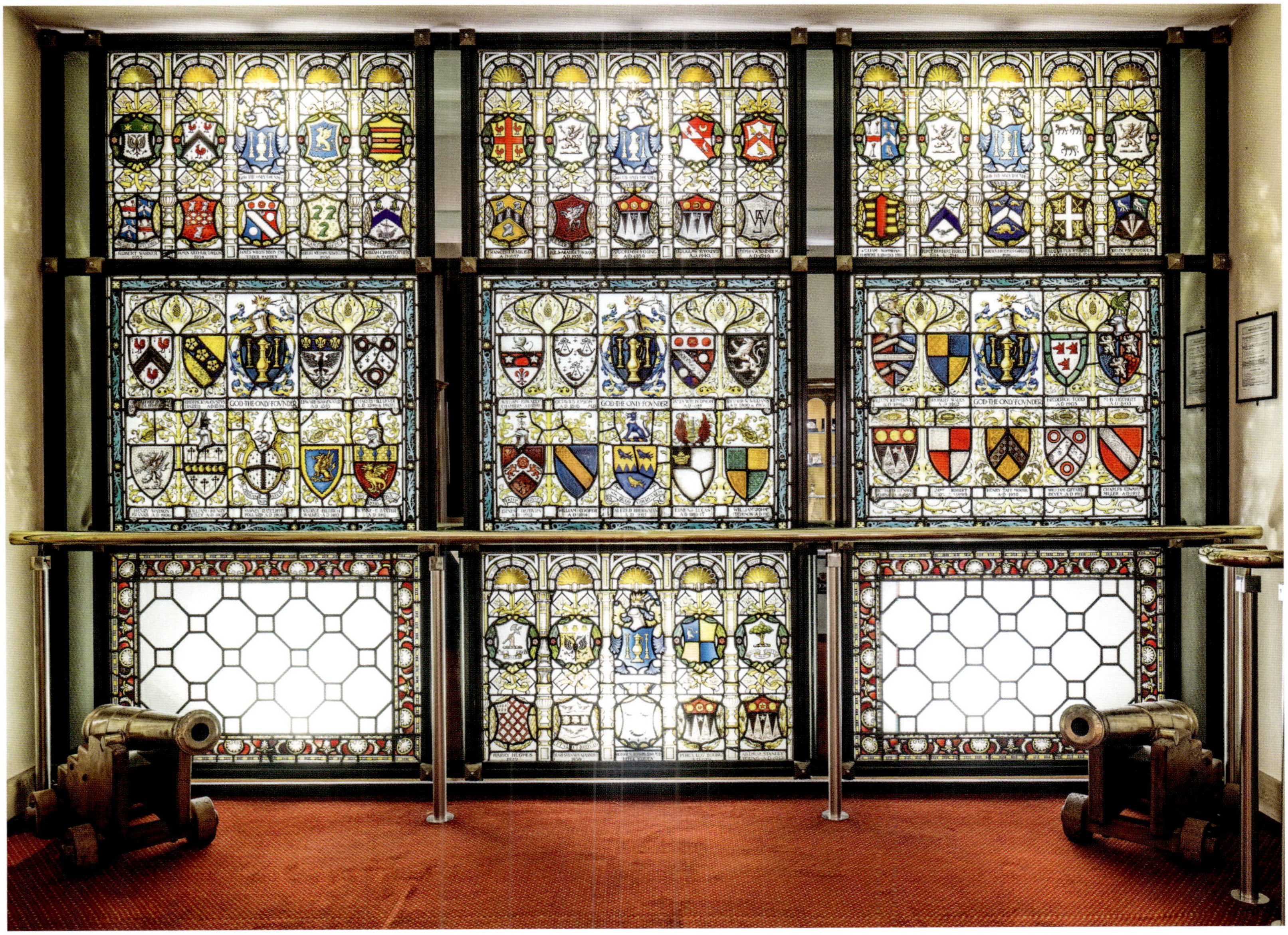

COOPERS' HALL

THE WORSHIPFUL COMPANY OF COOPERS
ORDER OF PRECEDENCE: 36TH

The frontage of Coopers' Hall is strongly suggestive of Fitzrovia and Bloomsbury, but the building lies only a short distance from Liverpool Street railway station.

Coopers – makers of casks – have been practising in London since Roman times. A tablet of between AD 80 and 95, discovered in the City in 2016, bears the Latin inscription '*dabes Iunio cupario contra Catullu*' (You will give [this] to Junius the cooper, opposite [the house of] Catullus). There are further references to coopers in the Mayor's Court of 22 May 1298 and again in 1396, when a fraternity of their number petitioned the Lord Mayor to help them prevent the use of inferior materials in the trade. In 1420 a City ordinance decreed that every barrel should have an official cooper's brand as an earnest of its authenticity. This empowered the fraternity to carry out spot checks to ensure conformity, and to sanction anyone who failed to comply. In the earliest reported raid, in 1464, substandard casks were seized and burnt next to the Standard, a fountain in Cheapside opposite Honey Lane. The casks thus destroyed were of all three main sizes: barrels (each with a capacity of 36 gallons [164 litres]), kilderkins (18 gallons [82 litres]), and firkins (9 gallons [41 litres]).

In 1490 John Baker bequeathed to the company of which he had been a member 'a piece of ground with buildings lying in Basinghall Street, between the Guildhall and the Church of St Michael Bassishaw'.[1] This legacy was subject to two stipulations: one, that Baker's widow should remain in residence as a life tenant; and two, that the coopers should acquire their own Charter. By 1522 both these conditions had been satisfied (the latter was granted to them by Henry VII in 1501); the property was henceforth unencumbered, and a quarter of a century later members of the Coopers' Company built themselves a new Hall next to the existing buildings on the land.

These building works were undertaken at a particularly inopportune moment: in the year of their completion, 1547, the Hall was confiscated by the Crown. This was ostensibly because it had been bequeathed to the Coopers for what were now termed 'superstitious uses', but was really because the Crown was broke. However, in a nice illustration of the truth of the adage 'You can always get out by paying', the Coopers reacquired their land and property for £19 'scraped together' in 1549.[2]

The Company managed to remove its valuables when its first Hall was destroyed in the Great Fire of 1666, but by 1670 replacement buildings had been completed on the same site by John Wildgos, Past Master of the Carpenters' Company. Comprising a central Hall, a Court Room, a Parlour, a kitchen and rooms for a Clerk or a Beadle, this was a grand edifice; indeed, it gradually emerged, rather too grand for the Coopers' realistic requirements. In the period 1865–68 they demolished it all and built a new Hall that occupied only one-third of the area of their old one. Their original intention was to rent out the remainder of the property to tenants, but when they found no takers they sold it to the Corporation of London for £21,000.

The third Coopers' Hall was designed by George Barnes Williams, the Company Surveyor. An unpretentious structure with a rectangular Court Room, a Clerk's office, domestic rooms, a strongroom and cellars, it remained the Coopers' home until it was all but completely destroyed by the Luftwaffe on the night of 29 December 1940. The Library and the strongroom survived the incendiaries, and in them some – but sadly not all – of the Company's plate and its historical records.

After the Second World War, the Coopers rented offices at No. 17 St Helen's Place, near Leathersellers' Hall, and later lodged for a time at Painters' Hall. They held their Court meetings and dinners first at

Carpenters' Hall and then at Vintners' Hall. In 1957 they sold the bomb site on which their third Hall had stood to the Corporation of London, which later installed there offices for Guildhall. In December 1957 the Company exchanged contracts to purchase its current building, a Queen Anne-style merchant's house a stone's throw from Liverpool Street railway station. The land on which it stands was the site of the home of the Earls of Devonshire until the mid-1670s, when it was purchased by the speculator Nicholas 'If-Christ-had-not-died-for-thee-thou-hadst-been-damned' Barbon (*c.* 1640–*c.* 1698), who began the process of turning this and the surrounding area into a square, which was completed in 1708. Barbon was also a builder and had been fined on numerous occasions by the Tylers' and Bricklayers' Company for poor-quality brickwork. This building – No. 13 Devonshire Square – and the adjacent No. 12 are thought to be the only surviving examples of his work.

Viewed from outside the south-facing frontage, at ground level the Hall has three windows and, between the first and second of these on the left, a door with a stone case, Ionic columns, a pulvinated frieze and a neat pediment. Above it are three further storeys, the top two of which are offices. On the ground floor are the Court Room and the Clerk's Office. On the first floor are the Dining Room, the Anteroom and the kitchens.

The half-basement of No. 13 Devonshire Square now contains cloakrooms and a small circulation area in which some of the Company's surviving treasures are displayed. Other treasures are on show throughout the Hall and include one of the oldest objects in the collection: a sixteenth-century chest that contained the pall cloth that every member of the Company was entitled to have draped over his coffin (an entitlement that was restricted to a liveryman or a liveryman's wife after August 1592).

In 1976 the whole Coopers' Hall, inside and out, was fully restored by J.S. Curtis & Sons, to something very like its appearance and condition in the 1740s.

NOTES

1 John Raithby, *The Statutes of the United Kingdom of Great Britain and Ireland*, London (G. Eyre and A. Strahan) 1822, vol. 8, p. 456.

2 Pamela Maryfield, *'Love as Brethren': A Quincentennial History of the Coopers' Company*, London (West Park Press) 2000.

The Dining Room mantelpiece is adorned with a selection of ornate miniature barrels.

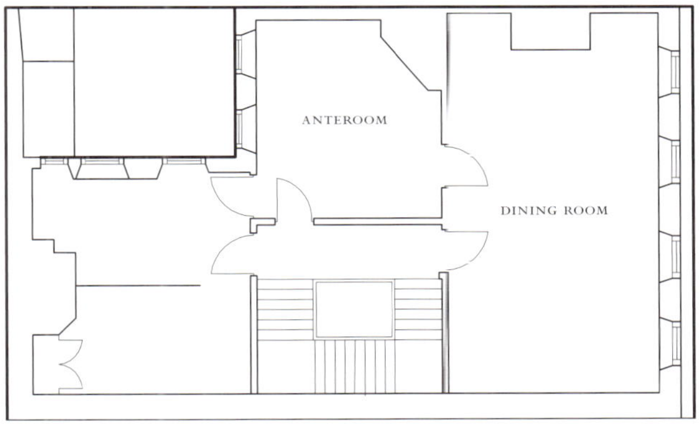

FIRST-FLOOR PLAN

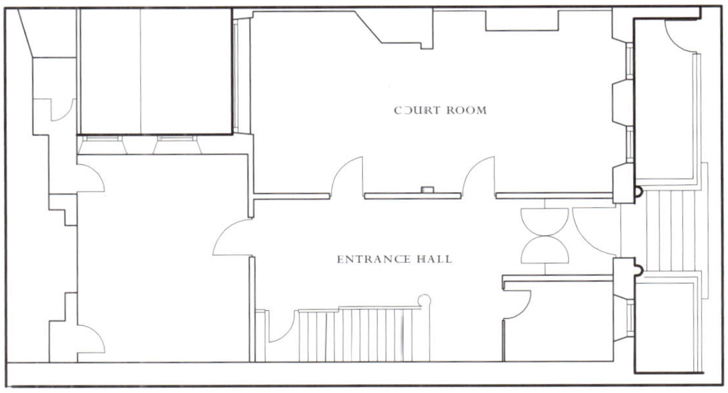

GROUND-FLOOR PLAN

Above and far right: The elegant ground-floor Court Room, prepared for a reception.

Right: The stairs in the Entrance Hall.

The first-floor Dining Room is decorated in a style appropriate to a pre-Georgian town house.

FARMERS' AND FLETCHERS' HALL

THE WORSHIPFUL COMPANIES OF FARMERS AND FLETCHERS
ORDER OF PRECEDENCE: 80TH AND 39TH

The dramatic spiral staircase is one of the focal points of the Hall. There is also a lift for full accessibility.

This well-appointed Hall is shared by the Farmers – one of the first of the modern Livery Companies, formed in 1952 and granted a Royal Charter three years later – and the Fletchers, one of the oldest such organizations, formed in 1371, who had a Hall in St Mary Axe for more than 400 years until it was sold in 1933. The current Hall was the first Livery Hall not actually constructed on the site of a previous Hall to be built in the City of London for 250 years.

The premises occupy the ground floor and basement of a red-brick building on the corner of Cloth Street and Middle Street, almost exactly 100 paces from the entrance to Barbican Underground station. Designed by Michael Twigg Brown & Partners, architects perhaps best known for the glass roof of Hay's Galleria, this place was originally opened in 1987. Bradley and Pevsner describe the Hall as 'undemonstrative', which it undeniably is, but its low-key exterior is a part of its charm, and part of its merit lies in the way in which the Companies and the constructors, Walter Lawrence, have cut their coat elegantly according to their cloth, having sympathetically blended in with older surrounding business and commercial premises: its frontage sits immediately to the rear of No. 140 Aldersgate Street, a seven-storey office block, but its simple lines help to prevent it going unnoticed by passers-by.

By the end of the first decade of the twenty-first century, the Companies had become aware that their amenities were showing signs of age; rental revenue was declining alarmingly, so, after adequate finance had been raised, the building was closed in 2013 for the conversion of the three upper floors into serviced apartments and the comprehensive modernization of the Companies' facilities on the lower levels. Supervision of this £1.8-million project was undertaken by the commercial real-estate service provider Cushman & Wakefield, which subcontracted various parts of the works to Edge architectural consultants. The refurbishment was completed early in 2015, and the Hall was officially reopened on 8 September of that year by the Princess Royal, Master of the Farmers in 2001.

From the main entrance, on Cloth Street, the visitor now enters a reception area that extends the whole length of the building and is lit along the right-hand (north) wall by two rectangular and two square windows and a smaller round window. To the left are a cloakroom and a lift to the basement; straight ahead is a spiral staircase that also leads down. This last, which replaced

The Master's chair lined up against the north wall of the basement. The head, shown in detail at left, features the Farmers' Company coat of arms above carvings of a pig, a cow and a sheep.

what Michael Fern, the director of Edge, described as 'a pokey set of stairs in the corner',[1] has been widely admired and is one of the focal points of the Hall.

To the left of the reception area is the Court Room, which measures 19 feet (5.8 m) by 23 feet 7 inches (7.2 m) and can be partitioned into two discrete sections. The whole is lit by two windows that look out on to Newbury Street, which runs along the southern flank of the building.

In the basement, the Great Hall extends along the whole 49 feet 2 inches (15 m) of the western side of the building. It is 24 feet 7 inches (7.5 m) across, a little less than 1 foot (0.3 m) wider than the Court Room, which stands directly above it. The Great Hall can accommodate up to 120 seated diners and 160 reception guests. The herringbone feature walls are fashioned from three types of oak – natural, fumed and teak-oiled – and embellished with brass detailing. Moveable partitions match the teal-painted wall panelling and allow for flexible use of space; the basement is extensively adaptable to the requirements of not only the Farmers and Fletchers themselves but also those wishing to hire the Hall.

To the left is the Meeting Room, which measures 15 feet 1 inch (4.6 m) by 11 feet 1 inch (3.4 m) and has a drinks bar along its northern edge. The bar may be hidden from view by a folding screen of perforated brass. Such fine detailing can be found throughout the Hall, complemented by distinctive pendant lamps – including, in the Great Hall, brass Up Pendants by Atelier Areti – and timber-effect floor tiling.

Also worthy of mention is the seating: after large-scale regeneration projects, chairs are too often chosen almost at random, an afterthought with scant regard to how well they fit into their context. Anticipating this danger, the Companies, after consultation with MB Furniture, commissioned upholstered Merano chairs from the Czech company Ton. These elegant and comfortable creations – with bent plywood seats and backrests, and with no screws or metal pieces – contribute significantly to the ambience of the Hall, which is intended to illustrate the design concept of 'our home in the city'.

NOTE

1 Quoted in 'Farmers & Fletchers in the City', http://premierconstructionnews.com/2015/12/29/25148/ (accessed June 2018).

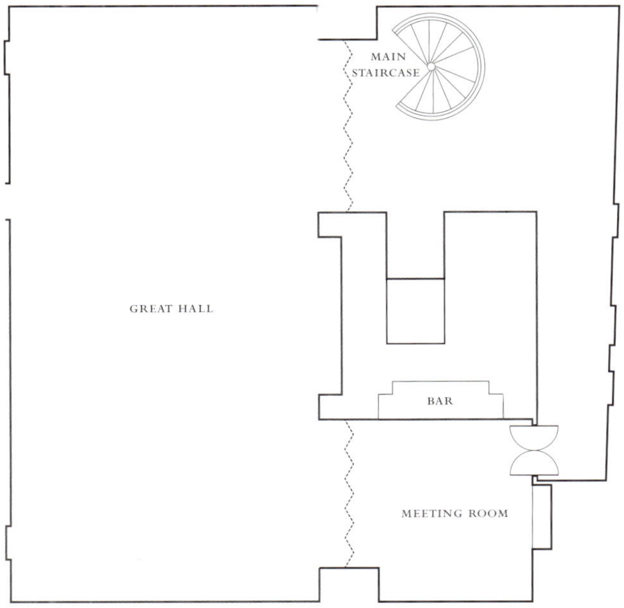

BASEMENT PLAN

Top: The top of the spiral staircase at ground-floor level.

Above: The ceramic floor in the reception area. Its pattern represents wheat for the Farmers or feathers for the Fletchers.

Right: The Great Hall. The retractable panelling on the left allows access to the adjacent Meeting Room.

PLAISTERERS' HALL

THE WORSHIPFUL COMPANY OF PLAISTERERS
ORDER OF PRECEDENCE: 46TH

Right: A view into the Reception from the Great Hall. The Company's coat of arms features some of the principal tools of the plasterer's trade: trowel, brush and hammers.

Below: Detail of the plasterwork in the Great Hall.

The plastering or rendering of building exteriors was practised in London before the Roman occupation. In the thirteenth century, plaster became fashionable in England as decoration, and during the late Middle Ages it was increasingly used as both an ornament and a safeguard against fire. In 1501 Henry VII granted the Plaisterers their first Charter. This was written in Latin, but the Charter granted by Elizabeth I in around 1596 is in English and features the now unusual spelling of the name, which the Company has retained to this day.

The Plaisterers' first Hall was bequeathed to them in 1556 by one of their own, William Elder; it may formerly have belonged to the by then defunct Pinners' Company. Unfortunately, the vaunted flame-retardant properties of plaster were insufficient to prevent this structure from being obliterated in the inferno of 1666.

The Hall's replacement, designed by Christopher Wren, was completed in 1669. This building featured sixteen rooms, most of which were ancillaries of the main function room, known as the Common Hall.

The whole structure was burnt to the ground in 1882, then rebuilt only to be flattened again during the Blitz on the night of 29 December 1940. After the Second World War, the site was acquired under a compulsory purchase order by the Corporation of London, which proceeded to redevelop the site so drastically that the roads on the junction of which the old Hall stood – Addle Street and Philip Lane – disappeared altogether.

In the early post-war period, the Company was homeless and had little hope of being rehoused until 1961, when a potentially suitable site became available on the corner of London Wall and Aldersgate Street. The planning application process was slow, and it was not until 1971 that the foundation stone of the new building was laid; after completion, the Hall was ceremonially opened on 29 November 1972.

The present Hall still occupies this site on the ground floor (entrance only) and basement of One London Wall, but the building above it is completely different from the 1970s original (designed by Ronald Ward and Partners), which had become inadequate for modern office use by the turn of the century. Work on its replacement began at the start of the new millennium and was completed in 2004. The Plaisterers' Company premises – a kitchen, three reception rooms and a Great Hall – now stand at the base of a twelve-storey block designed by Foster + Partners.

The interior of Plaisterers' Hall is substantially the work of Derek Robinson (Master of the Company in 1985, a founder member of the Worshipful Company of Chartered Architects and, at the time, a partner in the Ronald Ward office); the decor throughout was suggested by Harry Humber, Master of the Company in 1960. The former Court Room, now named in Humber's honour, features intricate plasterwork picked out in gold. The Mott Room – so called in memory of the family that provided Clerks to the Company for almost a century and a half – is unmistakably in the style of Robert Adam, with a plaster ceiling and frieze in the traditional pastel shades of the late eighteenth century.

The Livery Hall has walls of dark mahogany beneath an ornamental plaster frieze and ten basket-type chandeliers. It is grand, but it pales almost into

In common with all rooms in the Hall, the Reception is so brightly decorated and illuminated that it is easy to forget it is underground.

insignificance next to the Great Hall, the size of which alone is breathtaking: the largest room of its type in the City, it can accommodate up to 320 dinner guests and up to 600 for receptions. Its interior almost beggars description: the walls are lined panels punctuated by pairs of pilasters with capitals modelled on those of the Tower of the Winds in Athens; the intricately carved and subtly coloured entablature artfully conceals modern lighting; three huge chandeliers – each 12 feet (3.6 m) tall and 8 feet (2.4 m) in diameter – are suspended from a coved ceiling that stands 27 feet (8.2 m) above the floor.

Outside the Hall is the Jubilee Garden, which is laid out formally with stone steps leading up to a balustrade over the Roman Wall. The Plaisterers first obtained this area on licence from the City of London in 1977, the twenty-fifth year of the reign of Elizabeth II. Three years later they were further permitted to take over an additional strip of land that extends along the west side of Noble Street as far as an old watchtower. This is now a lawn and a wild flower garden with a beehive.

After three fires came a watery pestilence: on 24 March 2016 (Maundy Thursday), a burst main in Noble Street sent a torrent of water down the side of Jubilee Garden and into the Hall, flooding the whole area. It was the start of a public holiday; no one was around. By the time the leak was discovered, on Good Friday morning, the water was 4 inches (10 cm) deep throughout the floor. Drain covers and manholes were opened to let the water out, but the leak was not stemmed until 5 o'clock that evening. Furniture, tables and chairs were removed from the premises over the next forty-eight hours, and dehumidifiers were brought in, but catastrophic damage had already been caused, most noticeably to the carpets, which were beyond repair. The door panels, also saturated, warped as they dried. Also of concern was the wiring beneath the floor of the Great Hall, which, although encased in metal or plastic, was nevertheless underwater for more than two days; whether damaged or not, it would all have to be dug up for checking.

The Hall was subsequently closed for two days short of thirty-four weeks, during which period forty-two scheduled events had to be relocated. The anniversary of the reopening – 7 November 2016 – will forever be memorialized by the Plaisterers.

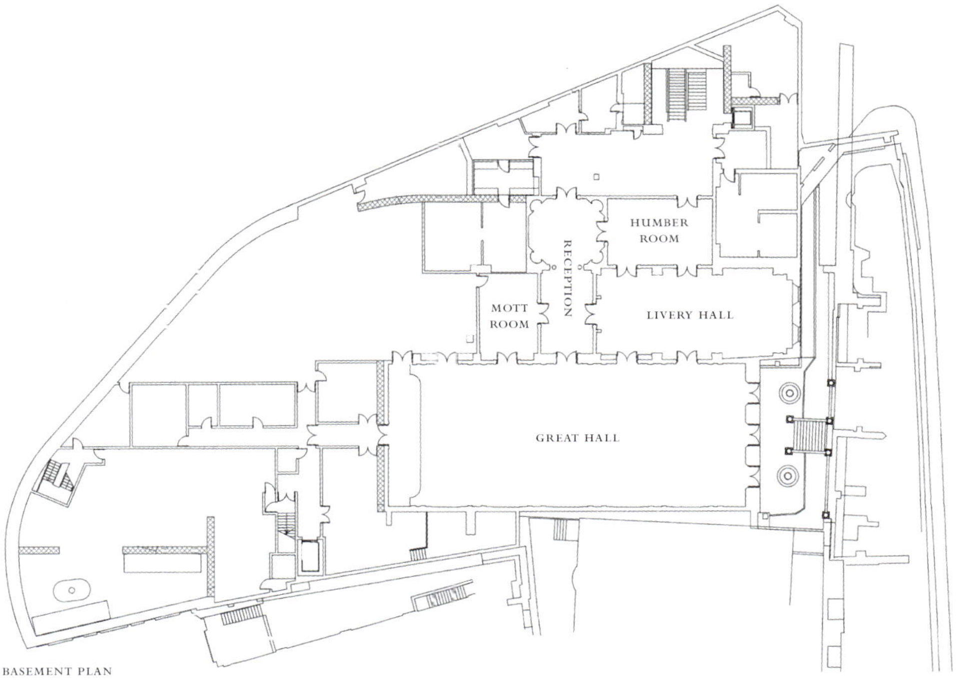

BASEMENT PLAN

Top: The Livery Hall. Its position between the Humber Room and the Great Hall makes it a route as well as a destination.

Above: A view from the Reception into the Humber Room.

Right: A view into the Humber Room from the Livery Hall.

Top: The Plaisterers' Great Hall is the largest of all the rooms of all the Livery Companies of London.

Left: A view from the Reception into the Great Hall.

Above: The Mott Room is unmistakably in the style of Robert Adam.

STATIONERS' HALL

THE WORSHIPFUL COMPANY OF STATIONERS AND NEWSPAPER MAKERS
ORDER OF PRECEDENCE: 47TH
GRADE I LISTED; SCHEDULED ANCIENT MONUMENT

Above: The hanging sign at the main entrance to Stationers' Hall.

Right: The processional door into the south end of the Livery Hall.

The modern home of the guild formed originally in 1403 to regulate the production and dissemination of manuscript books and writing materials, Stationers' Hall lies a little to the west of St Paul's Cathedral and to the north of Ludgate Hill, from which it may be reached either along a pedestrian alleyway (Stationers Hall Court) or via a left turn off Ave Maria Lane through a nameless passage beneath a modern office building. It is a distinctive combination of designs from the seventeenth, eighteenth, nineteenth and twentieth centuries.

After the previous buildings were destroyed in the Great Fire, reconstruction began in around 1669. The ground plan (described by Bradley and Pevsner as 'an elongated T-shape with the top aligned E–W and the Livery Hall N–S, making an inner and an outer courtyard') may be purely utilitarian: constructed within budgetary constraints to fit the pre-existent footprint. However, the 'open' layout – with front courtyard in plain view from the two proximate thoroughfares – is so unusual among the Livery Halls that it may have been stipulated by Charles II and his ministers; there is evidence to suggest that the king was anxious to prevent encroachments by subsequent building developments in the immediate surrounds that might have provided cover for the furtive publication of seditious material.[1]

The present Hall's foundations were surveyed in August 1669, but further progress was slowed by protracted disagreements within the Company's governing body; three years later the new buildings had been raised only to a single storey, where the kitchen, archive stores and reading rooms now are.

Thereafter, speed of reconstruction greatly increased: the frontage and Parlour of the Hall were completed

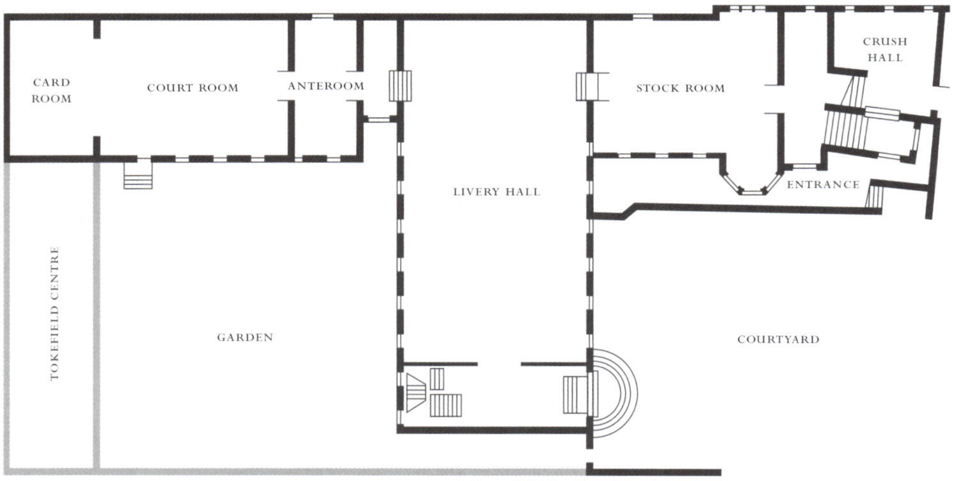

GROUND-FLOOR PLAN

by the end of 1673, although it was another year before the wainscot was fully installed by Stephen College (or Colledge). (College was a writer and illustrator as well as a carpenter-joiner: his verse satire *A Raree Show*, with accompanying cartoon showing a Janus-faced Charles II unable to make up his mind between popery and Protestantism, cost him dearly; in 1681 he became the last person in Britain to suffer capital punishment for a publishing-related offence.)

The next phase of development began in the late eighteenth century, when Robert Mylne, Company Surveyor, was charged with improving the appearance of the Livery Hall frontage. He preserved the seventeenth-century rendering on the western flank, but made the eastern and southern walls flat and astylar: part rendered, part stone-faced. Above the tall, round-headed windows on the eastern façade runs a fluted frieze with decorative Coade stone relief panels, some of which depict putti. This work was completed in 1800.

Twenty-five years later, Mylne's son and successor as Surveyor, William, improved the amenities of the Court Room; between 1877 and 1885 William's son and successor, Robert Mylne, partially rebuilt the east wing of the Hall, adding an off-centre canted window bay with a small spire. These last works involved the reshaping of the Stock Room in a design that retained the original 1670s wooden panelling and overmantel. The panelling is surmounted by a frieze bearing the coats of arms of Past Masters of the Company. The ceiling is a largely convincing Victorian pastiche of the work of Inigo Jones.

The roofs of the Livery Hall and the Court Room were severely damaged during the Blitz in the Second World War. Luftwaffe bombs also blew out the glass on the eastern side of the Livery Hall, but the Caxton window (a depiction of the printer showing his work to Edward IV and Elizabeth Woodville), at the north end, was unscathed, perhaps fortuitously but possibly because of the protection provided by steel trusses inserted into the roof in 1929. Stephen College's panels also remained intact, along with, at the south end, the minstrels' gallery above a carved oak screen. The latter – perhaps the work of Henry Foorde – was badly burnt in an electrical fire of 2010, but soon fully restored; the greater part of the Hall remains much as it was in 1674.

The stained-glass windows on the western side depict Shakespeare, Caxton (again), William Tyndale and Thomas Cranmer – stars of, respectively, literature, printing, biblical scholarship and Protestantism – along with St Cecilia, the patroness of musicians, who is featured in celebration of the Hall's magnificent acoustics. On 22 November 1692 the building was the venue for the first public performance of Henry Purcell's *Ode to St Cecilia*; the Band of the Royal Marines still plays here regularly.

Post-war restorative works were financed partly by the War Damage Commission and partly by the Stationers' sale of land on the corner of Ludgate Hill and Ave Maria Lane. The Hall was reopened in August 1951, during the Festival of Britain, although the Court Room was not fully restored until 1956.

From the courtyard today, the Livery Hall is reached via the Crush Hall staircase and the Stock Room. There is also a side entrance known as the Royal Door, used only on ceremonial occasions.

Beyond the Livery Hall, a small flight of steps leads up to the west wing, where the Court Room Suite – comprising a small Anteroom, the Court Room and the Card Room – evolved in distinct phases, at least one in each of the last three centuries. Particularly noteworthy in the Court Room are the modillion cornice and the Rococo plaster overmantel. The chimney piece dates from around 1730; the plaster ceiling, with a large central rose and slender scrolls and garlands in the

Detail of the stained-glass window in the Crush Hall, installed in 2003 to commemorate the 600th anniversary of the Company.

coving, was installed in 1757 and fully restored in the late twentieth century after damage in the Blitz. Adjoining the Court Room and fully open to it, the Card Room is an irregular octagon top-lit by a rectangular lantern.

In the garden to the west of the Livery Hall and south of the Court Room is the Tokefield Centre, named in honour of George Tokefield, the Clerk of the Company who saved its historic records from the Great Fire of London. Said to be the oldest book repository in London, this single-storey structure, with a tiled roof and wooden mullion and transom-cross window frames, has survived undamaged since the late 1700s. Unmodified, too, until 2017, when the interior was redeveloped into a resource centre to accommodate the Company's archive, which had previously been stored in the west wing's attic rooms (from which a door issues on to a flat roof around the Card Room lantern).

NOTE

1 See Anya Matthews, 'London's Livery Halls, *c.* 1603 to *c.* 1682: Their Architecture and Political Uses', PhD thesis, Courtauld Institute of Art, University of London, 2015, pp. 258–76, 'The Tory Watchdog and the Protestant Joiner: The Rebuilding of Stationers' Hall'.

Top and opposite: The Livery Hall, looking north towards the Caxton window (top) and south, towards the 17th-century screen (opposite).

Above: The Stock Room, looking west towards the Livery Hall.

Above, right: The view from the Court Room into the Card Room.

STATIONERS' HALL

GLAZIERS' HALL

THE WORSHIPFUL COMPANIES OF GLAZIERS AND PAINTERS OF GLASS, SCIENTIFIC INSTRUMENT MAKERS AND LAUNDERERS
ORDER OF PRECEDENCE: 53RD, 84TH AND 89TH
GLAZIERS' HALL OCCUPIES THE LOWEST TWO FLOORS OF HIBERNIA CHAMBERS, WHICH IS GRADE II LISTED

Glaziers' Hall, a former warehouse, is deemed to be within the City of London because it adjoins London Bridge on the south bank of the Thames.

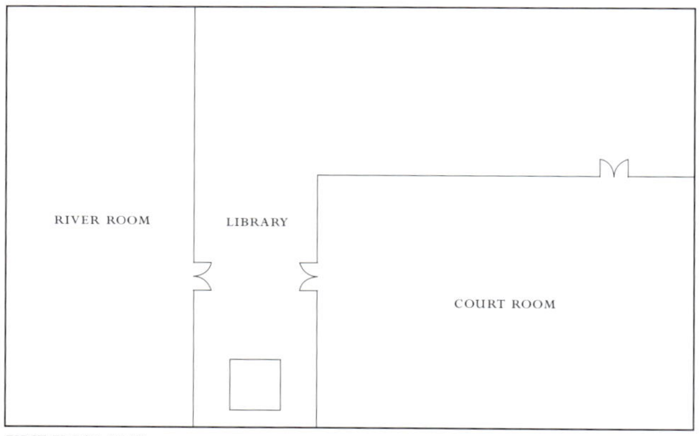

FIRST-FLOOR PLAN

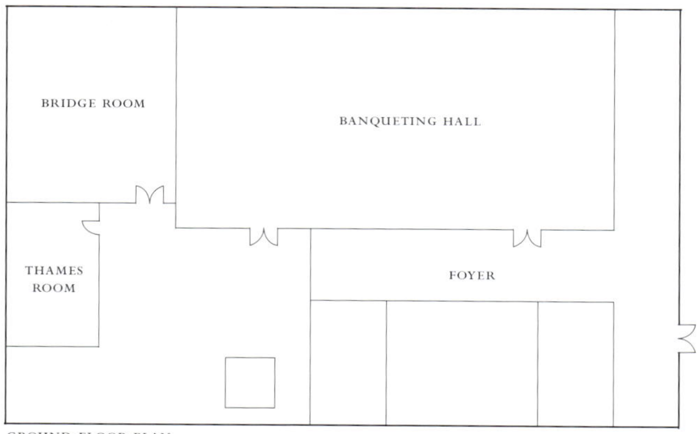

GROUND-FLOOR PLAN

It is clear from the map that the Glaziers' Hall lies to the south of the Thames and is therefore by all conventional definitions without the City. However, the building is bounded by, and attached to, London Bridge, which links the south and north banks of the river, and the foundations of the two structures are conterminous; the northern landside of this span is unequivocally in the City, and consequently the Hall is deemed to be in it, too.

Literalists may think that this is stretching a point, but it seems no more than historically just that the Glaziers should be permitted to retain a presence in that part of London in which they are known to have been based since at least 1328. Their first Hall was in Fye Foot Lane, which stood to the north of Upper Thames Street. The name of the thoroughfare may have been a corruption of 'Five Foot Lane', possibly in reference to its restricted width. The building was destroyed in the Great Fire of London; the lane was swept away in the nineteenth century by the construction of Queen Victoria Street.

For more than 300 years the Glaziers were peripatetic throughout the City: they remained homeless from 1666 until 1977, when they acquired their current premises on land with a remarkable and fascinating history. The original structure here was a riverside warehouse built in 1808 on what was then named Eagle Wharf; this was destroyed by fire in 1836 and rebuilt in 1850–51 by William Cubitt (1785–1861) as two storeys of offices above a double-height warehouse on the waterfront. The riverside exterior of Italianate yellow brick with stone dressings is a deliberate echo of Fishmongers' Hall, which stands directly opposite on the north bank of the river. The five doorways to the quay were later converted into round-arched windows; at what is now second-floor level are five windows with cornices on console brackets; above them is a row of five smaller windows with shouldered architraves; and at the top of the building is a balustraded parapet.

To coincide with Cubitt's new work, the dockside loading and unloading bay was renamed Hibernia Wharf and the building that stood on it was renamed Hibernia Chambers: both changes in reference to the fact that among the main commodities landed here at the time were imports from Ireland, particularly butter and cheese, which were stored in a coldroom in the basement.

Adjacent London Bridge has also changed a great deal during the last 200 years. Between 1967 and 1972, the structure completed by Sir John Rennie (1794–1874) in 1831 was replaced by a new span; the old one was

The River Room overlooks the Thames and offers spectacular views of the City. When the tide is low, the 'beach' beneath the windows can be seen, along with mudlarks on the other side of the river.

famously purchased by the American chainsaw magnate Robert P. McCulloch (who did not, it seems, in spite of the popular legend, mistakenly believe that he was buying Tower Bridge) and re-erected in Lake Havasu City, Arizona.[1]

The current London Bridge (the third stone version; Rennie's work replaced an earlier structure, completed in 1209) was designed by William Holford (1907–1975) in conjunction with the engineers Mott, Hay and Anderson. It is almost all new: the solitary external vestige of Rennie's structure is a granite arch that links London Bridge Walk and Montague Close; in the latter road is the current main entrance to Glaziers' Hall.

By the start of the 1970s the Port of London had lost much of its economic importance, since most cargo was now transported on container ships that were too big to navigate this far up the Thames. The cranes and hoists that had lined Hibernia Wharf were dismantled and removed; the building was gutted and the interiors modernized unsympathetically with steel and poured concrete; the only parts of Cubitt's work that remained visibly intact were the northern (riverside) and eastern façades.

When the Glaziers took up residence, they were joined by two other Livery Companies: the Worshipful Company of Scientific Instrument Makers and the Worshipful Company of Launderers. The building was officially reopened by the Duchess of Kent on 7 June 1978. Since then, Glaziers' Hall Ltd (the collective working body of all three Companies) has carried out an extensive restoration programme, among the many benefits of which has been the reappearance of the original barrel-roofed vaults and the eighteenth-century York stone paving below river level in the undercroft. Another highlight of the renovation works in the basement has been the installation, along the eastern flank of what is now a concourse, of a row of glass 'portholes', behind which a newly constructed wine store is backed by some more remaining stones of Rennie's old London Bridge, now again exposed to view.

The ground-floor entrance of Glaziers' Hall leads into a foyer that runs along the course of what was formerly Cock Alley, which linked Montague Close to the waterfront; here the removal of the 1970s concrete 'improvements' has revealed external brickwork of several vintages, which is now enclosed under a roof but has been left in plain sight. Off the concourse to the east is the Banqueting Hall, a large, double-height reception room with a black-painted concrete ceiling. For the most part artificially illuminated by pin spots and three great chandeliers, this room receives some natural light from glass panels in the skirting boards on the southern flank of the River Room above.

On the river-facing side of the ground floor are the Bridge Room and, next to it on the west, the Thames Room.

On the first floor are three rooms. The Court Room, with stained-glass windows and oak panelling, adjoins a small Library. The whole of the northern façade of the first floor is taken up by the River Room, the crowning glory of the Hall, with great views across the Thames through five floor-to-ceiling glazed arches. The two uppermost floors of Glaziers' Hall are occupied by the three Companies' offices.

NOTE

1 Before he became Clerk to the Worshipful Company of Chartered Architects (1989–95), Leonard Groome, OBE, was the City Engineer responsible for the sale of London Bridge to McCulloch. He attended the opening of the relocated bridge in Lake Havasu City, where he was treated as a guest of honour

Top: The Court Room, on the first floor, features stained-glass windows at its south end and on its oak panelling the names of the Past Masters of the Glaziers', Scientific Instrument Makers' and Launderers' Companies.

Above: The Foyer features exposed brickwork dating from the 18th century, from the original wall of the wharf (left), and windows that were bricked up to avoid the infamous 'window tax', which was based on the number of windows in a property during the 18th and 19th centuries (right).

Below: The Banqueting Hall, with its three bespoke chandeliers, is a versatile and flexible space for up to 300 guests.

Right: The Bridge Room, which adjoins London Bridge, is a multipurpose space providing views across the Thames towards the City.

APOTHECARIES' HALL

THE WORSHIPFUL SOCIETY OF APOTHECARIES
ORDER OF PRECEDENCE: 58TH
GRADE I LISTED; SCHEDULED ANCIENT MONUMENT

The Society's coat of arms in the pediment above the main entrance, on Black Friars Lane, dates from around 1780.

The site of Apothecaries' Hall was a Dominican priory from the early Middle Ages until the Dissolution of the monasteries during the reign of Henry VIII. Some of the buildings were a guest house for distinguished visitors, including Cardinal Campeggio, who came from Rome to negotiate the English king's divorce from his first wife, Catherine of Aragon. The Apothecaries bought the buildings in 1632, fifteen years after their Society split from the Grocers' Company.

The original structure was destroyed in the Great Fire of London, but a new Hall was in use by 1672 and completed in the following year. One of eight post-Fire Livery Company buildings designed by Edward Jerman, it was built by Thomas Lock. It is now widely believed to be the oldest standing Livery Hall (some people advance the counterclaims of the Tallow Chandlers; whatever the truth of the matter, there is little in it).

In the late eighteenth century there was an enormous increase in demand for pharmaceutical products, both in Britain itself and throughout the Empire, so the Apothecaries extended their buildings to the south and east. One of the new structures was the world's first large-scale drug factory, known as the Elaboratory. The Society also commissioned cosmetic improvements to the existing buildings, which had not been spruced up for a century. Completed in 1786 to a design by Richard Norris, the frontage on Black Friars Lane is still stuccoed at ground-floor level and stock brick on the upper storeys, of which there are two in the central bays and three at each end. The latter feature decorative sunken roundels, their shape picked out by circles of red bricks.

The main entrance protrudes slightly and issues through a portal on to a paved courtyard. Directly beneath the nineteenth-century lamp in the centre of this open space was a cistern (or possibly an ancient well) from which the friars drew water until they were banished at the Reformation.

Still in the courtyard, on the eastern side is the stuccoed exterior of the Great Hall, with four large oblong windows at the first-floor level and, above them, the same number of smaller circular windows. These features are roughly the same age as the frontage: 1787. The pediment and the wall clock are later additions: the former replaced a balustrade in 1793; the latter was installed in 1821.

Early twenty-first-century treatment of dry rot in the ground-floor windows of the southern side revealed that Roman floor tiles were reused around some of the frames as packing material. In the south-eastern corner is an external staircase leading into the south range, part of which was a magnesia warehouse until 1983, after which the walls were heightened and sash windows added.

Off the northern flank of the courtyard, the lobby is twentieth century, but the three-flight staircase behind it dates from the late 1660s. To the right off the first-floor landing is the Library, a long, thin corridor with a fireplace and panelling dating from 1672.

To the left, at the top of the stairs is first the Parlour. On its right-hand wall are glass cases displaying drug jars and other old glassware of the apothecaries' trade. On the left-hand wall is a mid-eighteenth-century fireplace that was donated in 1939 by the owner of West Harling Hall in Norfolk. During the Blitz a German bomb dropped right down the chimney; it had a delayed-action fuse, giving Sappers enough time to make it safe, but it still caused damage, which after the conflict was made good with concrete. This material turned out to be quite unsuitable for the purpose and had later to be replaced with mortar.

FIRST-FLOOR PLAN

Gideon de Laune, apothecary to Anne of Denmark, wife of James I. This bust of 1671 in the Great Hall is by Nicholas Young.

Apart from this incident, Apothecaries' Hall suffered less than many Livery Halls during the Second World War.

Next to the Parlour on the eastern side of the building is the Court Room, which is panelled in Irish oak. Both stained-glass windows here commemorate the Society's 350th anniversary in 1967. One features the Apothecaries' coat of arms – Apollo (the Greek god of healing) slaying a dragon (disease), supported by two unicorns (in deference to James I, whose own arms featured the mythical beast), and a rhinoceros as the crest. There are further images of rhinos throughout the state rooms and in the common parts of the building, in carpets, drawings, carvings and elsewhere. The association between the Apothecaries and these animals has persisted long after the old belief that rhino horn had medicinal properties was proven to be superstition.

The Library, Parlour and Court Room share a landing with the Great Hall, which stands on the foundations of the priory guest house and extends for 59 feet (18 m) – the length of the two previous rooms combined – and measures 29 feet 6 inches (9 m) across. The woodwork here is seventeenth century, by Robert Burges and Roger Davis (or Davies). At the north end is a minstrels' gallery; opposite is a reredos-like screen flanked by two pairs of Corinthian columns and a wide broken pediment. Below the coat of arms is a 1671 bust by Nicholas Young of Gideon de Laune, who led the Apothecaries' secession from the Grocers' Company. Also noteworthy is the large Muniment Chest, formed from six heavy chestnut planks with brass ornamentation and brass handles; it is probably Persian and was presented to the Society in the 1680s.

The kitchens are also on the first floor. The upper floors are offices. The buildings extend further east, and the Apothecaries own a considerable amount of the block encompassed by Black Friars Lane to the west, Playhouse Yard to the south, Church Entry to the east and Carter Lane to the north. The rotunda is the exterior of the magnesia repository; the other south-facing structure – described by Bradley and Pevsner as a 'crude warehouse' of 1927 – provides a memorable counterpoint to the stuccoed fronts of the Society's showpiece buildings.

NOTE

This entry was written with reference to Penelope Hunting, *A History of the Society of Apothecaries*, London (Society of Apothecaries) 1998.

Top: Apothecaries' glassware lines a display case in the Parlour.

Above: The magnificent staircase is a Stuart survival.

Above, right: The view from the first-floor landing into the Library. The Library floor follows the original course of the gallery between the guest house of the Dominican priory and Henry VIII's Bridewell Palace.

The Great Hall, with the de Laune bust beneath the broken pediment of the screen on the south-end wall.

THE PROOF HOUSE

THE WORSHIPFUL COMPANY OF GUNMAKERS
ORDER OF PRECEDENCE: 73RD
GRADE II LISTED

The Master's chair at the west end of the Court Room. The Company's coat of arms, on the wall behind, features three musket balls, two rifles and a powder barrel.

The Worshipful Company of Gunmakers is the only Livery Company with premises that have always been without the City wall. Several commentators – notably but not only W.A.D. Englefield and Peter J.A. Lubbock[1] – have taken this as somehow emblematic of what they regard as the Company's aloofness. However, the rationale for keeping firearms as far as reasonably possible away from densely populated urban areas really requires little explanation: the Gunmakers' detachment is no selfish affectation; it attests nothing but benevolence and a survival instinct. Moreover, it is important to note that the Gunmakers are one of the few Companies that have not diversified their activities. They still perform exactly the same function as that for which they were granted their Royal Charter by Charles I in 1637: testing and inspecting guns. Security is thus of paramount importance, perhaps never more than now in the early twenty-first century.

After their original Proof House in Aldgate, 'next to the Bulwarke under the Citty Wall',[2] was seriously damaged in 1663 by an explosion, the Gunmakers moved their premises in 1675 to what was then described as the 'Physic Garden in or near the back lane in the parish of St Mary Whitechapel'[3] – a site that is now on the south side of Commercial Road between Gower's Walk to the east and Goodman Stile to the west.

No part of the present complex is older than 1757, in which year the Company's governors gave orders that the dilapidated pre-existent buildings should be 'speedily taken down and rebuilt'.[4] Their original intention was that the old walls should be preserved if at all possible, but it seems unlikely that anything of the original edifice survived: according to a surveyor's report of 1760, 'the charging house, marking house and compting house were in ruinous condition and not fit to be repaired'.[5]

The reconstruction, which was extensive even if it was not total, was carried out under the supervision of John Buckmaster and completed by New Year's Day 1761.

Today, the oldest part of the northern façade of the buildings stands out from its surroundings by being single-storey next to two- and three-storey neighbours. It has three bays of stock brick divided by stuccoed stone pilasters. At its centre, between two windows, the main entrance has a consoled architrave and a segmental pediment. At parapet level, a raised central panel bears the name of the Company and the year of its incorporation.

Immediately inside the doorway, the Receiving Room – gaunt, functional and highly protected – backs on to an open courtyard. This paved quadrangle abuts the surrounding walls on three sides at ground level. The interiors here contain loading rooms, firing chambers, shooting ranges and laboratories in which all kinds of tube-fired artillery pieces are rigorously proofed (stress- and safety-tested). By striking contrast, along the north wall, beneath the Receiving Room, the courtyard issues on to a ledge above a semi-basement. Here is located the Court Room with, on its eastern side, the Anteroom, to the south of which is a small kitchen.

With windows on only its southern flank, the Court Room almost always needs artificial lighting, but that does nothing to diminish its tranquil quality amid a ballistic

Left: The Courtyard, looking south from the window of the Court Room.

Left, bottom: In the Court Room is a portrait of Charles I, who in 1637 granted the Gunmakers their first Royal Charter.

storm. As might be expected in view of its low elevation, the enduring historic enemy of this structure is damp, which required serious remedial treatment in 1984.

Although the focus of the Proof House remains the core activity of proofing, the Court Room is available for hire by approved visitors. The space can accommodate twenty-four guests for meals at a great mahogany table. The Master's chair is at the west end of the room.

The Proof Master's House, the three-storey building to the east of the Receiving Room, was designed by the Company Surveyor, Robert Turner Cotton, built in 1826 and acquired by the Gunmakers in the following year; it currently houses the Company's offices. At the rear of this building, visible from Gower's Walk, is the windowless brick flank of what was until 1994 the Proving Chamber. The wall – double thickness for soundproofing – has arched openings on high: some of these are blank; others have iron louvres that could be shut while weapons were tested and then opened to allow smoke to clear. The roof is made of fireproof iron.

The two-floor structure to the west of the Receiving Room, Gunmakers' Hall, was built in 1871–72; beyond that, its exact origins are uncertain. It may have been designed by John Jacobs, a builder from nearby Leman Street, perhaps because the Company did not want to pay for a qualified architect, but it is at least possible that G.H. Simmonds, the Company Surveyor, was involved in the design. The Italianate façade is of brick and Portland stone; Cherry, O'Brien and Pevsner describe it as 'pompous',[6] which seems harsh. Inside is a neo-Jacobean staircase installed in 1893 by W.J. Lambert and, on the ground floor, the old Court Room – decorated with elaborate plasterwork and a glazed panel in the ceiling – which was designed to accommodate the fifty liverymen who made up the Company in the late nineteenth century.

Unable to afford the necessary repairs, the Gunmakers sold their Hall in 1927 for £5750. In 2007 they repurchased it; the premises are currently leased to tenants. In the intervening eighty years, the two buildings retained by the Company were damaged in Luftwaffe raids on 8 September and 1 November 1940, and again by incendiary devices on 14 March 1944. Restoration was not completed until 1953.

NOTES

1 W.A.D. Englefield, *The Halls of the Livery Companies of the City of London*, ed. Peter J.A. Lubbock, London 1981, p. 163.
2 Quoted in Derek Stimpson (ed.), *The Worshipful Company of Gunmakers: A History*, London (The Worshipful Company of Gunmakers) 2008, p. 3.
3 Quoted *ibid.*
4 Committee meeting minutes, 27 January 1757; quoted *ibid.*, p. 32.
5 Committee meeting minutes, 26 June 1760; quoted *ibid.*
6 Bridget Cherry, Charles O'Brien and Nikolaus Pevsner, *London 5: East* (Pevsner Architectural Guides: Buildings of England), New Haven, Conn., and London (Yale University Press) 2005, p. 484.

Here and in adjoining rooms are tested most of the firearms issued or legally sold in the United Kingdom. (The remainder are tested at the Gun Barrel Proof House in Birmingham.)

The Court Room. The left-hand shield on the wall in the image to the left depicts the arms of Air Commodore and Alderman the Hon. Sir Peter Vanneck, GBE, CB, AFC, DL, *who in 1977 became the first Gunmaker Lord Mayor of London.*

HQS *WELLINGTON*

THE HONOURABLE COMPANY OF MASTER MARINERS
ORDER OF PRECEDENCE: 78TH

The sloop is moored facing upstream on the River Thames, between Waterloo Bridge and Blackfriars Bridge.

The Master Mariners have bucked trends since 1932, when they became the first new Livery Company since the Carmen in 1746. They were also the first – and until 2014, when Elizabeth II granted a Royal Charter to the Honourable Company of Air Pilots, the only one – of their kind to be styled 'Honourable' rather than 'Worshipful', a title bestowed on them in 1928 by George V in tribute to the losses sustained by Royal Navy and merchant seamen during the First World War.

Moreover, the Master Mariners are the only Livery Company with a permanent residence that is not a piece of real estate. Their offices are on board a decommissioned warship moored and facing upriver on the north bank of the Thames. The vessel is deemed to be within the City of London, even though it is to the west of the boundary stone on the Embankment pavement, because its after moorings are on the riverbed on the 'right' (eastern) side of the line.

Launched in Devonport in 1934, *Wellington* is a Grimsby class sloop. (A sloop was originally any single-masted boat with a fore-and-aft rig and no boom on the foresail; since the end of the age of sail, the term has been used more loosely to describe any small warship.) The vessel weighs 1300 tons, measures 266 feet (81 m) from stem to stern and is 34 feet (10.4 m) broad in the beam.

Wellington has a distinguished history. It was designed as a patrol vessel and was first based in Auckland, New Zealand (hence the ship's name, after the capital city), from where it patrolled British island protectorates in the South Pacific. During the Second World War, it served mainly as an anti-submarine escort, first for Atlantic convoys on the Western Approaches, later for Allied shipping off the north-west coast of Africa, and finally in the Mediterranean.

At the end of the war, the ship was transferred to the Reserve Fleet and lay in a mud berth in Milford Haven in Wales until purchased in 1947 by the Master Mariners, who had previously been based in offices on land in Leadenhall Street. (They had tried to get back on to the water before, and were in the process of purchasing *Archibald Russell*, a full-rigged sailing ship, when war broke out in 1939. By the end of the conflict this vessel had fallen into disrepair and the Mariners had decided that an ex-Royal Navy warship was more appropriate for their purposes than a merchantman.)

Towed to Chatham Dockyard in Kent and there converted for civilian use, *Wellington* ceased to be HMS (His Majesty's Ship) and became the first and

Left: The gangway seen from the starboard side of the vessel.

to date still the only HQS (Head Quarters Ship). The vessel was installed in its present location near Temple Underground station in December 1948.

Of the numerous differences between HMS *Wellington* and HQS *Wellington*, the most readily apparent is the absence of armaments: the two 4.7-inch guns, one forward, one aft, and the anti-aircraft gun amidships were removed at the time of decommissioning, along with the radar and the engines.

While the refit was underway, the Master Mariners became aware of a passenger ship that was being broken up in a yard at Port Glasgow on the River Clyde. The vessel in question had started out as RMS *Viper*, a Scottish steam packet that was launched in 1906 and worked the Ardrossan–Belfast route until 1914 but was sold in 1920 to the Isle of Man Steam Packet Company, under whose aegis it became the *Snaefell*. The Mariners approached the final owner, Burns & Laird, and purchased from it the ship's main passenger staircase, a magnificent teak artefact that is now at the heart of the *Wellington*.

Below the Reception Deck is the Model Deck, so named for the displays here of magnificently detailed scale miniatures of historic ships. Among the most striking exhibits are very fine models of HMS *Wellington* as originally built and the tea clipper *Cutty Sark*. A model of the Cunard liner RMS *Aquitania* occupies a glass case close to some of the chairs and a card table that were among the luxury furnishings of the full-size original that plied the Atlantic between 1914 and 1950. Behind glass doors painted with a striking Turneresque seawater design is a small but comprehensive Library.

The Medal Room is on the port side in an alcove, on one bulkhead of which are displayed some of the medals awarded to members of the Company, including a Victoria Cross and two George Crosses.

A further flight downstairs, the Court Room occupies the space formerly taken up by the engine and boiler rooms. At the entrance are two paintings. *The First Court*, by Maurice Randall (1865–1950), shows David, Prince of Wales, at the meeting in September 1926 at which the Master Mariners' Company was founded. The other is a portrait by John St Helier Lander (1868–1944) of the same royal, now Edward VIII. This is the only full-length painting made of that monarch during the eleven months in 1936 between his accession and his abdication.

Above the Reception Deck on the Foc'sle Deck are the Committee Room and the Master Mariner's accommodation.

In 1991 HQS *Wellington* was towed to Sheerness dry dock in Kent for an extensive refit: the Foc'sle and Upper Decks were replated, the office space was extended, and the galley enlarged. More recently, the Court Room has been repanelled and now has air conditioning and greatly improved lighting.

Below: In more clement weather than shown here, the after end of the Boat Deck may be used for social gatherings.

Opposite and left: The teak staircase was due to be scrapped, but was saved by the Master Mariners and restored to its original glory.

Below: Model ships are displayed on the Reception Deck as well as on the Model Deck.

Bottom: The Company's collection of plate is displayed in cabinets set in the panelling of the Court Room, which occupies the space previously taken up by the ship's engine and boiler rooms.

FURNITURE MAKERS' HALL

THE WORSHIPFUL COMPANY OF FURNITURE MAKERS
ORDER OF PRECEDENCE: 83RD
GRADE II LISTED

A 2-inch (5-cm) diameter plaque records that this console table by Matthew Burt was awarded the Master's Jubilee Prize in 2001.

Formed as a guild in 1952, the Furniture Makers' Company became the 83rd Livery Company of the City of London in 1963. That such an ancient craft should have been so late in collectivizing may be a surprise to some, but it is explicable by the fact that historically the practice was often undertaken by members of numerous other established guilds, most notably the Worshipful Company of Carpenters, the Worshipful Company of Joiners and Ceilers, the Worshipful Company of Upholders and the Worshipful Company of Turners. During the two periods when the furniture makers were at their most prosperous and influential – after the Restoration in 1660 and during the career of Thomas Chippendale (1718–1779) – they were perhaps too busy with their work to concern themselves with forming a Company.

The Company merged with the Furnishing Trades Benevolent Association in 2012; in the following year, to coincide with its fiftieth anniversary, it was granted a Royal Charter by Elizabeth II.

Meanwhile, after a year as leaseholders of No. 12 Austin Friars, the Furniture Makers had purchased the freehold of the building in 2006. The name of this street is taken from the Augustinian friary that was founded here by Henry III in 1253. Rebuilt after 1354, the friary church later lost all but its nave during the Dissolution of the monasteries under Henry VIII. In 1550 what remained of it was given to Flemish Protestant refugees from persecution by the Spanish Roman Catholic occupiers of The Netherlands; it henceforth became known as the Dutch Church. Destroyed by bombs during the Second World War, it was afterwards rebuilt and is now the world's oldest Dutch-language Protestant church. The current church sits immediately opposite the Furniture Makers' building.

Nos. 12 and 14 Austin Friars were both designed by E.A. Gruning in what is sometimes known loosely and not enormously helpfully as Queen Anne Revival style. This was the vernacular approach widely adopted by the Scottish architect Richard Norman Shaw (1831–1912), whose work on a range of important buildings, including the first New Scotland Yard, Albert Hall Mansions and the Kate Greenaway House in Frognal, was popular and influential in the late nineteenth century. Gruning's work in Austin Friars began in 1881; No. 12 was ready in 1882, and the project as a whole was completed in the following year.

The first occupants of No. 12 were Frühling & Goschen, German merchant bankers who came to England from Leipzig in around 1800. They had long been interested in property in this part of the capital: work on this very site had been started in 1853 by George Goschen, who later became Viscount Goschen, MP for the City of London, First Lord of the Admiralty and a director of the Bank of England.

Unlike the church on the opposite side of the road, Furniture Makers' Hall got through the Second World War with no more than superficial damage to the windows and the façade. Consequently, it still has

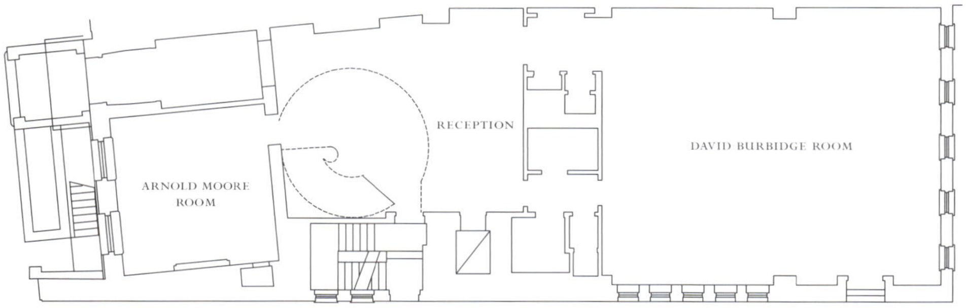

GROUND-FLOOR PLAN

many original external Victorian features, including the red-brick frontage, the deep, square-headed door canopy and the tall windows. The terracotta frieze between the second and third floors is a repetition of the adornment applied by Gruning to his earlier work a quarter of a mile away on No. 11 Tokenhouse Yard, currently a rentable business centre.

Beyond the main entrance of Furniture Makers' Hall, visitors enter a spacious reception area with a sweeping spiral oak staircase to the right and straight ahead a concierge's desk flanked by two doors: these both lead into the David Burbidge Room, which is named after the Master of the Company in 2004 and the founding chairman of the Hall. Here, as throughout the premises, are numerous bespoke fittings and items of furniture all made from the Company's most essential raw material: wood. The rear windows admit natural light, but there is little space between them and the back of the buildings in Great Winchester Street.

At the south-facing front of the ground floor, with an outlook on to the Dutch Church, is a wooden-panelled room named in memory of Arnold Moore (1916–2000), the businessman and philanthropist who founded Furniture Productions (now Knightsbridge Furniture).

On the first floor, immediately above, is the Mike Clare Room. Named after the entrepreneurial founder of a major British bed and mattress retailer, it has even better views of the church from its three tall sash windows. Also noteworthy here are the high ceiling with its ornate cornicing, the fireplace made of marble and carved wood, and the beautifully crafted boardroom table and chairs. The Mike Clare Room is used by the Company for small committee meetings.

All other parts of Furniture Makers' Hall – a total of five floors above ground and a basement – are let to tenants.

The reception area is dominated by the magnificent spiral staircase of oak.

Below: In the Arnold Moore Room is one of three cabinets made by Liveryman George Feeny to display the Company's treasures.

Right: In the same room hangs a tapestry made by the textile designer Lucienne Day and presented by her husband, the furniture designer Robin Day, an honorary liveryman.

Right: In the David Burbidge Room, the Wardens' chairs, made and presented by Ercol, are positioned either side of the Master's Jubilee Prize-winning console table by Matthew Burt.

The Hall's main space, on the ground floor, is named after David Burbidge, Master of the Company in 2004 and founding chairman of the Hall.

INFORMATION TECHNOLOGISTS' HALL

THE WORSHIPFUL COMPANY OF INFORMATION TECHNOLOGISTS
ORDER OF PRECEDENCE: 100TH

The façade of the Information Technologists' Hall is an outstanding example of late 19th-century Queen Anne Revival style.

This modern Livery Company was the 1980s brainchild of Alan Benjamin and Bernard Harty, IT professionals who believed that their industry should have the same standards and safeguards, and develop along the same lines as the great guilds of every vintage, from the oldest, the Weavers (1155), to the professional body that was then the most recent to be granted livery status, the Environmental Cleaners, who became the 97th Company in 1986.

In 1987 the Information Technologists took a significant step towards their ultimate goal when they became a City Company without Grant of Livery. Two years later they received their coat of arms and a motto, *CITO*, the Latin for 'swiftly', which is how the best computers perform and happily includes the letters I and T within the C–O abbreviation for 'Company'. The Information Technologists then deliberately waited until the Chartered Architects and the Constructors had taken the 98th and 99th positions respectively in the order of precedence before applying for livery status so that, in 1992, they themselves became the City of London's 100th Livery Company (receiving its Royal Charter in 2010). The number 100 seemed particularly apposite to them because it looks like, or could be taken as, binary notation (for the number four).

The Company then sought a permanent base, but lacked the funds to do so until 1998, when it received a donation of £5 million from the Shirley Foundation. This charitable fund was set up by Dame Stephanie Shirley, who had made her fortune at the head of Freelance Programmers, a software company she founded in 1962 with £6 capital and which by the end of the 1960s was producing, among other things, the black boxes used on Concorde, the Anglo-French supersonic airliner.

Almost immediately the Information Technologists took £1 million of this money, matched it with the same amount from their own members, and used the total to purchase a property midway between Smithfield and the Barbican in a street that Bradley and Pevsner describe as 'a straggling backwater', but which seems today more atmospherically picturesque – an olde worlde oasis of calm in the eye of a storm of busy-ness and modernity.

The earliest recorded use of this building, dated 1737, is as an inn, The Rose and Crown. It goes almost completely unmentioned in history, apart from in 1887, when there was some limited news coverage of the death of its landlord, Charles Shaw, who drowned while swimming in the Vale of Health Pond, Hampstead.[1]

The Livery Roll, which is signed by all liverymen and officers of the Company. The open page is inscribed by Honorary Freeman William (Bill) Gates, the principal founder of Microsoft.

Although Dear & Winder, the architects who refitted the building in 1897, described it as 'an asymmetrical former pub',[2] it was taken over in the following year by Benskins Brewery and seems to have continued serving alcohol until 1923. It then became the premises of one catering butcher, E. (Ernie) Russell Ltd, and in 1954 of his successor in business, Tim Stone. During this period the front door on the left of the building was the entrance to the office; that on the right led into the cutting room. In 1978 it became the premises of a security firm; two years later a new twenty-five-year lease explicitly proscribed the use of the place 'for the manufacture consumption or sale of meat (whether cooked or uncooked) beer wine or spirituous liquors'.[3]

Shortly after the Information Technologists bought the Hall and moved into it, they moved out again for two years so that it could be fully refurbished. It was formally reopened on 20 September 2001.

Today the façade of the Information Technologists' Hall epitomizes the Queen Anne Revival style of the late nineteenth century: red brick with stone facings and three arched entrances beneath a tripartite oriel with twelve windows crowned by the Company's arms. The top floor has a single window with six sections, capped off by a gable roof.

On either side of the partly glazed central entrance are two large square windows. Both windows and the door sit within a wide overall arch enclosing a wooden frame that houses thirty-one panes of glass. The door on the left as one faces the building leads to a staircase that is lit by a tall, thin eight-pane window; the door on the right now leads into a cloakroom.

Inside the Hall, the basement contains the main computer system and an archive room. The ground floor houses the Reception and the administration offices of the Information Technologists' Trust. At the rear of the building is a stained-glass window bearing the Company's coat of arms.

On the first floor are the Livery Hall, the kitchen and the Treasures Area. Among the most striking displays are a glass appliqué panel bearing the arms of the City of London and a bronze bust of Dame Stephanie, who in addition to being a benefactor was Master of the Company in 1992.

At the top level are the Gold Room, the Blue Room (both named for the main colours of their respective decor) and the Members' Room (formerly the Green Room). In the Gold Room, the largest of the trio, is another representation of the Company's arms, this one carved in teak.

NOTES

1 See *The Illustrated Police News*, 2 July 1887, p. 4.

2 Quoted in Joan M. Smith, *A History of the Information Technologists' Hall*, London (The Worshipful Company of Information Technologists) 2008.

3 Quoted *ibid*.

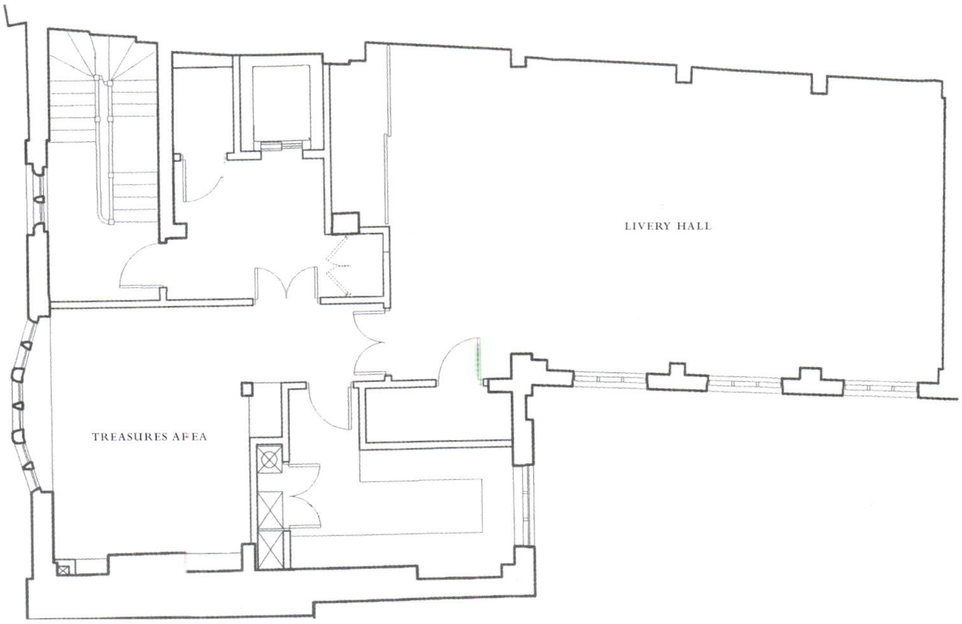

FIRST-FLOOR PLAN

Below: Detail of the Millennium Plate, which records the engraved names of all liverymen of the Worshipful Company of Information Technologists at 1 January 2000, a gift to the Company from Peter Cropper, who was Master at that time.

Right: Nine separate portraits in a work entitled Five Masters, Three Wardens and the Clerk *and the Master's chair, incorporating symbols from the telecommunications industry.*

Left: The Livery Hall, in which Court meetings are held.

Below: Among the artefacts in the Treasures Area is a bronze bust of Dame Stephanie Shirley (seen in detail at opposite, bottom right), the first female Master of the Company.

WATERMEN'S HALL

THE COMPANY OF WATERMEN AND LIGHTERMEN OF THE RIVER THAMES
GRADE II* LISTED; SCHEDULED ANCIENT MONUMENT

Right: The original 18th-century frontage of Watermen's Hall at No. 18 on the west side of St Mary at Hill.

Right, bottom: A model ship made of bone, presented to the Company in 1842, at the entrance to the Parlour Room on the ground floor.

First regulated by Act of Parliament in 1514 during the reign of Henry VIII and granted permission to hire apprentices during the reign of Mary I in 1555, this is a City Company without Grant of Livery for historic reasons and therefore does not feature in the order of precedence. However, it warrants inclusion in the present volume because it is one of the forty Companies that own their own Hall. Moreover, the Watermen's is the only property of its type in the City of London that is still today substantially as it was in the eighteenth century.

The guild was the Company of Watermen alone until 1700, when its members (who were providers of passenger ferriage) were joined in enterprise by the Lightermen (carriers of goods and cargo).

The Watermen's original sixteenth-century building, the Mansion of Cold Harbour, lay to the south of Upper Thames Street, closer to the river than the current premises. Perhaps the only surviving contemporary image of this place is a detail in *Long View of London from Bankside* (1647), a panoramic etching by Wenceslaus Hollar (1607–1677).

The mansion was destroyed in the Great Fire of 1666, then rebuilt twice, in 1670 and 1720. In 1780 the Company moved to a new building at No. 18 St Mary at Hill. This was the first work by William Blackburn (1750–1790), the architect who went on to become his generation's leading designer of prisons (his *chef-d'œuvre* was the old City Gaol in Oxford Castle).

The east-facing stone frontage of Watermen's Hall is elegantly classical, with Ionic pilasters supporting an entablature and pediment, and Doric columns within a three-part first-floor window surmounted by a lunette. The external details – frieze, plaques and carvings in the capitals – are commonly agreed to show the influence of Samuel Wyatt (1737–1807), designer in 1780 of the new façade and portico of the Theatre Royal, Birmingham.

Watermen's Hall was damaged in the Second World War, but not too badly; it was fully repaired by 1951. There were major refurbishments in 1961, and in the early 1980s the Company doubled its usable space by taking over adjacent properties. No. 17, the building to the right as one faces the original Watermen's Hall, was constructed in 1786 and had been the Fellowship Porters' Hall until 1894, when that Company had been forced to vacate it. Made of stock brick, the façade of this building is less ornate than that of its neighbour.

Right: A collection of historic backboards in the groin-vaulted entrance passage of No. 18.

Right, bottom: The view from the Entrance Hall into the Parlour Room.

Here another lunette sits above an elliptically headed triple first-floor window with a fanlight. The arcading along the ground-floor exterior was installed in 1983 by Cluttons to an eighteenth-century design. The same architects were also responsible for the neo-Georgian frontage of No. 16 (further right again, up the hill), which the Watermen took over at the same time.

The modern public entrance is through the door of No. 17 via the Silver Room, which is panelled with timber salvaged from some of the nineteenth-century riverside warehouses that were pulled down during the late twentieth-century deindustrialization of the Port of London.

The Parlour Room, on the ground floor of No. 18, the original building, has a beautiful low-relief plaster ceiling and a stained-glass window.

At the rear of the building on the interior west wall is a stone staircase cantilevered around a semicircular stairwell and, above its head, a domed oval skylight with a garlanded frieze and a lower band of Vitruvian scroll.

The Court Room now extends slightly more than 20 feet (6 m) across the whole of the first floor of No. 18. Its oval ceiling, with festoons and scalloped fluting arranged concentrically, is mounted on pendentives. There are also lunettes with circular reliefs and scrolls, and a festooned frieze, which is stepped down where it passes between the top of the window and the bottom of a lunette. On the south wall, the marble fireplace has a relief carving of a river god. Above the mantelpiece is an attention-grabbing relief sculpture of the Company's coat of arms: a boat on six silver and blue wavy bars and, in chief, a pair of crossed oars between two cushions. The crest is an arm holding an oar upon a wreath of silver and red; the supporters are two dolphins; the Latin motto, *Jussu superiorum*, is usually rendered in English as 'At the commandment of our superiors'.

Occupying the whole of the 1983 extension across the first floor of Nos. 16–17, the Freemen's Room is taller, wider and longer than the Court Room. Its most striking features are its neo-Georgian ceiling and the silverware and old uniforms in glass display cases around the walls.

The basement, all decked out in modern tiling, has cloakrooms and, along its corridor, further glass-case exhibits of cups, model boats and other valuables and memorabilia.

Right and below: The Freemen's Room, occupying the first floor of Nos. 16 and 17, is part of the 1983 extension to the Hall.

Opposite, top and bottom right: The Court Room features pilasters and pendentives supporting a delightfully enriched oval ceiling. The Company's coat of arms sits above the marble fireplace.

Opposite, bottom left: The Parlour Room is dominated by a round-arched window with stained glass and an elegant plaster ceiling with a large central oval.

THE LOST HALLS

Anya Lucas

One of the observations most commonly made about the Livery Halls is their capacity for absorbing, accommodating and surviving changes and disruption. 'The wonder is', noted W.A.D. Englefield in his introduction to a picture book on the Halls, 'that so many have resisted the combined efforts of time and history, war, fires and other calamities to efface them.'[1] Similarly, Bradley and Pevsner have observed that 'Their survival against the odds is a remarkable feature of the City's history.'[2] Evidence of this capacity for survival can be found across the City today: in Mincing Lane, for example, there have stood six incarnations of Clothworkers' Hall; Thames Street has had three different Fishmongers' Halls, and Gresham Street five Wax Chandlers' Halls. Not even topographical continuity has been necessary to the survival of the type; there have been six Salters' Halls on three different City sites (Bread Street, St Swithin's Lane and Fore Street), for example (figs. 1 and 2). There have been repeated rebuildings and substitutions, but the chain has, more often than not, remained unbroken. This chapter offers an account of the Halls' development: from the mid-fourteenth

century (when the Merchant Taylors first occupied Threadneedle Street) to the present day – via Tudor expansion, Caroline beautification and Carolean reconstruction.

RETRIEVING THE LOST HALLS: FINDING THE EVIDENCE

An essential source for studying the lost Halls is the large corpus of Livery Company records held at the Guildhall Library. All but nine of the seventy-seven ancient Companies (that is, those founded in or before the seventeenth century) have placed their records in care of the City of London Corporation. Most Companies possess unbroken runs of Court minutes and accounts, but the survival rate for building papers such as committee minutes, fabric accounts, craftsmen's quotes, bills and articles of agreement, promissory books and subscription lists, still less plans, surveys and designs, is much lower. The archives of the Mercers', Goldsmiths', Brewers', Cutlers' and Tallow Chandlers' Companies are the exceptions that prove this rule. A particularly valuable survival is a pen-and-wash drawing dated 1669: a proposal for the street frontispiece of the Brewers' post-Fire Hall. This is the earliest architectural drawing relating to a Hall building that we possess (fig. 3).

The combination of a paucity of extant pre-twentieth-century fabric and voluminous archival material means there is an obvious danger of over-privileging literary sources. The documentary evidence needs to be handled cautiously, however. Sometimes Court minutes can be obligingly specific and highly evocative, at others infuriatingly cryptic and vague. Although they can read as compelling statements of overall corporate intent, it is also important to remember that the minutes record the discussions only of the governing body – the 'ancientest' of the Company,

Fig. 1 (page 224) The loggia at the entrance to Salters' Hall off St Swithin's Lane, built in 1668 to designs by John Wildgos; pen and ink with colour wash by 'Wilson', c. 1780.

Fig. 2 (previous page) Salters' Hall in Fore Street, completed in 1976 to designs by Sir Basil Spence.

Fig. 3 (left) Platforme for the Hall Front, Brewers' Hall, 1669 *by Thomas Whiting; the earliest surviving architectural drawing relating to a Livery Hall.*

as they were described. The Court should never be confused with the body of freemen as a whole, whose opinions on building were not documented.

The position regarding visual evidence is no more straightforward. Most of the Livery Halls that existed in the first half of the seventeenth century were destroyed in 1666. Some, such as Skinners' Hall in Dowgate Hill, were by then buildings of considerable antiquity, while others had only recently been completed: a new Cutlers' Hall had been erected at great and futile expense from 1661, for example. The few Halls that survived the Fire are nevertheless mostly lost to us; Ironmongers' in Fenchurch Street, for example, escaped the flames but was rebuilt in 1748–50, apparently without any visual record having been made of its sixteenth-century predecessor. Leathersellers' Hall in Bishopsgate is the single exception: a series of views of this building, which was extensively rebuilt and extended in the 1620s, was made prior to its destruction in 1799, providing us with the only visual record of a pre-Fire Livery Hall interior (fig. 4). Pre-Fire topographical surveys and accounts of London are of no help as far as visual material is concerned; neither John Stow's *Survey of London* (1598, 1603, 1633) nor James Howell's *Londinopolis* (1657) offer any kind of pictorial representations of the Halls. The Copperplate Map of London (*c.* 1560), of which three sheets survive, hints at the appearance of some of the pre-Fire Halls, but its small scale means that it is not a reliable source for the appearance of individual buildings.

A far better visual record exists for the post-Fire Halls (built *c.* 1668–75), yet here, too, the picture is incomplete. Fourteen survived into the twentieth century, when the Halls were recorded and photographed for a series of articles published in *The Builder* between 1916 and 1920 and for the City of London volume of the Royal Commission on Historical Monuments (1929).[3] These photographs and survey drawings are a precious record of buildings that, in most cases, would be destroyed during the Second World War.

Prints and drawings are often the only visual sources available, and these tend to date from the nineteenth century.[4] The sites and basic ground plans of the Halls are recorded in John Ogilby and William Morgan's *Large and Accurate Map of the City of London* (1676), but topographical works such

Fig. 4 (top) The Leathersellers' main Hall, remodelled 1610, depicted by James Peller Malcolm just before demolition in 1799.

Fig. 5 (above) A 17th-century print of Mercers' Hall, built by John Oliver, 1668–82, to outlines suggested by Edward Jerman.

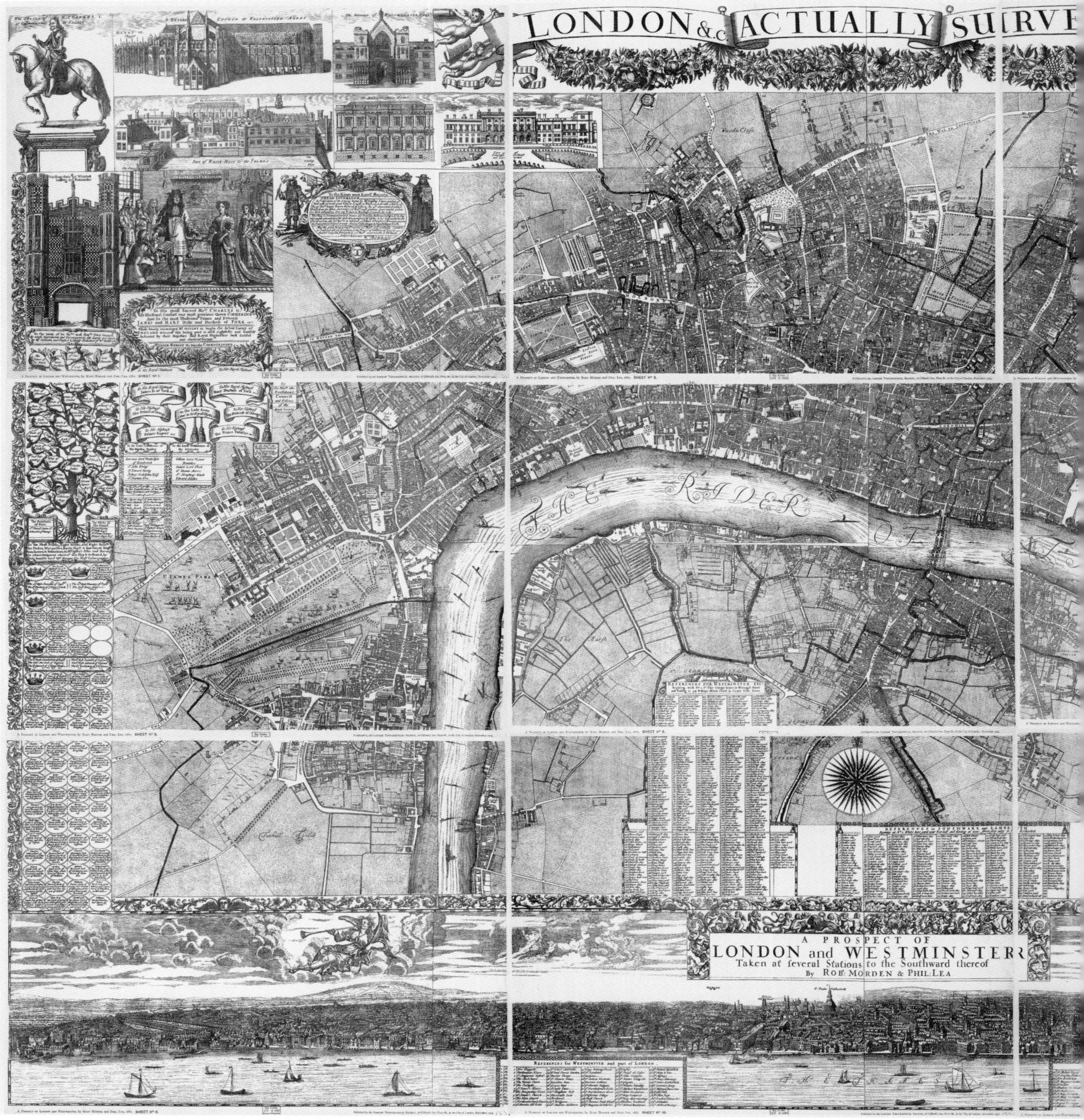
LONDON &c. ACTUALLY SURVE
THE RIVER OF
A PROSPECT OF
LONDON and WESTMINSTER
Taken at several Stations to the Southward thereof
By ROB^T MORDEN & PHIL:LEA

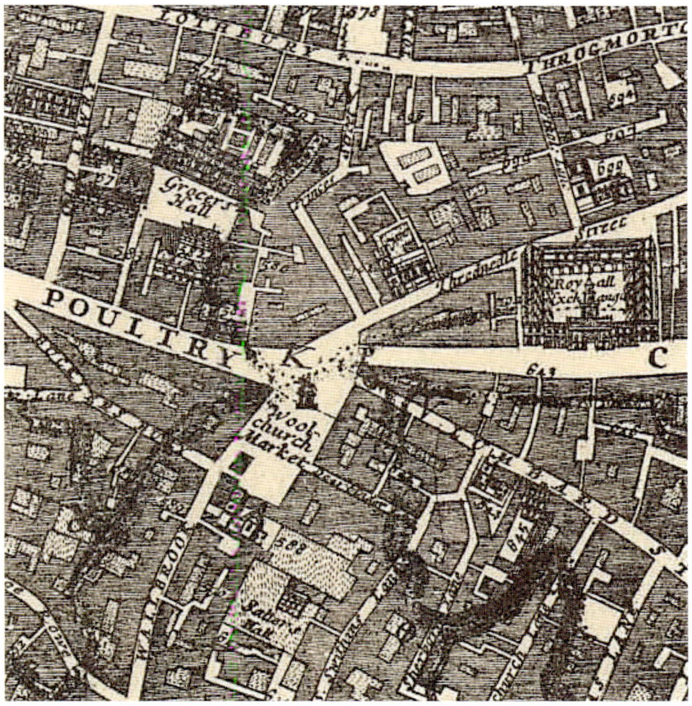

Fig. 6 (left) London Actually Survey'd *by William Morgan, 1682.*

Fig. 7 (above) London Actually Survey'd *by William Morgan, 1682; detail showing Grocers' Hall.*

Fig. 8 Engraving by Benjamin Cole of Stationers' Hall for William Maitland's The History and Survey of London from Its Foundation to the Present Time, *1756.*

Fig. 9 Exterior of the Carpenters' 1664 Court Room block; engraving by Thomas H. Shepherd, c. 1830.

Fig. 10 Brewers' Hall, Addle Street, *watercolour by Samuel Ireland*, c. *1794*.

as Edward Hatton's *New View of London* (1708) and John Strype's 1720 edition of Stow's *Survey*, despite describing the Halls in some detail, include no views. William Morgan's 1682 map, *London Actually Survey'd* (fig. 6), does include bird's-eye views of key new buildings, including Livery Halls, but, again, the scale is too small to convey much detail (fig. 7). Detail is provided in an early view of Mercers' Hall made shortly after its completion in 1682 (fig. 5). Otherwise, William Maitland's *The History and Survey of London from Its Foundation to the Present Time* (1756) provides the first known detailed views of the post-Fire Halls (fig. 8). With the exception of these engravings, the buildings were largely ignored by topographical artists and printmakers until 1827, when the watercolourist Thomas H. Shepherd was commissioned to produce a series of views for inclusion in printed volumes celebrating the capital (fig. 9). The discovery, in the collection of the Yale Center for British Art, of hitherto unpublished watercolour views of the Halls from c. 1794 has shed new light on the appearance of several lost Restoration livery buildings (fig. 10).[5]

TUDOR AND JACOBEAN BUILDING ACTIVITY

As the Introduction explained, the Companies began acquiring and adapting buildings from which to operate with particular intensity from c. 1390. These were typically medieval courtyard town houses (the westward drift of nobility away from the City ultimately freed up many such buildings). It was primarily around this courtyard house type – with a dominating hall and withdrawing apartments opening off it – that corporate activities and rituals therefore evolved. By the sixteenth century the Companies were upgrading their premises, and the decades preceding the accession of James I were by no means characterized by a lack of building activity at the Halls; work to expand or create specialized rooms within the buildings was routinely undertaken by Companies at different points on the scale of precedence and wealth at this point in their history.

The release of monastic property in the City on to the open market after the Dissolution of the monasteries provided a number of smaller Companies with the opportunity to acquire premises for the first time, and gave more well-established Companies the chance to expand: in 1542 the City's premier Company, the Mercers, had been able to increase its foothold in Cheapside by subsuming the church and conventual buildings belonging to the dissolved Hospital of St Thomas of Acre (see Introduction, fig. 13), and in the following year the Leathersellers' Company acquired St Helen's Priory in Bishopsgate.[6] A degree of repair and alteration naturally followed, although in some cases relatively little work was needed to effect a change of use: the former nuns' dormitory of St Helen's provided the Leathersellers with a banqueting hall without the need for major alterations (fig. 4).[7] Other upgrading and expansion that took place in the sixteenth century included the rebuilding of the Clothworkers', Fishmongers' and Merchant Taylors' hall ranges in 1548, 1581–82 and 1586–90 respectively, and the complete rebuilding of Coopers' Hall (1547), Cordwainers' Hall (1577) and Ironmongers' Hall (1578–87). In 1592 the Vintners rebuilt their street gates and the Grocers wainscoted their main Hall. Two years later the Merchant Taylors rebuilt their fifteenth-century King's Chamber.[8] John Schofield has partially explained the rebuilding of the Halls in the sixteenth century as the result of the Companies' expanding role as landlords and charitable trustees, and diminishing role in the regulation of trade.[9]

By far the most common category of building activity between 1536 and 1603 was the addition or expansion of the parlour for the use of the Court of Assistants or, in some cases, the creation of a second parlour. This kind of work was undertaken by ten companies, including the Skinners, Bakers, Tallow Chandlers and Carpenters.[10] The increasing withdrawal of Courts into newly created private rooms away from the nucleus of the hall mirrored the trend at the time in royal palaces and great houses, which saw the dais end of the hall increasingly abandoned for a great or privy chamber beyond or above it.[11]

The specialization and ordering of space within the Livery Hall continued into the seventeenth century as this building type emerged from its domestic and monastic origins and was refined and adjusted. After 1603, however, Hall-building activity became more ambitious and self-conscious, and there was a greater drive towards symmetry and stylistic homogeneity. Courts were increasingly aware of architectural fashions, and building was repeatedly connected in their discussions with such values as honour and credit, which were of central importance to citizen identity in the period.

In early Stuart London, the 'notion that London's relationship with the crown was one of mutual benefit and interdependence' was still current,[12] and the mere anticipation of a new reign might, therefore, induce a Company to attend to its buildings. For example, as Elizabeth I's health began to wane in autumn 1602, the Worshipful Company of Merchant Taylors, apparently concerned that its Hall on Threadneedle Street was 'unfit furnished', was galvanized into a busy programme of repairs and decoration. This began in October, when the Hall gates were replastered and repainted with 'white lead, red lead, oyle, size, Spanish white, russet and yellow oker'.[13] This striking combination of colours is found in the crest and mantling of the Company's coat of arms, which almost certainly adorned the centre of the gates. The following month, William Olyver, freemason, was paid £24 for paving and making a stone mantel and chimney piece in the King's Chamber, the room above the dais end of the Great Hall that had been rebuilt just a few years before.[14] Investment in these areas – the street gates, through which all who entered the complex passed, and the one room in the Hall dedicated for royal use – perhaps indicates that the City's sixth (alternately, seventh) Company felt that it was in with a chance of attracting the next monarch as an honorary freeman.

Elizabeth died on 24 March 1603, and with near-indecent haste the Merchant Taylors began further embellishments. First, the windows in the King's Chamber were decorated with '3 newe armes' for 24*s*. Panes of Normandy glass 'with armes' were fitted in the Great Hall window, on the staircase and in the gallery.[15] The amount of heraldic glass painting specified is noteworthy and reminds us that Livery Halls were relatively flexible fields for display; with a few judicious scene changes important statements about Company allegiances could be made rapidly. The three new arms in the King's Chamber were, according to the common formula, likely to have been those of the Company, the City and the new Stuart king. By the summer, the Merchant Taylors had also paid £8 for 'a great banner of the kings armes wrought in oyle and fine golde' and a further £21 for 'gilding and workmanship for armes and badges about the kings chamber as well over the too portals'.[16] Joiners and carvers were paid a total of £35 for making a plate cupboard and for 'wainscotting in the chamber next the kings chamber'.[17] The Merchant Taylors were displaying loyalty to the new dynasty using a decorative language they had been accustomed to for more than 200 years: painted heraldic devices, displays of plate, and the paraphernalia of civic pageantry, such as banners. The Halls were also increasingly spaces for the display of a new and fashionable form of portraiture by foreign-trained artists rather than native painter-stainers.[18]

The corporation that in fact won James I as a freeman (in 1606) was the Clothworkers' Company, which occupied a mid-sixteenth-century Hall in Mincing Lane. Competition between these two Companies for royal favour as King James and Prince Henry's freedoms were being settled appears to have found an outlet in a spate of rival building activity: a new gallery in the Clothworkers' garden and a new banqueting house in the Merchant Taylors' garden.

Even when the king was not, and in all likelihood never would be, physically present at a Hall, his royal favour might still precipitate building activity. The acquisition of a Royal Charter, which confirmed or restyled a Company's material and constitutional resources, was an obvious cue for a Livery Company to build anew or to renovate existing premises, not least because the benefactions needed to finance such activity flowed more freely with incorporation.[19] The Turners' Company, fifty-first in order of precedence, protected the interests of London craftsmen who turned and shaped wood on a lathe. When James I issued the Turners with a Charter in 1604, the Company immediately began rebuilding the large house it had first leased in Philpot Lane in 1591.[20] The project was finally complete in summer 1606 and included fine carving by 'Mr Carter'. In all likelihood this was the young Francis Carter, the carpenter by trade who would become Clerk of Works to Prince Henry in 1610. Carter had just completed the wainscoting in the hall of Trinity College, Cambridge – another high-status project on a building type with obvious similarities to a Livery Hall.[21]

Inter-Company rivalry may have taken a particularly focused form in the case of the bids by the Merchant Taylors' and Clothworkers' Companies' for royal approbation, and perhaps preferment, through the fabric of their Halls, but competitive emulation also provided a general impetus behind Halls' enlargements and embellishments in the period. The Leathersellers' Company, first chartered in 1444 and fifteenth in order of precedence, had, through good management, amassed wealth comparable to that of any of the Great Twelve by the time its second Charter was granted in 1604.[22] By this time the Company had long abandoned and rented out its first Hall, on London Wall near Moorgate, a two-storey town house, for more prestigious premises on the City's eastern edge.[23]

The Leathersellers undertook fairly considerable building activity before the renewal of their Charter, in the dissolved Benedictine priory of St Helen's, which they acquired in 1543. Records suggest that the building work undertaken after 1604 was designed to serve reputational needs as well as functional requirements. The main Hall's elaborate redecoration was, suggestively, accompanied by urgent Court discussions about the apparel of members; complaints registered under the heading 'Foynes' (the fur that adorned livery gowns) in July 1611, for example, deplored the 'undecent manner of dress' of the Company's senior membership.[24] The comeliness and decency of 'fabric' (in both modern senses of the word) was a growing preoccupation for the Companies in the seventeenth century. Indeed, the idea of architectural sumptuousness, one so appropriate to corporations whose members were defined by the costly livery they wore, is a particularly productive way of thinking about the architecture of the Halls both then and still now; these were buildings conceived as carcasses to be dressed with ornament. In 1608 the Leathersellers' hall range received a new roof and an elaborate fretwork ceiling with pendants and the badges of the City of London and the Company.[25] Such a commission would certainly have helped to place the Leathersellers' Hall on a par with those of the Great Twelve, which were also investing in this kind of display.

A new gate on Bishopsgate in 1619 of 'brick and stone with the companies armes in stone' contributed to James I's ambition to turn a 'London of Sticks' into a 'more durable, safe from fire, beautiful and magnificent' one of bricks.[26] The next decade saw the Leathersellers' Company return its focus to the inner complex and the rebuilding of the kitchen or service block. The result was a range with a handsome three-gabled brick elevation to Little St Helen's with rubbed brick dressings in the form of lugged window architraves and a thick string course

Fig. 11 The Leathersellers' service range in Little St Helen's depicted by John Thomas Smith just before demolition in 1799.

(fig. 11). By producing a flat-fronted, comparatively uniform building of brick, the Company was responding to new building rules. The plentiful options for articulating the surfaces of timber-framed buildings – pargeting, canting, jettying, carving – were now unavailable, but such devices as the lugged architrave or the cutting of 'wedges Archwise' over entries (as in the case of the rusticated gate in fig. 11) provided a new, decorative vocabulary with which to animate a brick elevation.[27] The sculpted gables on the courtyard façade of the same range were of the fashionable 'Holborn' type, with alternately triangular and segmental pediments, as a view of *c.* 1794 illustrates (fig. 12). The same view shows the stone porch added to the Hall's main entrance at the time that the service range was reconstructed. Here, at a particularly important threshold within the complex, full advantage was taken of the potential for contrasting stone and brick, as well as of the amenability of stone to informative carving. Superimposed on a rusticated entrance archway similar to that on the service block, Ionic columns – a prelude to those that adorned the screen inside – supported the figures of Charity and Justice, carved scrolls and the Company's coat of arms.[28] The porch deployed elements of the fashionable classicizing designs then in circulation through Continental (and some English) pattern books, but these were not allowed to eclipse the structure's primary function: to signal corporate virtue, antiquity and authority in the form of the carved figures and the oversized heraldic display that dominated its centre.

The Leathersellers' building activity encapsulates that of the Companies more generally in the early modern period: an interest in privacy, functional distinction and competitive comparison; the pursuit of honour and decency; and the need to respond to a new regulatory context.

BUILDING, REPAIR AND BEAUTIFICATION UNDER CHARLES I

The next key phase in the Halls' development centres on the story of how the Livery Companies became embroiled in the politicization of building under Charles I's Personal Rule (1629–40). In 1630 Inigo Jones, along with Jones's friend and patron Thomas Howard, 14th Earl of Arundel, became members of a reconstituted and more exacting Commission for Buildings. For the duration of Charles's Personal Rule these two men, along with other prominent courtiers, would deploy architecture as an instrument of 'social engineering' in their pursuit of an architecturally harmonious city that was also politically compliant.[29] Stuart royal interest in London's fabric amounted to more than a series of individual projects and proposals, such as the portico of St Paul's Cathedral, the laying-out of Lincoln's Inn Fields or the redevelopment of London Bridge along more modish lines; these were components in a concerted and ambitious master plan for a royal capital city (one in which a wide range of citizen-led building projects, such as the rebuilding of St Michael-le-Querne church and Goldsmiths' Hall, were caught up).[30]

Beautification initiatives in the 1630s City, such as the reformation of Cheapside, Jones's refacing of St Paul's and the rebuilding of St Katharine Cree and other churches – all projects to which the Livery Companies contributed financially – have been well documented by historians and understood, to a greater or lesser extent, to be the result of pressure applied by Charles I's Privy Council or William Laud, Archbishop of

Fig. 12 Leather Sellers' Hall, St Helen's, *watercolour by Samuel Ireland,* c. *1794.*

Fig. 13 South side of St Katharine Cree, Leadenhall Street, with its original crest- and saddle-stone battlement; etching, 1740.

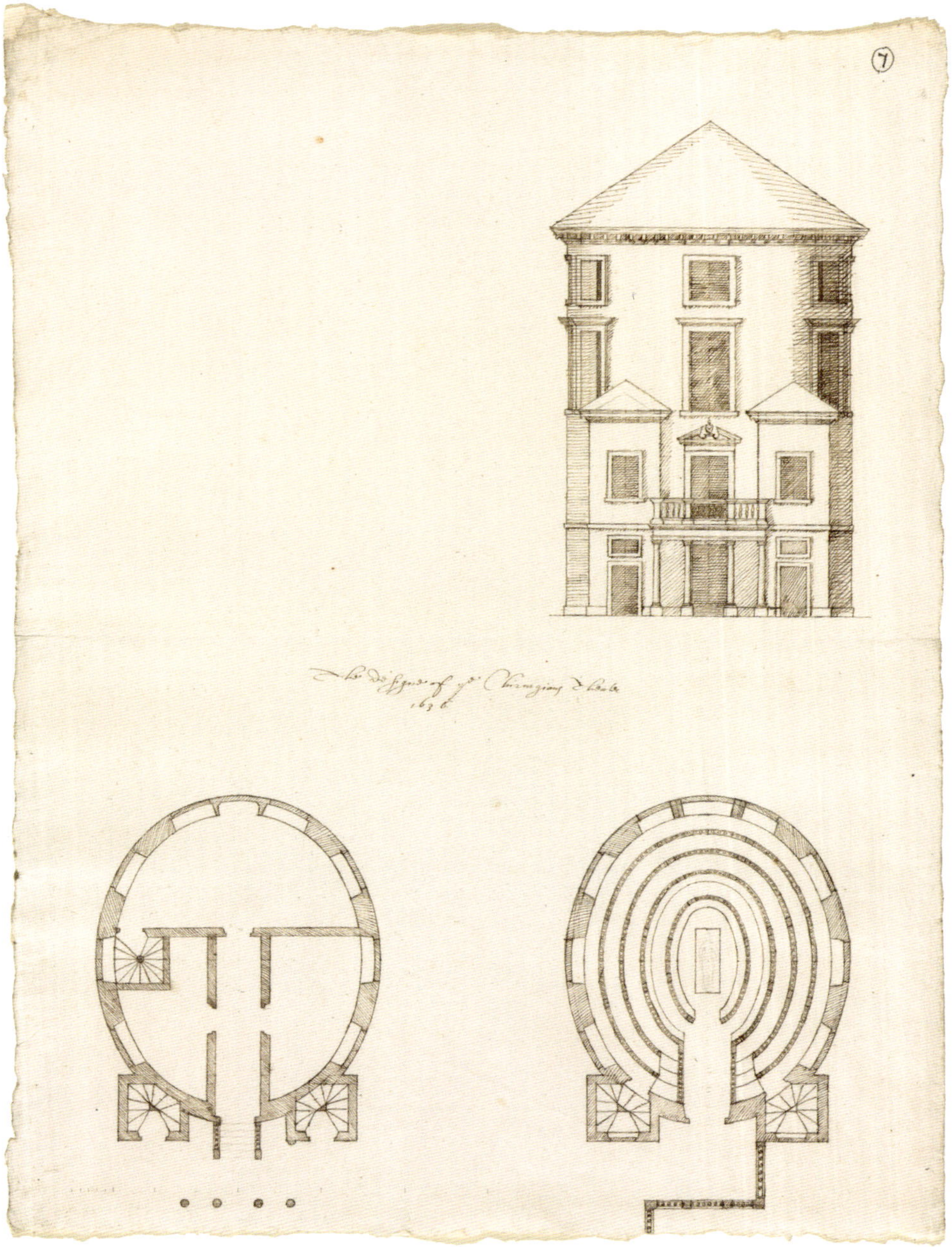

Fig. 14 The designe of ye Chirugeons Theater, 1636; *plans of ground floor (lower left) and first floor (lower right) and elevation of the entrance front of Barber-Surgeons' Hall by John Webb; reproduced in John Harris and A.A. Tait,* Catalogue of the Drawings by Inigo Jones, John Webb and Isaac de Caus at Worcester College, Oxford, *1979.*

Canterbury from 1633 (fig. 13). Little attention has been paid to the way in which Livery Halls might have been enlisted in the service of the 'City beautiful' plan. However, rebuilding and beautification projects at Mercers' Hall (1632–40), Clothworkers' Hall (1633), Apothecaries' Hall (1633), Barber-Surgeons' Hall (1633–37; fig. 14) and Goldsmiths' Hall (1634–36) all fall into this category. The first of these projects is particularly characteristic of this phase in the Halls' history.

Mercers' Hall was built between 1517 and 1522 on the site of the Hospital of St Thomas of Acre between two houses on the corner of Ironmonger Lane to the west and the Mitre Tavern and St Mary Colechurch on the corner of Old Jewry to the east. The new building cost the Company £2700 and had a vigorous battlemented front elevation on to Cheapside and an ornate frontispiece in the centre of its five bays, as the Copperplate Map of London faintly shows (Introduction, fig. 13).[31] The building soon became a landmark in this most important City thoroughfare at the centre of an area dominated by the mercery trade in such fine cloths as silk and linen.

By 1630 the building's fabric was in need of attention, but what began as a straightforward stonework repair soon escalated into a beautification project of considerable scope, expense and sophistication. The Company Wardens, along with the Company Surveyor, Daniel Gorsuch, were appointed as a committee to organize repairs, 'the stone work of the Companies Chappell and hall being growne much into decay'.[32] A direct link between the Company and the Commission for Buildings makes it likely that the Mercers' building activity was related to the Crown's wider beautification agenda: both Inigo Jones and the Earl of Arundel were liverymen (fig. 15).[33] A further clue to Jonesian influence is the identity of the mason whom the Mercers appointed to carry out work on their Hall: Edmund Kinsman, a leading City craftsman who had already worked for Jones and would be employed by him on repairs to St Paul's.[34] The agreement bound Kinsman and his apprentice Robert Dodson to 'take downe the whole battlements or forefront of Mercers hall London towards the streete', to build it anew in 'sufficient substantiall and workemanlike manner with the hardest Portland stone' and to 'cause a frontispiece of the hardest Portland stone to be raysed above the said Battlements'. Each window was to be adorned with sundials rising above the battlements, an arrangement that must have closely resembled that made by John Young, Kinsman's collaborator, at Holy Trinity, Berwick-upon-Tweed (fig. 16). Kinsman's task appears to have been to refine and regularize a somewhat irregular and patched construction. He completed the work in February 1633 and in May of that year was paid an extra £100 in recognition of the high quality of his stonework repairs and mouldings.[35]

The battlements were evidently central to this programme of work; their decorative and symbolic potential was strong in this context. The juxtaposition of the Hall's castellated skyline with functioning shops at street level was a curious one, but the effect created must have been as close to that of a castle as it was possible for a building in such a confined urban setting to get, and the City's premier Livery Company presumably enjoyed the lordly associations, as well as the decorative qualities, of this architectural form. The battlements may have been an allusion to the crown worn by the Mercers' 'Maiden', the device that had adorned the Company's coat of arms since the early fifteenth century (fig. 17), and to the mural crown, the antique emblem for a city. Although the City of London's jurisdictional boundary spread beyond the gates to the inner suburbs, in the early modern imagination the walls were still the Square Mile's most potent symbol (Introduction, fig. 7).[36] The prominent Cheapside location of Mercers' Hall placed on it a dramatic burden, too; the street elevation formed part of the backdrop to a space used for public events such as proclamations, exemplary punishments, pageants and processions. A run of polished and gleaming battlements made of the finest Portland stone can only have enhanced the building's contribution: as Vanessa Harding has observed, 'When something was done in Cheapside, it was done for effect, and with an eye to its audience.'[37]

By 1637 the Company was involved in the rebuilding of yet another part of its large Hall complex, for in January of that year the parishioners of St Mary Colechurch appealed to the Mercers' Court of Assistants for an 'order for repaire of the church'.[38] This project brought the Mercers into official contact with the Commission for Buildings.[39] Colechurch occupied the first

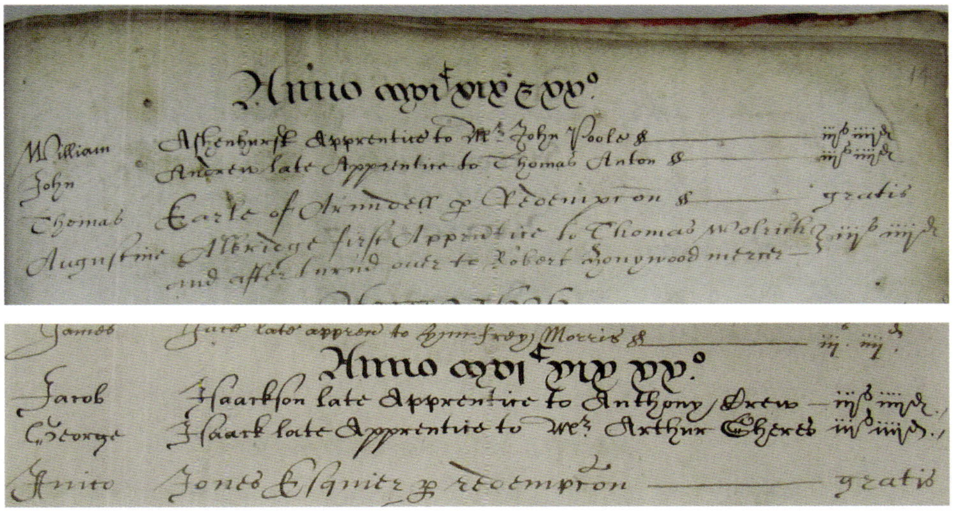

Fig. 15 (top) The Mercers' Company Register of Freemen; entries for the admission of Thomas, Earl of Arundel, and 'Inico' Jones 'gratis', 1620.

Fig. 16 (above) A sundial is set within the battlements of the church of the Holy Trinity, Berwick-upon-Tweed. The church was built by Edmund Kinsman's collaborator, the London mason John Young of Blackfriars, in 1650–52.

Fig. 17 Arms of the Mercers' Company, as recognized and authorized by Sir Henry St George, Richmond Herald, following the visitation of 1634.

Fig. 18 Design for a window depicting the arms of the King (centre), the Prince of Wales (left) and the Mercers' Company (right), attributed to Edward Pearce the Elder, c. 1638.

floor of the south-eastern corner of the Mercers' complex, sandwiched between shops and cellarage below and a tenement owned by the Company above. Its chancel and east end – the upkeep of which was the responsibility of the Mercers – faced Old Jewry on the corner of Cheapside. The rectory and advowson of the church were purchased by the Company in 1542 after the dissolution of the Hospital of St Thomas of Acre. The costly repair of this church brought the Mercers into direct contact with Inigo Jones, following whose intervention a new east window was ordered at the Company's expense. What had been planned as a window of plain lights 'white within' now became an expensive one with an elaborate and politically freighted painted scheme containing 'the Kings armes the Princes armes and their owne Armes'.[40]

The Mercers' complex was destroyed in the Great Fire, so the exact appearance of their east window would have remained a mystery but for the existence of a design for a three-light stained-glass window bearing the Mercers' Maiden emblem, the arms of Charles I and the Prince of Wales's feathers in the RIBA Drawings Collection (fig. 18). This drawing has now been convincingly attributed to Edward Pearce the Elder (*fl.* 1630–d. 1658), a leading decorative designer who worked closely with Inigo Jones; it is here linked with the Mercers' rebuilding project for the first time.[41]

The very considerable building activity undertaken by several of the Livery Companies in the 1630s has been obscured by the drama and disruption of the wholesale rebuilding that took place after the Great Fire. During the Civil War and later, until government was seized and held by Oliver Cromwell, parliamentary committees held great sway, and they chose Livery Halls as their meeting places: the Committees of the Commons at Grocers' Hall, and the Committee for the Advance of Money at Haberdashers' Hall; the estates of the delinquents were sequestered at Clothworkers' Hall; and the powerful Committee for Compounding found its permanent home at Goldsmiths' Hall.

The power reversal between king and state was played out in miniature in these 'turncoat' Halls, rather as it was – albeit in a more dramatic way – at the Banqueting House in 1649, when the building that Charles I had made a monument to the Stuart monarchy became the setting of his own execution. Royal coats of arms were removed from the Halls by the Companies during the early 1640s and were just as predictably replaced in 1660 in anticipation of the return of Charles Stuart. The image of the two-faced turncoat, so prominent in political discourse of the period and so appropriate to a discussion of institutions that were defined by dress, can help us to understand the Livery Halls' capacity to survive political upheaval. Buildings, like men, were capable of changing sides. By the Restoration, the urban ambitions of James I and Charles I for a royal capital city were forgotten; the construction of the post-Fire Halls was very much a City enterprise, and Crown involvement in the shaping of their architecture was the exception, not the rule.[42]

WITH HONOUR YET FRUGALITY: RECONSTRUCTION AFTER THE GREAT FIRE, *C.* 1668–75

In just a few days the Great Fire of September 1666 destroyed forty-four Livery Halls;[43] buildings that by this point had in many cases, like 'so many hives of bees', been the focus of uninterrupted corporate activity for more than two centuries.[44] A common theme of much providentially minded post-Fire verse and sermon-making was the purgative effect of the flames both on the City's sinful population and on its buildings, which were condemned either as architecturally irregular 'dross' or as sullied by association with the events of the Civil War and Interregnum.[45] For some contemporaries, their association with the parliamentary committees rendered the Halls, too, tarnished and in need of purification.[46] In the midst of the Fire, John Evelyn mourned the loss of the Halls, but did so in terms of their ornamental contribution to the City's fabric: 'all the rest of the Companies Halls, sumptuous buildings, arches, entries, all in dust'.[47] But the loss of meeting places in which to foster fraternal love and unity was perhaps the more devastating aspect of the disaster for the Companies.

The Companies' records for the period immediately after the Fire unsurprisingly indicate a profound sense of shock and corporate dislocation. The minutes of their first Court meetings following the Fire typically list property burnt in addition to the Hall: sad litanies of loss.[48] The Companies were experiencing what Cynthia Wall has described as the 'terrifying difference' of a post-Fire City in which spaces once fixed and stable were now shifting and treacherous.[49]

Interim measures were taken remarkably swiftly. Some Companies moved Court meetings to one of the few unburnt Halls, and others met at private houses and taverns that had escaped the Fire. The Court of the Pewterers' Company, for example, met at the Mitre in Aldgate, 'since it hath pleased God to destroy ye hall by Fire soe that at this tyme ye company are destitute of a place to meet in as well as ye Beadle of a habitacion'.[50] The Clothworkers' Company, coming to terms with the loss of its Hall as well as a property portfolio across the City worth £540 per annum in rent, met first at Lamb's Chapel by Cripplegate and then made arrangements to use the Leathersellers' Hall.[51]

The lack of a Hall might, then, be felt for a variety of practical reasons: it made officers homeless; it deprived the Company of the income that could be made from renting rooms; and it meant that valuable Company records and paraphernalia, where these indeed survived, had to be carted about the City.[52] Until its Hall was reconstructed, a Company would struggle to discharge its civic duties to the dishonour of both itself and the City. But the conceptual implications might have been still more damaging. As Ian Archer has observed, the Companies liked to invoke the 'rhetoric of antiquity' in order to defend their prerogatives.[53] Without a venerable Hall in which to reverberate, that rhetoric must have felt strangely empty. In any case, exposed and vulnerable in the fragile and fickle political environment of the Restoration, each of those Companies that had lost its Hall in the Fire faced a stark decision after September 1666.[54] Delaying the reconstruction of a Hall or discounting it altogether might have been a sensible course of action in the weakened financial state that resulted from loss of rental income in the Fire and enforced loans and gifts to Charles II since 1660. Such a decision would, however, have carried the risk of corporate extinction.

A map of the City etched by Wenceslaus Hollar for Charles II in 1666 conveys some idea of the vacuum created by the Great Fire and the enormity of the task of rebuilding (fig. 19). This plan and others like it were not only mapping the trauma of the Fire, they were also topographical chessboards that invited speculation about who was going to make the first move towards reconstruction. Before Hollar's etching was published, there had been several proposals for filling the vacuum. Plans submitted to Charles II by Christopher Wren and John Evelyn in the week following the Fire would have seen the City's erratic medieval street plan swept away in favour of a more uniform street plan of straight avenues, *ronds-points* and piazzas. The manoeuvring and manipulation of the Livery Halls' sites were key to the realization of both. According to *Parentalia*, Wren's design (fig. 20) would have seen the Halls of the Great Twelve grouped 'into one regular Square annexed to Guild-hall'.[55] Evelyn's design, recorded in a late eighteenth-century etching (fig. 21), would have placed the Halls around the City on the main axes '[b]etween the piazzas, market places and churches ... fronted ... with stone [and] adorned with statues'.[56] The Halls were thus treated as moveable elements in proposals that reveal little understanding of the Companies' long-standing connection to certain sites.

In the immediate aftermath of the Fire, the Companies were respectful of interventions made by the authorities to prevent unregulated and hasty building. The proclamation that Charles II issued on 13 September to impede hurried and unlawful rebuilding appears to have made a powerful impression on, for example, the Courts of the Tallow Chandlers' and Clothworkers' Companies, both of which happened to meet that day. The former received petitions from its tenants asking for repayment of their leases, but dismissed them 'until his Majestie's pleasure shall be fully knowne'.[57] In line with the royal proclamation and precepts issued by the Court of Common Council, the Companies did, however, start to clear their land of rubbish.[58] Securing the site and protecting the integrity of vaults and cellarage were vital considerations. Consolidation and clearing were, for the present, the only legitimate activities. The Mercers appointed labourers under the supervision of the Beadle and the Company Bricklayer to sort lead, iron and stone from the debris of their Hall in Cheapside. More than 16 tons of lead were retrieved and melted down before being removed for safe storage at Gresham College in Bishopsgate.[59]

Fig. 19 (right) A Map or Groundplot of the Citty of London and the Suburbes thereof ... by which is exactly demonstrated the present condition thereof since the last sad accident of fire. The blanke space signifeing the burnt part ..., *etching by Wenceslaus Hollar, 1666.*

Fig. 20 (opposite, top) Christopher Wren's plan for rebuilding the City of London, 1666.

Fig. 21 (opposite, bottom) John Evelyn's plan for rebuilding the City of London; late 18th-century etching published by Alexander Hogg.

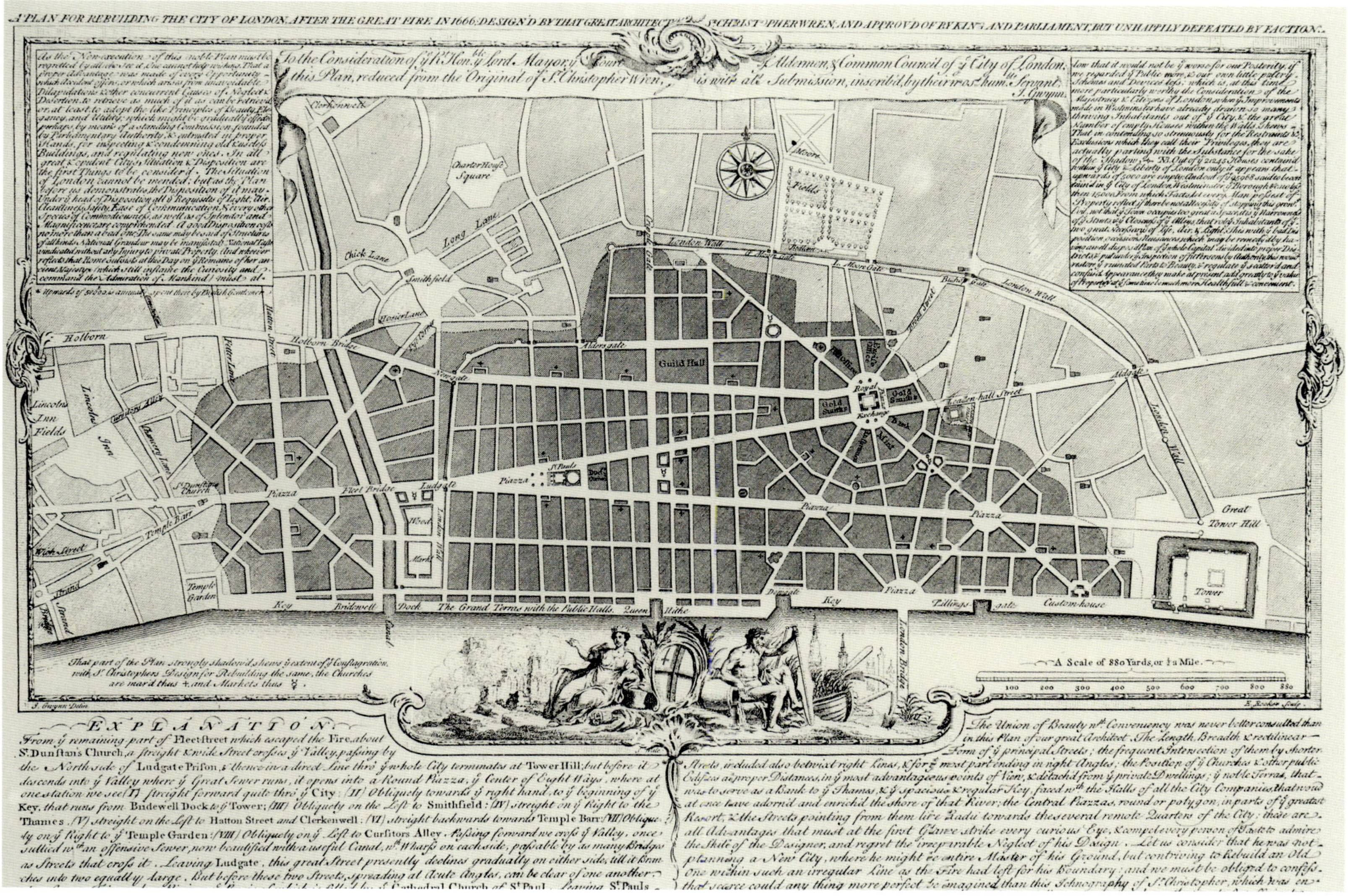

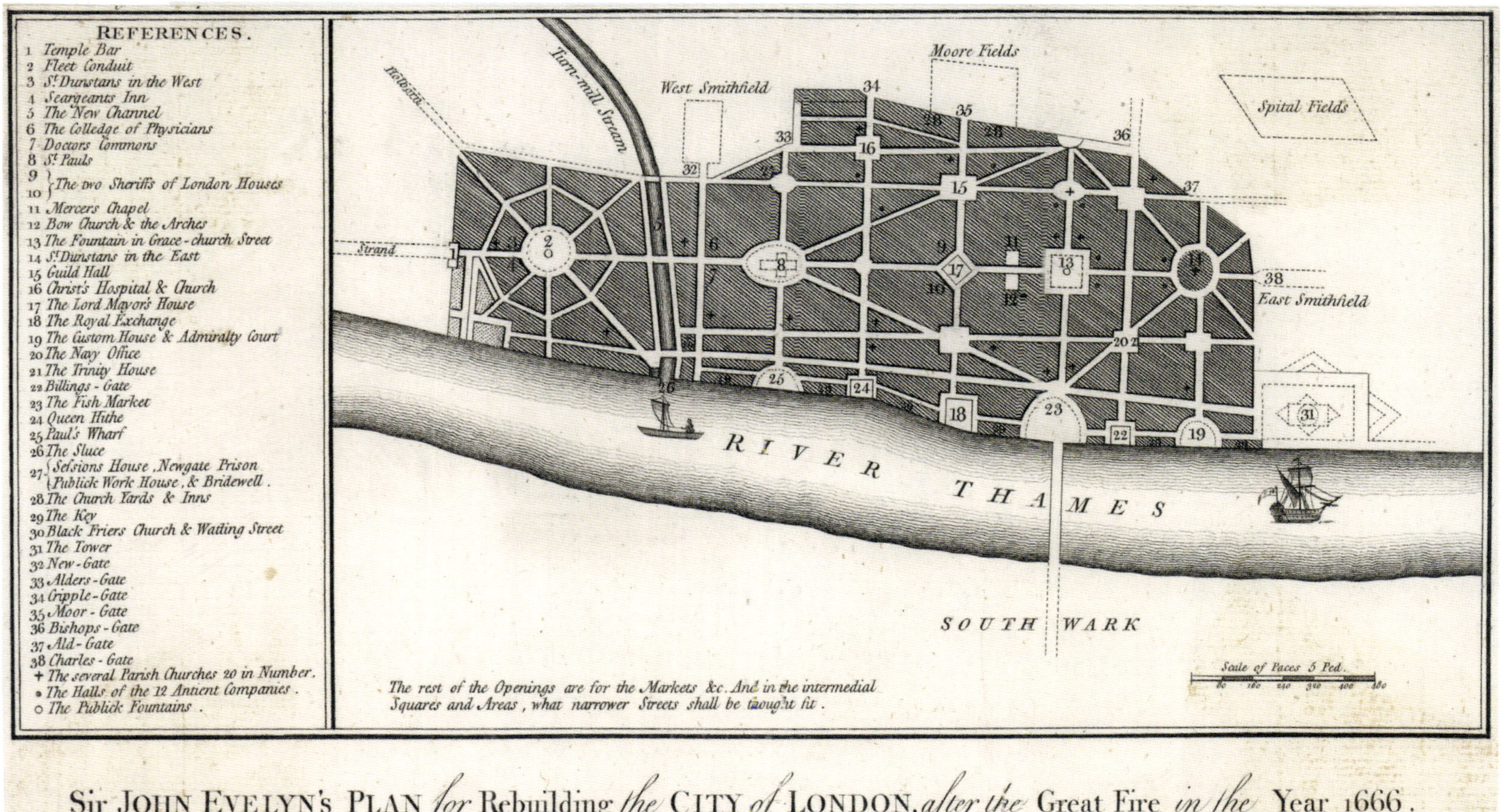

Sir JOHN EVELYN's PLAN *for* Rebuilding *the* CITY *of* LONDON, *after the* Great Fire *in the* Year 1666.

These injunctions to sift sites for the transmogrified remains of the old Halls, prosaic though they are, contain echoes of John Evelyn's dramatic description of lead 'mealting downe the streets in a streame' on the second day of the Fire, and of Samuel Pepys's diary entry for 5 September, in which he recalls taking up 'a piece of glasse of Mercers' Chappell in the streete, where much more was, so melted and buckled with the heat of the fire like parchment'.[60] The sale of some of the salvaged materials from the old Halls would help to fund reconstruction, but reclaimed materials were also stored in anticipation of the time when rebuilding could begin and they could be incorporated in the new structure.[61]

Once they were sifted and secured, there was little to be done on Livery Hall sites until the King's Commissioners and City Surveyors had made their surveys and decided on a model for reconstruction. Both Wren and Evelyn had envisaged the manoeuvring of the Livery Halls, but even once their plans had been abandoned resiting remained a possibility. This question was one of a number discussed as part of negotiations between the City authorities and the king following the Fire.[62] Charles II suggested resiting the Halls of the lesser Companies along the riverfront, although his wishes were not acted upon by Corporation officials or the Companies.[63] The Companies' records demonstrate undoubted awareness of and adherence to the 1667 Act for Rebuilding, but their building projects proceeded with only minimal involvement from the City Corporation, the King's Commissioners and City Surveyors. There are but two exceptions. The Fishmongers' new Hall, designed by Edward Jerman, infringed the river quay in a manner proscribed by the 1667 Act (Introduction, fig. 32).[64] This project had to be granted a certificate of indemnity by Wren in 1669.[65] The rebuilding of Stationers' Hall (fig. 8) attracted royal intervention for political reasons and, as I have argued elsewhere, some of its design features can be linked to a campaign by Charles II's Surveyor of the Imprimery, Roger L'Estrange, to suppress seditious publications.[66]

Fig. 22 Relief sculpture on the Monument's pedestal by Caius Gabriel Cibber, completed 1677.

REBUILDING THE HALLS

An inscription on the south face of the pedestal supporting the Monument erected to the Fire, which was finished in 1677, declares rather optimistically: 'Haste is seen everywhere, London rises again, whether with greater speed or greater magnificence is doubtful, three short years complete that which was considered the work of an age' (as translated from the Latin). The relief sculpture by Caius Gabriel Cibber on the same structure depicts Charles II directing the reconstruction and the beleaguered figure of London being comforted by Time against a backdrop of smoking buildings (fig. 22). In reality, what had been completed three years after the Fire was the surveying of 5000 plots, the construction of 4000 houses, the reconstruction of a single public building (the Royal Exchange) and the start of work on two churches.

The reconstruction of the Livery Halls did, however, justify some of the hyperbole of the Monument's inscription, and deserves that double distinction of speed and magnificence. Of the forty-four Livery Halls burnt in the Fire, eight had been rebuilt by 1669, ten had more or less been completed by 1670, and three-quarters were structurally complete by 1673.

That the Livery Companies were so energetic is surprising and initially hard to account for, given their financial situation. Whereas successive parliamentary Acts for Rebuilding the City

Fig. 23 Loyal London at the Entrance to the Thames and Medway, *oil on canvas by Isaac Sailmaker*, c. *1666*.

provided a formal funding mechanism for the reconstruction of the churches and such 'public' buildings as the prisons, that of the Livery Halls was funded entirely privately. Heavy demands had been placed on their finances in the preceding decades, and, by destroying rental property across the City, the Fire had robbed the Companies of a vital source of income.[67] The Companies had helped the City to loan the Crown £100,000 in 1664 and funded the building of a ship called the *Loyal London* to be deployed in the Second Anglo-Dutch War in summer 1666 (fig. 23). These loans were meant to be repaid with interest, but rarely were.

It is worth our notice that in that relief sculpture on the Monument the figure of Plenty hovers non-committally over the two camps of the King and the City: from where is the bounty she is so liberally pouring on the reconstruction enterprise supposed to be coming? Plenty is shown supported by Peace, but the Fire occurred in the midst of a war. For the Companies at this time, plenty was elusive, and the Court of the Brewers' Company spoke for most when, in 1667, it cursed 'the destruccion & unsettledness of the tymes'.[68]

Unlike the heralds at the College of Arms – also a corporate body rebuilding its headquarters in the City after the Fire – the Companies were not able to collect subscriptions from wealthy individuals outside the Square Mile. They were generally limited to levying small subscriptions from freemen – the Company rank and file. However, they did this extremely efficiently and assiduously, and the ability to extract subscriptions and donations effectively became key to the progress of Hall reconstruction. These contributions can be found in a handful of surviving subscription lists and promissory books. Occasionally a particularly wealthy or ambitious member of the livery offered to defray, or at least temporarily cover, the cost of wainscoting or plastering a room. But with the shell of an average Livery Hall costing at least £3000, for the most part the Companies faced a shortfall that could be met only with high-interest loans.

Starts to most rebuildings faltered because of a lack of cash, and many Court minutes record the increasingly desperate measures taken to raise funds. The Tallow Chandlers, for example, decided in January 1668 to build four houses on the street front of their Hall complex to designs by Edward Jerman and John Caine.[69] Once rented, these houses provided an income to fund reconstruction of the rest of the complex. Even so, the Company was forced to borrow £1000 at a high interest rate.[70]

The Brewers' Company, meanwhile, had been led to believe by Sir Samuel Starling, an Alderman and Past Master, that he would finance rebuilding, but the Court was told that 'his mind was altered'.[71] The Brewers borrowed less than the Tallow Chandlers, but their fundraising methods were no less painful; Company plate was sold, but it was compulsory subscriptions that brought in the sums needed. The diligence of the Wardens

Fig. 24 Early 20th-century photograph of the Court Room of Brewers' Hall (now destroyed).

Fig. 25 East door of the Parlour at Tallow Chandlers' Hall with inscription recording Sir Joseph Sheldon's donation of wainscoting, completed 1675.

and the Court of Assistants meant that £1879 was soon gathered in this way, along with an in-kind offer of 50,000 bricks.[72] Starling eventually contributed towards the new Brewers' Hall by covering the costs of wainscoting the Court Room (fig. 24), while Sir Joseph Sheldon (nephew of Gilbert, Archbishop of Canterbury, who commissioned and funded the construction of the Sheldonian Theatre at Oxford) defrayed the cost of wainscoting the Parlour at Tallow Chandlers' Hall (fig. 25 and Introduction, fig. 31).

Each Company appointed a committee for rebuilding comprising four to six members of the Court of Assistants (with a minimum quorum of three). Decisions to be made by this committee ranged from choosing the form of the Hall roof (flat and leaded, hipped and tiled, or topped with a lantern) to selecting models for plasterwork or wainscoting. It was empowered to borrow money at interest using the Company's common seal, to negotiate and direct craftsmen, and to 'peruse the workemens bills and accompts'.[73]

After the dislocation created by the destruction of the Halls in the Fire, the Companies' response to the completion of their new buildings was, unsurprisingly, one of enormous relief. The Halls were at the centre of restored civic order and ritual, and the Court of the Tallow Chandlers noted proudly on 30 October 1671: 'The Master Wardens and Livery of this Company attended the Right Hon[oura]ble Lord Mayor ... to and from Westminster it being his oath day; And att their Returne dyned att and in their new rebuilded Comon Hall att a dyner.'[74] While the Halls might be 'new rebuilded', as far as the Companies were concerned they were still 'ancient' in essence.[75]

From the perspectives of both income generation and cost saving, rebuilding on old foundations and replicating the traditional courtyard plan had much to recommend it as an approach to reconstruction of the Halls after the Great Fire. As the 1667 poem 'On the Rebuilding of London' explains:

> More sumptuous Buildings in Retirement
> plac'd
> Are the Emblem of the wary Citie's trade;
> Their Streets and Shops much better lin'd than
> fac'd,
> Costly without, but richlier inlaid.[76]

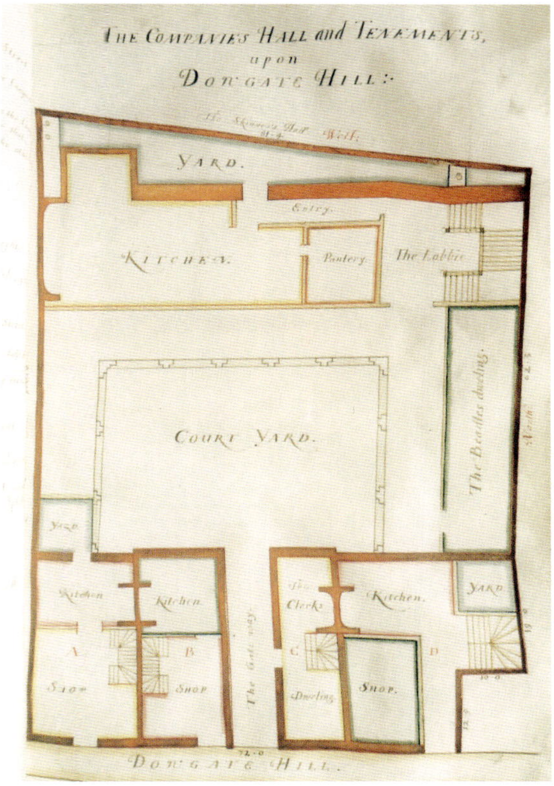

Most of the Companies adopted this policy of 'retiring' from the street and investing the greater part of the ornament within the complex in their rebuildings. A selection of post-Fire Hall plans is illustrative of the tendency (figs. 26 and 27). A mid-nineteenth century painting provides a sense of what might be glimpsed of a hall range and courtyard from the street in this type of courtyard arrangement (fig. 28).

There were some exceptions to the 'retirement' rule. The Vintners' Company, for example, decided after a lengthy discussion not to rebuild a street range, but to leave it 'open with a hansome bricke wall'.[77] The result was a building around '3 sides of a Quadrangle', separated from the street by the brick wall mentioned.[78] Entry was through an iron gate flanked by freestone piers topped with a Bacchus sitting on three tuns – the tuns being a device found on the shield of the Company's coat of arms. The hall range could, therefore, be easily viewed from Thames Street (fig. 29). Mercers' Hall had always enjoyed a powerful presence in Cheapside, and no courtyard intervened to lessen its impact. Like its predecessor, the post-Fire Hall (1668–82) combined shops at ground level with a highly ornamental central frontispiece (figs. 5 and 30).

When the street range of a Hall was rebuilt, decisions had to be made about what should

Fig. 26 (above, left) Plan of Goldsmiths' Hall in Foster Lane by John Ward, 1692.

Fig. 27 (above) Ground-floor plan of the post-Fire Tallow Chandlers' Hall, 1678.

Fig. 28 The Brewers' hall range seen through the Addle Street range; oil on canvas by Henry Pether, 1857.

Fig. 29 Vintners' Hall, built 1671–75, seen from Thames Street; pen and ink with colour wash by 'Wilson', c. 1780.

appear there, and what ornaments and marks of distinction should be reserved for the inner complex – the process of facing and lining described in the poem quoted above. Obscurity was a risk, but – with limited resources – so was spending vast sums. The result was a degree of focused investment on the street range, with the rest of the display reserved for the exterior of the main hall range and, in particular, the interiors. It is this phenomenon of recessive display that led Strype to observe of the post-Fire Halls that many were 'little inferior to some Princes Palaces' but 'lie for the most part backwards, and cannot be taken notice of by strangers'.[79]

Gates were the natural focus of the street range; in addition to securing the Hall complex, they had an important function as objects that 'structured ... performances of welcome and hospitality' throughout the City.[80] This symbolic function carried with it an expectation of ornament, and so scrollwork, festoons, swags, garlanded Ionic capitals, swan necks, oversized coats of arms under shell hoods or breaching segmental pediments, and other ornaments were deployed on this pinch point in the plan (fig. 31). Sometimes the architectural emphasis given to a Hall's door or gate extended the full height of an otherwise plain brick elevation, creating a vertical 'sliver of splendour'.[81] Such frontispieces operated as an index of what lay beyond. Indeed, Strype likened the relationship of Hall complex to street gate to the way 'Hercules Body may be judged by his Foot'.[82] Thomas Whiting's early design for a frontispiece for the Brewers' Company is illustrative of the way in which the contrivers of some post-Fire Halls were forced to think vertically and to pile up this signifying ornament on the street range (fig. 3).

The exterior elevations of the Halls, aside from the gates and frontispieces, were often relatively plain; typically brick elevations with stone dressings. One recurring component of the post-Fire Hall courtyard, however, was the open arched loggia or arcade, a classicizing feature and prestige architectural component found, for example, at Brewers' Hall and Tallow Chandlers' Hall (fig. 33 and Introduction, fig. 8). Elsewhere, a loggia covered the entrance to John Wildgos's Salters' Hall – this time one with square fluted columns and coffering in the soffits of the arches (fig. 1). Hatton also noted an Ionic 'Piazza' in the inner courtyard of Fishmongers' Hall.[83] Exterior elevations were frequently animated with *oeil-de-boeuf* windows – an oval or round light – as a design accent. These adorned a large proportion of the Halls, either singly or in rows, as in the case of

Fig. 30 Stone carvings from the doorcase of the post-Fire Mercers' Hall (formerly in Cheapside, London, now in Swanage, Dorset), 1668–82.

Fig. 31 (clockwise, from top left) Shell hood over the entrance to Barber-Surgeons' Hall in a 19th-century etching; main gates of the Haberdashers', Innholders' and Saddlers' Halls, as illustrated by Thomas H. Shepherd in the 19th century.

Fig. 32 Black-Smiths' Hall, *watercolour by Samuel Ireland, c. 1794.*

the Stationers' main Hall elevation (fig. 8) and on Blacksmiths' Hall (fig. 32).[84]

Ornamental loggias and gates apart, greater decorative investment was undoubtedly expended by the Companies on the interiors of their Halls, particularly when it came to wainscoting and plastering. Fine wainscoting in the hall and Court room and carved screens and chimney pieces abound in these buildings, and could be said to be their defining feature. Such wainscoting offered opportunities for an enormous number of combinations of motifs, which typically incorporated those devices and symbols that represented the Company in question. One notable joiner who worked at the Halls of both the Vintners and the Tallow Chandlers was John Symes (or sometimes Symms).[85] His carved festoons, volutes and classical ornament in the Livery Hall and Court Room of the former (see p. 101) and in the Banqueting Hall and Parlour of the latter (figs. 34 and 35) are extant. Symes had also been employed at Brewers' Hall once that building was structurally complete in early 1672 and the job of decorating and ornamenting had begun. In October of that year the Company appointed Symes for the sum of

Fig. 33 Early 20th-century photograph of the Brewers' post-Fire hall range.

Fig. 34 The screen in the Tallow Chandlers' Banqueting Hall, carved by John Symes in 1674–75.

£355 to wainscot their main Hall.[86] The result was perhaps one of the finest (and now lost) wainscoted Restoration interiors in the City (figs. 36 and 37). Interestingly, the Tallow Chandlers instructed Symes to give the screen in their Banqueting Hall 'a front in the middle as is in the Middle of the plot drawne for the Upper end of Gouldsmiths Hall and then shewed unto the said Committee'.[87] In so doing, the Company was aspiring to one of the City's most prestigious models. The Goldsmiths' grand screen can be seen in a view of the Hall interior made in 1692 by the Company Surveyor, John Ward (fig. 38). Elsewhere, Joiners' Hall, a building with a restrained and barely ornamented exterior (fig. 39), was 'richlier inlaid' with a fine display of wainscoting and carving in cedar.[88] At Clothworkers' Hall, wainscoting was carried out by the joiners 'Day' and 'Kedge'.[89] This was dismantled and auctioned off in 1856 (Introduction, fig. 1), but two swags and two festoons survive in the collection of the Victoria and Albert Museum (fig. 40). The Mercers' Company also invested heavily in fine wainscoting and carving.[90] Nor were

Fig. 35 (above) Wainscoting in the Parlour of Tallow Chandlers' Hall, made by John Symes and paid for by Sir Joseph Sheldon, whose arms appear over the door.

Fig. 36 (left) Wainscoting on the north side of the Brewers' main Hall by John Symes (now destroyed); cartouches over the pedimented door held the arms of the Company's Wardens for 1673.

Fig. 37 Measured drawing of the wainscoting on the south side of the Brewers' main Hall, from The Builder, *December 1916.*

Fig. 38 Interior of the Goldsmiths' main Hall; watercolour by John Ward, 1692.

Fig. 39 Joiners' Hall, Thames Street, *watercolour by Samuel Ireland,* c. *1794.*

staircases neglected, as an ornate extant example at Vintners' Hall by a Mr Woodroffe demonstrates (fig. 43).

Aside from wainscoting, plasterwork offered the greatest opportunities for ornament in the post-Fire Halls, although Hatton noted it less often. An outstanding but now lost ceiling was that in the Court Room of Edward Jerman's repaired Goldsmiths' Hall (1669), which can be appreciated in a nineteenth-century survey drawing by the architect Philip Hardwick (fig. 42). This shows a graceful pattern of beams with a central quatrefoil, the soffits of which were covered with swirling foliage. Hardwick replaced the post-Fire Hall in 1835, but largely replicated the Court Room ceiling and incorporated the elaborate cornice from the original (fig. 41). The gilded and silvered cornice stages a parade of herms, unicorns, swags and scrolls.

An analysis of the lost Halls' impasted fronts and gates, and the ornament inlaid in their principal rooms, certainly takes us closest to an understanding of these buildings' use and function, and to what mattered to the Companies as architectural patrons then – and indeed now. Over the centuries the Halls have increasingly been the recipients of forms of ornamentation that are fashionable, and to that extent generic; but fashion has never been allowed to eclipse their primary function of communicating corporate virtue, antiquity and authority.

Of the handful of Halls that survived the Fire, nearly all were lost by the nineteenth century. The Leathersellers' building, as has already been noted, was replaced as part of a speculation by William and Thomas Roper in 1799 (although not before careful recording by antiquarians). The Armourers' venerable building, which had occupied Coleman Street since the fourteenth century, was finally replaced in 1835–41, despite attempts to bring it up to date with a new street front in the 1790s. Cooks' Hall in Aldersgate Street escaped the Great Fire and provided a base for several homeless Companies in the 1670s; it succumbed to a more localized conflagration in 1771, however, and was not rebuilt. In Leadenhall Street, the mid-sixteenth century Hall of the Tylers and Bricklayers fell out of use by that Company in the eighteenth century and became a synagogue for Dutch Jews; it was demolished by developers just two decades before the widespread destruction of 1941.

The Halls reconstructed in the wake of the Great Fire encountered mixed fortunes. That of the Wax Chandlers lasted barely more than a century, being replaced in 1792–93. The 1820s and 1830s saw several Restoration buildings swept

Fig. 40 (above) Carved festoon from the post-Fire Clothworkers' Hall, c. 1668.

Fig. 41 (left) The cornice of the Goldsmiths' post-Fire Court Room, c. 1669, reincorporated in Philip Hardwick's replacement building of 1835.

Fig. 42 The ceiling of the Goldsmiths' post-Fire Court Room, depicted in a survey drawing by Philip Hardwick shortly before demolition in 1829.

away, including John Wildgos's Salters' Hall in St Swithin's Lane (rebuilt 1823–27), Nicholas Stone and Edward Jerman's Goldsmiths' Hall (replaced 1829–35 by the leading architect Philip Hardwick), and the Fishmongers' imposing riverside building (which had required that special dispensation from Christopher Wren). Others enjoyed greater longevity: in 1929 the Royal Commission on Historical Monuments was able to record in the City of London volume of its *Inventory of Historical Monuments* such treasures as the Corinthian screen of Girdlers' Hall in Basinghall Street (now Basinghall Avenue; 1680–81) and the interiors of Brewers' Hall discussed in this chapter. The authors were able to capture, too, the main entrance to Pewterers' Hall in Lime Street, which had moulded plinths inscribed 1668 and acanthus capitals bearing the date 1669. Just three years later that building was demolished; the post-Fire gate was saved and relocated to the campus of University College London in Bloomsbury, while 1670s panelling and plasterwork from the Master's Parlour found their way into the collection of the Geffrye Museum.

Fig. 43 Carved staircase at Vintners' Hall, 1673.

Until 1752, the civil calendar began on Lady Day (25 March). To avoid ambiguity, dates between 1 January and 24 March are given in the notes using both the old-style and the new-style year, e.g., 17 January 1666/67; dates in the essay are new style.

BS Archives of the Worshipful Company of Barbers

CL Archives of the Clothworkers' Company

GL Guildhall Library, London

LMA London Metropolitan Archives

LS Archives of the Worshipful Company of Leathersellers

MC Archives of the Worshipful Company of Mercers

ST Archives of the Worshipful Company of Stationers and Newspaper Makers

1 W.A.D. Englefield, *The Halls of the Livery Companies of the City of London*, ed. Peter J.A. Lubbock, London 1981, p. 13.
2 Simon Bradley and Nikolaus Pevsner, *London 1: The City of London* (Pevsner Architectural Guides: Buildings of England), Harmondsworth (Penguin) 1997, pp. 373–412, on p. 373.
3 Royal Commission on Historical Monuments (England), *An Inventory of the Historical Monuments in London*, vol. 4: *The City*, London (HMSO) 1929, p. xxvii.
4 See Bernard Adams, *London Illustrated, 1604–1851: A Survey and Index of Topographical Books and Their Plates*, London (Library Association) 1983. Adams lists a total of 175 prints of the Halls.
5 These were prepared for, but not included in, Samuel Ireland, *Picturesque Views, with an Historical Account of the Inns of Court in London and Westminster*, London (R. Faulder and J. Egerton) 1800.
6 See Jean Imray, *The Mercers' Hall*, ed. Ann Saunders, with an introduction by Derek Keene, London (London Topographical Society) 1991, p. 16; Robert Scourfield, 'The Livery Company Hall, 1536–1666', MA diss., Courtauld Institute of Art, University of London, 1993, pp. 1–3. See also John Schofield, 'The Topography and Buildings of London, ca. 1600', in *Material London, ca. 1600*, ed. Lena Cowen Orlin, Philadelphia (University of Pennsylvania Press) 2000, pp. 296–321, on p. 313.
7 See Scourfield, 'The Livery Company Hall', p. 3.
8 *Ibid.*, pp. 6–46; Schofield, 'Topography and Buildings of London', pp. 311–12.
9 Schofield, 'Topography and Buildings of London', pp. 311–12.
10 See Scourfield, 'The Livery Company Hall', pp. 4–51.
11 See Mark Girouard, *Life in the English Country House: A Social and Architectural History*, New Haven, Conn., and London (Yale University Press) 1978, p. 110.
12 Ian W. Archer, 'Discourses of History in Elizabethan and Early Stuart London', *Huntington Library Quarterly*, vol. 68, nos. 1–2, March 2005, pp. 205–26, on p. 218.
13 GL MS 34348, fols. 91–94, October 1602.
14 *Ibid.*, fol. 98, November 1602; this arrangement survives in Merchant Taylors' Hall today. The King's Chamber is now known as the King's Gallery.
15 *Ibid.*, fols. 106–107, April 1603.
16 *Ibid.*, fol. 109, [between April and August] 1603.
17 *Ibid.*, fols. 112–20, April–August 1603.
18 See Robert Tittler, 'Portraiture, Precedence and Politics amongst the London Liveries, *c.* 1540–1640', *Urban History*, vol. 35, no. 3, December 2008, pp. 349–62, on pp. 356–57.
19 See Phil Withington, *The Politics of Commonwealth: Citizens and Freemen in Early Modern England*, Cambridge (Cambridge University Press) 2005, p. 8; Richard Grassby, unpublished history of the Leathersellers' Company, Archives of the Worshipful Company of Leathersellers, p. 149.
20 See Roland Champness, *The Worshipful Company of Turners of London*, 2nd edn, ed. Brian Burnett, London (The Worshipful Company of Turners) 2004, p. 36.
21 See Howard Colvin, *A Biographical Dictionary of British Architects, 1600–1840*, 4th edn, New Haven, Conn., and London (Yale University Press) 2008, p. 230.
22 See Grassby, unpublished history of the Leathersellers' Company, p. 148.
23 *Ibid.*, p. 155.
24 LS GOV/1/1, fol. 45, July 1611.
25 *Ibid.*, fol. 1, [early months of] 1608; Claire Gapper, 'Plasterers and Plasterwork in City, Court and Country, *c.* 1530–*c.* 1660', PhD thesis, Courtauld Institute of Art, University of London, 1998, chapter 5, 'The London Evidence': http://clairegapper.info/the-london-evidence.html (accessed June 2018).
26 LS GOV/1/1, fol. 134, 11 June 1619; C.C. Knowles and P.H. Pitt, *The History of Building Regulation in London, 1189–1972*, London (Architectural Press) 1972, p. 19.
27 See Knowles and Pitt, *History of Building Regulation in London*, p. 20. A building proclamation of 1619 specified that cutting 'wedges Archwise' would contribute to the 'ornament of the Streets'.
28 See the account of the Hall in *The Gentleman's Magazine*, 20 November 1798, vol. 68, part 2, p. 924, just prior to its demolition.
29 Kevin Sharpe, *The Personal Rule of Charles I*, New Haven, Conn., and London (Yale University Press, 1992, p. 411.
30 See James C. Robertson, 'Stuart London and the Idea of a Royal Capital City', *Renaissance Studies*, vol. 15, no. 1, March 2001, pp. 37–58.
31 See Imray, *Mercers' Hall*, pp. 15–16.
32 MC, Acts of Court 1631–37, fol. 19v, 16 February 1631/32.
33 They were made or became members of the Company in 1620; the usual redemption fee was waived in both cases.
34 See Colvin, *Dictionary*, pp. 620–21.
35 See MC, Acts of Court 1631–37, fol. 73v, 2 May 1633.
36 See Vanessa Harding, 'City, Capital, and Metropolis: The Changing Shape of Seventeenth-Century London', in *Imagining Early Modern London: Perceptions and Portrayals of the City from Stow to Strype, 1598–1720*, ed. J.F. Merritt, Cambridge and New York (Cambridge University Press) 2001, pp. 117–43, on p. 135.
37 Vanessa Harding, 'Cheapside: Commerce and Commemoration', *Huntington Library Quarterly*, vol. 71, no. 1, March 2008, pp. 77–96, on p. 77.
38 MC, Acts of Court 1631–37, fol. 234r, January 1636/37.
39 For a detailed account of this commission and its political context, see Anya Matthews, 'London's Livery Halls, *c.* 1603 to *c.* 1684: Their Architecture and Political Uses', PhD thesis, Courtauld Institute of Art,

University of London, 2015, pp. 124–33, '"In a workmanlike and gracefull manner": The Mercers' Colechurch Window'.

40 MC, Acts of Court 1637–41, fol. 54r, 4 July 1638.

41 The attribution will be discussed in a forthcoming article for the *Volume of the Walpole Society* by Gordon Higgott and A.V. Grimstone: 'Drawings by Edward Pearce the Elder (*fl.* 1630–d. 1658)'. I am grateful to Gordon Higgott for bringing this design to my attention.

42 See Robertson, 'Stuart London', p. 58.

43 See Walter George Bell, *The Great Fire of London in 1666*, 3rd edn, London (Bodley Head) 1923, p. 337.

44 James Howell, *Londinopolis*, London (printed for H. Twiford *et al.*) 1657, p. 41.

45 Jacob F. Field, 'Reactions and Responses to the Great Fire: London and England in the Later Seventeenth Century', PhD thesis, Newcastle University, 2008, p. 329.

46 See, for example, Henry Hesketh, *A Sermon Preached … upon the Second of September, 1679 … in Memory of the Late Dreadful Fire*, London (printed for Will. Leach) 1679, pp. 13–14.

47 John Evelyn, *The Diary of John Evelyn*, ed. E.S. de Beer, Oxford (Clarendon Press) 1955, vol. 3, p. 460.

48 See, for example, the Tallow Chandlers' Court Book, GL MS 6153/3, fol. 116r, 13 September 1666, and fol. 117v, 18 October 1666.

49 Cynthia Wall, *The Literary and Cultural Spaces of Restoration London*, Cambridge (Cambridge University Press) 1998, p. 3.

50 GL MS 7090/6, unfoliated, 18 September 1666.

51 See CL/B/1/10, fol. 32v, 13 September 1666, and fol. 46v, 17 January 1666/67.

52 See, for example, the Barber-Surgeons' accounts, which note £3 'for carrying of the Companyes goods by Porters to Moore Fields'; BS D/2/2, unfoliated, 1666–67 [*c.* 5 September 1666].

53 Archer, 'Discourses of History', p. 207.

54 See N.H. Keeble, *The Restoration: England in the 1660s*, Oxford and Malden, Mass. (Blackwell) 2002, p. 46.

55 Christopher Wren (ed.), *Parentalia: or, Memoirs of the Family of the Wrens … Chiefly of Sir Christopher Wren …*, London (printed for T. Osborn and R. Dodsley) 1750, pp. 268–70, on p. 268.

56 John Evelyn, *London Revived: Consideration for Its Rebuilding in 1666*, ed. E.S. de Beer, Oxford (Clarendon Press) 1938, p. 41.

57 GL MS 6153/3, fol. 116r, 13 September 1666.

58 See CL/B/1/10, fol. 31r, 13 September 1666.

59 See Imray, *Mercers' Hall*, p. 25.

60 *Diary of John Evelyn*, vol. 3, p. 448; Samuel Pepys, *The Diary of Samuel Pepys: A New and Complete Transcription*, vol. 7: *1666*, ed. Robert Latham and William Matthews, London (Bell & Hyman) 1972, p. 277.

61 The Mercers' Company sold all of the iron stored at Gresham College for a total of £52 4*s*. 6*d*. in 1671; see Imray, *Mercers' Hall*, p. 30.

62 See T.F. Reddaway, *The Rebuilding of London after the Great Fire*, reprint [1940], London (Edward Arnold) 1951, p. 105.

63 See LMA, COL/CC/01/01/044, Journal of the Court of Common Council, no. 46, 1665–69, unfoliated, 6 March 1666/67.

64 See Helen Collins, *Edward Jerman, 1605–1668: The Metamorphosis of a Master-Craftsman*, Cambridge (Lutterworth) 2004, p. 93.

65 GL MS 6762, 'Dr Wren's Certificate for ye Hall', May 1669.

66 See Matthews, 'London's Livery Halls', pp. 258–76, 'The Tory Watchdog and the Protestant Joiner: The Rebuilding of Stationers' Hall'.

67 See Valerie Pearl, *London and the Outbreak of the Puritan Revolution: City Government and National Politics, 1625–43*, Oxford (Oxford University Press) 1961, p. 75; Robert Ashton, *The City and the Court, 1603–1643*, Cambridge and New York (Cambridge University Press) 1979, p. 70.

68 GL MS 5445/20, fol. 21r, 2 May 1667.

69 See GL MS 6153/3, fols. 134r–135v, 10 January 1667/68.

70 See GL MS 6153/4, fol. 5r, 29 April 1668.

71 GL MS 5445/20, fol. 8r, 22 November 1666, and fol. 10v, 19 December 1666.

72 *Ibid.*, fol. 242r, 8 March 1669/70.

73 GL MS 7151/1, fol. 414r, 1 February 1660/61.

74 GL MS 6153/4, fol. 54r, 30 October 1671.

75 GL MS 7090/6, unfoliated, 11 August 1670.

76 Reprinted in Robert Arnold Aubin (ed.), *London in Flames, London in Glory: Poems on the Fire and Rebuilding of London, 1666–1709*, New Brunswick, N.J. (Rutgers University Press) 1943, pp. 122–33, verse 29 on p. 127.

77 GL MS 15201/5, fol. 165r, 20 February 1672/73.

78 Edward Hatton, *A New View of London; or, An Ample Account of That City*, London (printed for John Nicholson *et al.*) 1708, vol. 2, p. 621. The Vintners adorned their three-sided courtyard with a stone balustrade from the demolished York House on the Strand.

79 John Stow, *A Survey of the Cities of London and Westminster … Brought down from the Year 1633 … to the Present Time by J. Strype*, London (printed for A. Churchill *et al.*) 1720, vol. 1, p. 235.

80 Christine Stevenson, *The City and the King: Architecture and Politics in Restoration London*, New Haven, Conn., and London (Yale University Press) 2013, p. 8.

81 *Ibid.*, p. 57.

82 Strype, *Survey*, vol. 1, p. 235.

83 Hatton, *New View*, vol. 2, p. 605.

84 Mr Pollard the painter was paid 4*s*. for painting the 'bars in the 12 Ovall windows' (that is, six on each side of the hall range) at Stationers' Hall in 1675; ST M992/5/101, Box G.

85 Symes was a freeman of the Tallow Chandlers' Company rather than of the Joiners; see GL MS 6153/4, fol. 79r, 9 July 1674.

86 See GL MS 5502.

87 GL MS 6153/4, fol. 79r, 9 July 1674.

88 Hatton, *New View*, vol. 2, p. 610.

89 CL/D/5/10, fol. 26r, 1668–69. These were probably Stephen Day (*fl.* 1653–62) and George Kedge (*fl.* 1669–93), members of the Joiners' Company.

90 Imray, *Mercers' Hall*, p. 48.

GAZETTEER

This Gazetteer provides a list of Livery Companies occupying the extant Livery Halls featured in this book, presented in order of precedence. Where a Hall is occupied by more than one Livery Company, each Company is listed separately.

1
MERCERS' HALL
The Worshipful Company of Mercers
Ironmonger Lane
London EC2V 8HE
www.mercers.co.uk
pp. 40–45

2
GROCERS' HALL
The Worshipful Company of Grocers
Princes Street
London EC2R 8AD
www.grocershall.co.uk
pp. 46–51

3
DRAPERS' HALL
The Worshipful Company of Drapers
Throgmorton Avenue
London EC2N 2DQ
www.thedrapers.co.uk
pp. 52–57

4
FISHMONGERS' HALL
The Worshipful Company of Fishmongers
London Bridge
London EC4R 9EL
www.fishhall.org.uk
pp. 58–63

5
GOLDSMITHS' HALL
The Worshipful Company of Goldsmiths
Foster Lane
London EC2V 6BN
www.thegoldsmiths.co.uk
pp. 64–69

6 or 7
SKINNERS' HALL
The Worshipful Company of Skinners
8½ Dowgate Hill
London EC4R 2SP
www.skinners.org.uk
pp. 70–75

7 or 6
MERCHANT TAYLORS' HALL
The Worshipful Company of Merchant Taylors
30 Threadneedle Street
London EC2R 8JB
www.merchant-taylors.co.uk
pp. 76–81

8
HABERDASHERS' HALL
The Worshipful Company of Haberdashers
18 West Smithfield
London EC1A 9HQ
www.haberdashers.co.uk
pp. 82–87

9
SALTERS' HALL
The Worshipful Company of Salters
4 London Wall Place
London EC2Y 5DE
www.salters.co.uk
pp. 88–93

10
IRONMONGERS' HALL
The Worshipful Company of Ironmongers
Shaftesbury Place
London EC2Y 8AA
www.ironmongers.org
pp. 94–99

11
VINTNERS' HALL
The Worshipful Company of Vintners
68 Upper Thames Street
London EC4V 3BG
www.vintnershall.co.uk
pp. 100–105

12
CLOTHWORKERS' HALL
The Clothworkers' Company
Dunster Court
Mincing Lane
London EC3R 7AH
www.clothworkers.co.uk
pp. 106–111

13
DYERS' HALL
The Worshipful Company of Dyers
11–13 Dowgate Hill
London EC4R 2ST
www.dyerscompany.co.uk
pp. 112–15

14
BREWERS' HALL
The Worshipful Company of Brewers
Aldermanbury Square
London EC2V 7HR
www.brewershall.co.uk
pp. 116–19

15
LEATHERSELLERS' HALL
The Worshipful Company of Leathersellers
7 St Helen's Place
London EC3A 6AB
www.leathersellers.co.uk
pp. 120–23

16
PEWTERERS' HALL
The Worshipful Company of Pewterers
Oat Lane
London EC2V 7DE
www.pewterers.org.uk
pp. 124–27

17
BARBER-SURGEONS' HALL
The Worshipful Company of Barbers
Monkwell Square
Wood Street
London EC2Y 5BL
www.barberscompany.org
pp. 128–31

18
CUTLERS' HALL
The Worshipful Company of Cutlers
4 Warwick Lane
London EC4M 7BR
www.cutlerslondon.co.uk
pp. 132–35

19
BAKERS' HALL
The Worshipful Company of Bakers
9 Harp Lane
London EC3R 6DP
www.bakers.co.uk
pp. 136–39

20
WAX CHANDLERS' HALL
The Worshipful Company of Wax Chandlers
6 Gresham Street
London EC2V 7AD
www.waxchandlers.org.uk
pp. 140–43

21
TALLOW CHANDLERS' HALL
The Worshipful Company of Tallow Chandlers
4 Dowgate Hill
London EC4R 2SH
www.tallowchandlers.org
pp. 144–47

22
ARMOURERS' HALL
The Worshipful Company of Armourers and Brasiers
81 Coleman Street
London EC2R 5BJ
www.armourershall.co.uk
pp. 148–51

23
GIRDLERS' HALL
The Worshipful Company of Girdlers
Basinghall Avenue
London EC2V 5DD
www.girdlers.co.uk
pp. 152–55

24
BUTCHERS' HALL
The Worshipful Company of Butchers
87 Bartholomew Close
London EC1A 7EB
www.butchershall.com
pp. 156–59

25
SADDLERS' HALL
The Worshipful Company of Saddlers
40 Gutter Lane
London EC2V 6BR
www.saddlersco.co.uk
pp. 160–63

26
CARPENTERS' HALL
The Worshipful Company of Carpenters
1 Throgmorton Avenue
London EC2N 2JJ
www.carpentersco.com
pp. 164–67

28
PAINTERS' HALL
The Worshipful Company of Painter-Stainers
9 Little Trinity Lane
London EC4V 2AD
www.painter-stainers.org
pp. 168–71

32
INNHOLDERS' HALL
The Worshipful Company of Innholders
30 College Street
London EC4R 2RH
www.innholders.org.uk
pp. 172–75

33
FOUNDERS' HALL
The Worshipful Company of Founders
Number One, Cloth Fair
London EC1A 7JQ
www.foundersco.org.uk
pp. 176–79

36
COOPERS' HALL
The Worshipful Company of Coopers
13 Devonshire Square
London EC2M 4TH
www.coopers-hall.co.uk
pp. 180–83

39
FARMERS' AND FLETCHERS' HALL
The Worshipful Company of Fletchers
3 Cloth Street
London EC1A 7LD
www.fletchers.org.uk
pp. 184–87

46
PLAISTERERS' HALL
The Worshipful Company of Plaisterers
One London Wall
London EC2Y 5JU
www.plaistererslivery.co.uk
pp. 188–91

47
STATIONERS' HALL
The Worshipful Company of Stationers and Newspaper Makers
Ave Maria Lane
London EC4M 7DD
www.stationers.org
pp. 192–95

53
GLAZIERS' HALL
The Worshipful Company of Glaziers and Painters of Glass
9 Montague Close
London SE1 9DD
www.glazierscompany.org.uk
pp. 196–99

58
APOTHECARIES' HALL
The Worshipful Society of Apothecaries
Black Friars Lane
London EC4V 6EJ
www.apothecaries.org
pp. 200–203

73
THE PROOF HOUSE
The Worshipful Company of Gunmakers
48–50 Commercial Road
London E1 1LP
www.gunmakers.org.uk
pp. 204–207

78
HQS *WELLINGTON*
The Honourable Company of Master Mariners
Temple Stairs
Victoria Embankment
London WC2R 2PN
www.hcmm.org.uk
pp. 208–11

80
FARMERS' AND FLETCHERS' HALL
The Worshipful Company of Farmers
3 Cloth Street
London EC1A 7LD
www.farmerslivery.org.uk
pp. 184–87

83
FURNITURE MAKERS' HALL
The Worshipful Company of Furniture Makers
12 Austin Friars
London EC2N 2HE
www.furnituremakers.org.uk
pp. 212–15

84
GLAZIERS' HALL
The Worshipful Company of Scientific Instrument Makers
9 Montague Close
London SE1 9DD
www.wcsim.co.uk
pp. 196–99

89
GLAZIERS' HALL
The Worshipful Company of Launderers
9 Montague Close
London SE1 9DD
www.launderers.co.uk
pp. 196–99

100
INFORMATION TECHNOLOGISTS' HALL
The Worshipful Company of Information Technologists
39a Bartholomew Close
London EC1A 7JN
www.wcit.org.uk
pp. 216–19

WATERMEN'S HALL
The Company of Watermen and Lightermen of the River Thames
16–18 St Mary at Hill
London EC3R 8EF
www.watermenscompany.com
pp. 220–23

ACKNOWLEDGEMENTS

The Worshipful Company of Chartered Architects and the authors and photographer would like to thank the Masters, Prime Wardens and Wardens of all forty Companies with Hall for agreeing to take part in this project; they are grateful to the following for their generous help in opening their buildings and sharing their archives and records with us.

The Worshipful Society of Apothecaries: Nick Royle, *Clerk*; Nick Wood, *Curator and Past Master*; Dr John Ford, *Historian*; Andrew Wallington-Smith, Hon. LMSSA;

The Worshipful Company of Armourers and Brasiers: Peter Bateman, *Clerk*;

The Worshipful Company of Bakers: Alan Willis, *Clerk*;

The Worshipful Company of Barbers: Col. Malachy Doran, *Clerk*;

The Worshipful Company of Brewers: Col. Michael O'Dwyer, OBE, *Clerk*; Jerome Farrell, *Archivist*; James Fitzgerald, *Beadle*;

The Worshipful Company of Butchers: Maj. Gen. Jeff Mason, MBE, RM, *Clerk*;

The Worshipful Company of Carpenters: Brig. Tim Gregson, MBE, *Clerk*; Julie Tancell, *Archivist*;

The Clothworkers' Company: Joss Stuart-Grumbar, *Clerk*; Jessica Collins, *Senior Archivist*;

The Worshipful Company of Coopers: Lt Col. Adrian Carroll, *Clerk*;

The Worshipful Company of Cutlers: Rupert Meacher, *Clerk*;

The Worshipful Company of Drapers: Col. Richard Winstanley, OBE, *Clerk*; Penny Fussell, *Archivist*;

The Worshipful Company of Dyers: Russell Vaizey, *Clerk*;

The Worshipful Company of Farmers: Graham Bamford, *Clerk*;

The Worshipful Company of Fishmongers: Peter Capon, *Head of Collection*;

The Worshipful Company of Fletchers: Kate Pink, *Clerk*; Clive Coward, *Past Master*;

The Worshipful Company of Founders: Andrew Bell, *Clerk*;

The Worshipful Company of Furniture Makers: Jonny Westbrook, *Clerk*; George Cooper, *Marketing and Communications Manager*;

The Worshipful Company of Girdlers: Brig. Ian Rees, *Clerk*; Robert Young, *Beadle*;

The Worshipful Company of Glaziers and Painters of Glass: Alison Evans, *Clerk*; Samantha Enstone, *Managing Director*;

The Worshipful Company of Goldsmiths: Sir David Reddaway, KCMG, MBE, *Clerk*; Eleni Bide, *Librarian*; Richard McCrow, *Hall Keeper*;

The Worshipful Company of Grocers: Brig. Greville Bibby, MBE, *Clerk*; Lisa Miller, *Executive Assistant*;

The Worshipful Company of Gunmakers: John Allen, *Clerk*;

The Worshipful Company of Haberdashers: Dr David Bartle, *Company Archivist*;

The Worshipful Company of Information Technologists: Mike Jenkins, *Clerk*; Jonathan Soar, *Past Master*;

The Worshipful Company of Innholders: Dougal Bulger, *Clerk*; Gillian Croxford, *Assistant Clerk*;

The Worshipful Company of Ironmongers: Teresa Waller-Bridge, *Assistant Clerk*;

The Worshipful Company of Leathersellers: Brig. David Santa-Olalla, DSO, MC, *Clerk*; Jerome Farrell, *Archivist*;

The Honourable Company of Master Mariners: Cdre Angus Menzies, RN, *Clerk*;

The Worshipful Company of Mercers: Rob Abernethy, *Clerk*; Jane Ruddell, *Company Historian*; Stephen McNally, *Hall Manager*;

The Worshipful Company of Merchant Taylors: Rear Adm. Nick Harris, CB, MBE, *Clerk*; Danielle Haeger, *Event Co-ordinator*;

The Worshipful Company of Painter-Stainers: Christopher Twyman, *Clerk*;

The Worshipful Company of Pewterers: Capt. Paddy Watson, RN, *Clerk*; Eleanor Mason Brown, *Assistant Clerk*;

The Worshipful Company of Plaisterers: Nigel Bamping, *Clerk*;

The Worshipful Company of Saddlers: Brig. Philip Napier, OBE, *Clerk*; Sue Hurley, *Archivist*; Keith Marsh, *Beadle and Hall Manager*;

The Worshipful Company of Salters: David Morris, RN, *Clerk*;

The Worshipful Company of Skinners: Maj. Gen. Andrew Kennett, CB, CBE, *Clerk*; Nick Tyson, *Historian*; Paul Richards, *Hall Manager*;

The Worshipful Company of Stationers and Newspaper Makers: William Alden, MBE, DL, *Clerk*; Kevin Dewey, *Past Master*; Keith Fletcher, *Liveryman*;

The Worshipful Company of Tallow Chandlers: Brig. David Homer, MBE, *Clerk*; Richard Kennell, *Beadle and Hall Manager*;

The Worshipful Company of Vintners: Brig. Jonathan Bourne-May, *Clerk*; Stephen Freeth, *Company Archivist*;

The Company of Watermen and Lightermen of the River Thames: Colin Middlemiss, *Clerk*;

The Worshipful Company of Wax Chandlers: Georgina Brown, *Clerk*; Stanley Liu, *Beadle and Hall Manager*;

City of London Corporation and Guildhall: Nick Bodger, *Head of Cultural and Visitor Development*; Amy Poole, *Research and Development Officer*.

ANYA LUCAS wishes to thank Professor Christine Stevenson of the Courtauld Institute of Art, University of London, for supervision of her 2015 PhD thesis (as Anya Matthews), 'London's Livery Halls, *c.* 1603 to *c.* 1684: Their Architecture and Political Uses', from which her two chapters in this book derive.

ANDREAS VON EINSIEDEL wishes to thank Ian Headland, who did an extraordinary job in producing brilliant finished files from the originals, which were often far from perfect owing to the challenging lighting conditions in many of the Halls.

With thanks to David Cole-Adams, Dr Mervyn Miller and Michael Welbank, MBE, Past Masters of the Worshipful Company of Chartered Architects, for their reading of the draft texts and their helpful comments.

SPONSORS

The following organizations and individuals have made this book possible through their generous donations.

CITY OF LONDON

LIVERY COMPANIES

THE WORSHIPFUL COMPANY OF ARTS SCHOLARS

THE CLOTHWORKERS' COMPANY

THE WORSHIPFUL COMPANY OF COOKS OF LONDON (ANONYMOUS DONATION)

THE WORSHIPFUL COMPANY OF DRAPERS

THE WORSHIPFUL COMPANY OF FARMERS

THE WORSHIPFUL COMPANY OF GOLDSMITHS

THE WORSHIPFUL COMPANY OF HORNERS

THE WORSHIPFUL COMPANY OF INFORMATION TECHNOLOGISTS

THE WORSHIPFUL COMPANY OF INNHOLDERS

THE WORSHIPFUL COMPANY OF INSURERS

THE WORSHIPFUL COMPANY OF LEATHERSELLERS

THE WORSHIPFUL COMPANY OF MERCERS

THE WORSHIPFUL COMPANY OF PARISH CLERKS

THE WORSHIPFUL COMPANY OF PLAISTERERS

THE WORSHIPFUL COMPANY OF TALLOW CHANDLERS

CITY-BASED COMPANIES

Brookfield Properties

THE COOK & THE BUTLER EVENT COMPANY

ARCHITECTURE PRACTICES

Allies and Morrison

Assael

BuckleyGrayYeoman

CDA Chris Dyson Architects LLP

dMFK

Eric Parry Architects

Gensler

Hawkins\Brown

Hopkins Architects

Mæ

MatthewLloydArchitects LLP

PITMAN TOZER ARCHITECTS

SOM

Stiff + Trevillion

tp bennett

WestonWilliamson+Partners

MEMBERS OF THE WORSHIPFUL COMPANY OF CHARTERED ARCHITECTS

Denise Bennetts, Freeman
Rab Bennetts, OBE, Freeman
Richard Brindley, Master 2016
David Cole-Adams, Master 1995 and Clerk Emeritus
Karen Cook, Liveryman
Philip Cooper, Renter Warden 2018
Professor James Stevens Curl, Liveryman
Rosemary Curry, Liveryman and Senior Steward
Roger France, Master 2009
Cristina Garcia, Liveryman
Dr Stuart Le Sage, Almoner
Valerie Owen Le Vaillant, OBE, Upper Warden 2018
Jonathan Louth, Freeman
Dr Mervyn Miller, FRIBA, Master 2012
Barry Munday, Master 2018
Giles Murphy, Court Assistant
Peter Murray, FRIBA, Master 2015
Brian Prideaux, Liveryman
Canon Dr Geoffrey Purves, Master 2014
Ian Ritchie, CBE, RA, Liveryman
David Rolfe, Liveryman
Nigel Thomson, Master 2004
Stephen Wagstaffe, Master 2017
Paul Weston, Court Assistant

OTHER
Dr Peadar O'Mórdha

INDEX

Page numbers in *italic* refer to the illustrations.

C

H

T

PICTURE CREDITS

All illustrations copyright © 2018 Andreas von Einsiedel, with the exception of the following (key: l = left, r = right, t = top, c = centre, b = bottom):

Antiqua Print Gallery/Alamy Stock Photo: 230b; Artokoloro Quint Lox Limited/Alamy Stock Photo: 31t; Colin Michael Baker/Alamy Stock Photo: 247; blickwinkel/Alamy Stock Photo: 14br; David Borland – VIEW/Alamy Stock Photo: 251t; The Brewers' Company: 27tr, 244t, 245b, 249b, 251b; The Trustees of the British Museum: 25b, 246; Don Brownlow/Alamy Stock Photo: 237b; CC0 1.0 Mike Calder via Wikimedia: 25t; CAMimage/Alamy Stock Photo: 8; CC0: 19t; Chronicle/Alamy Stock Photo: 29b, 230t, 241b, 248bl; The Clothworkers' Company: 12, 26tr, 26b, 30; The Drapers' Company: 28b; Keith Fletcher www.hmfletcher.co.uk: 24t; The Goldsmiths' Company: 24b, 245tl, 252c, 253b, 254; Granger Historical Picture Archive/Alamy Stock Photo: 248tr, 248br; Guildhall Library & Art Gallery/Heritage Images/Getty Images: 240; The Haberdashers' Company: 18; Heritage Image Partnership Ltd/Alamy Stock Photo: 15b, 227b, 235b; Jeremy Hoare/Alamy Stock Photo: 16b; Angelo Hornak/Alamy Stock Photo: 242; Lambeth Palace Library, London, UK/Bridgeman Images: 20t; The Leathersellers' Company: 23, 27tl, 227t, 234; PD-US Library of Congress, Geography and Map Division: 228–29, 229; London Metropolitan Archives: 22; Dr Anya Lucas/The Brewers' Company: 226; Phil McCarthy/The Butchers' Company: 156l, 156r, 157t, 157b, 158b, 158–59; Base map © maproom.net: 36–37; The Mercers' Company: 237t, 238t; CC0 1.0 from The Metropolitan Museum of Art, New York, Gift of Sarah Lazarus, 1891: 21t, 21b; Museum of London: 19b; Museum of London/PLA Collection: 243; B. O'Kane/Alamy Stock Photo: 14bl; The Painter-Stainers' Company: 20b; The Print Collector/Getty Images: 16tl; Private collection/Bridgeman Images: 224; RIBA Collections: 238b, 252t; By kind permission of the Society of Antiquaries of London: 29t; CC BY-SA 4.0 Spudgun67 via Wikimedia: 15tl, 15tr; The Stationers' Company: 26tl; Edmund Sumner – VIEW/Alamy Stock Photo: 158t; The Tallow Chandlers' Company: 245tr; Joanne Underhill/Alamy Stock Photo: 225; Victoria and Albert Museum, London: 253t; CC BY 4.0 The Wellcome Collection: 17, 28t, 241t, 248tl; Provost and Fellows of Worcester College, Oxford/Colin Dunn (Scriptura Ltd), H&T 1: 236; Photo courtesy Yale Center for British Art: 14t; Photo courtesy Yale Center for British Art, Paul Mellon Collection: 16tr, 27b, 31b, 231, 235t, 249t, 252b

The publishers have made every effort to trace and contact copyright holders of the illustrations reproduced in this book; they shall be happy to correct in subsequent editions any errors or omissions that are brought to their attention.

First published 2018 by Merrell Publishers, London and New York

Merrell Publishers Limited
70 Cowcross Street
London EC1M 6EJ

merrellpublishers.com

in association with

The Worshipful Company of Chartered Architects
The Old Vicarage
Anchor Road
Calne
Wiltshire SN11 8DR

architectscompany.org

British Library Cataloguing in Publication Data. A catalogue record for this book is available from the British Library.

ISBN 978-1-8589-4670-2

Produced by Merrell Publishers Limited
Designed by Nicola Bailey
Project-managed by Claire Chandler
Picture research by Nick Wheldon
Proofread by Barbara Roby
Indexed by Hilary Bird

Printed and bound in China

JACKET, FRONT: The Caxton window in the Livery Hall, Stationers' Hall; see pp. 192–95.
JACKET, BACK (CLOCKWISE FROM TOP LEFT): The first-floor landing, Tallow Chandlers' Hall (see pp. 144–47); The Livery Hall, Armourers' Hall (see pp. 148–51); The Livery Hall, Cutlers' Hall (see pp. 132–35); By the foot of the main staircase, Fishmongers' Hall (see pp. 58–63).
PAGE 258: The Livery Hall, Cutlers' Hall; see pp. 132–35.
PAGES 262–63: The spiral staircase, Leathersellers' Hall; see pp. 120–23.
OVERLEAF: Detail of the marble chimney piece in the Court Room, Goldsmiths' Hall; see pp. 64–69.